Motorcycling

Across

Michigan

Motorcycling Across Michigan

by William M. Murphy

Arbutus Press, Traverse City, MI

ISBN 0-9766104-6-9

Manufactured in the United States of America
Second Edition

Photos are by the author unless otherwise noted.
Maps designed by Burdick Consulting, Rob Burdick, Grand Rapids, Michigan
  616-458-6981
Maps © Arbutus Press
Interior design and layout by Julie Phinney, Bozeman, Montana
  (406-586-1297 – mjphinney@msn.com)

Dedicated to my sister, Helen, whose ride through life

was much too short; to my wife, Susan;

my children, Diana, Billy and Helen;

and to all riders seeking the joys of the open road.

Contents

Preface

Aफ्टेर हाविंग स्पेंट over thirty years and well over 100,000 miles riding motorcycles over much of the United States and Canada, I've been fortunate enough to ride on some of the most exciting and beautiful roads North America has to offer. My motorcycling experience has brought me more enjoyment and excitement than I could possibly articulate and has broadened my knowledge and appreciation of this land and its people. I couldn't count the number of times that I've witnessed absolutely jaw-dropping beauty, experienced exhilaration beyond description, and met the most wonderful and friendly people that you're likely to find anywhere. I know I've only scraped the surface, however. There are thousands of miles of "made-in-motorcycle-heaven" roads that I've yet to experience, there are hundreds or thousands of wonderful places yet to visit, and there are untold numbers of great people that I have yet to ride with, meet on the road, share stories with and hear all about their adventures.

One of my only regrets about this wonderful activity is that it is misunderstood by far too many people. Maybe its vestigial "outlaw' image is part of the charm. Who knows? But the fact is our sport, which could more correctly be described as a lifestyle for many enthusiasts, has been badly tainted in the minds of many whose image of motorcycling and motorcyclists was formed by movies that portrayed us as outlaws or of suspect character, at best. Truth is most motorcyclists are quite mainstream, in the sense that its devotees represent a cross-section of society. Now, I do believe that this cross-section has certain traits and qualities that make us somewhat different. We motorcyclists are willing to accept an increase in potential danger and discomfort for the incredible adventure and freedom that are its rewards. Blue-collar, white-collar or pink-collar, cowboy boots, wing-tips or high-heel shoes, it doesn't matter what we wear when we aren't riding. It's our love of the sport and the adventure and joy it brings us that counts and that makes us one community.

And a community we are. Though there are many types and brands of machines available to meet the differing desires of enthusiasts, when you get right down to the basics, there are common threads that all bikers will list when asked. These qualities include the incredible sense of freedom, an exhilaration that is very hard to describe or quantify, a very real sense of adventure, and of course, the gut-level enjoyment that comes from being one with a most remarkable machine capable of providing the same thrills that many seek at amusement park rides—only the ride never ends.

The motorcycling family in Michigan is growing steadily. The period from 1997 to 2002 saw a forty-five percent increase according to the Michigan Secretary of State. The SOS also said that over 6,000 students per year complete the motorcycle rider and safety education program. Currently, there are slightly over 200,000 registered motorcycles in Michigan—a significant and growing number of intelligent folk who know a great thing when they see it.

One of the most gratifying recent developments in motorcycling is the remarkable increase in the number of female riders. Women are now becoming a part of the motorcycling scene, and I'm not talking about riding on the pillion seat. As new owners of motorcycles, they account for a significant part of the recent upsurge in motorcycle ownership and are as enthusiastic about their machines and what they represent as male riders. The number of organizations and web sites devoted to female owners and operators is nothing short of amazing. As the father of two daughters, who I hope can be whoever and whatever they want to be, this illustrates still another positive step in the ability of women to live full lives per their choosing, not society's. I think it's just great when I see a woman's long hair flying in the wind behind her as she's roaring down the road on her bike.

As is true for most enthusiasts, I derive a great deal of enjoyment reading about my sport in books and magazines. Vicarious enjoyment of motorcycle rides of others is very real—especially on a cold winter night when my own bike is hibernating in the garage, waiting for the next warm day. Coming from the Midwest, however, I must admit to feeling pangs of jealousy and a desire to shout out "Hey, take a look at us!" whenever I read yet one more story in still another motorcycle magazine about wonderful mountain roads in the west or east. I guess stories about riding Michigan's roads just can't compete for readers the way a story about winding and hilly blacktop in the Appalachians, or traversing 9,000-foot passes in the western mountains can.

So I've decided to write a book extolling the joys of riding in Michigan. Having ridden in Michigan for well over thirty years, I know it has many great motorcycling roads and even more wonderful places to see and things to do. The purpose of this book is to share what I've learned from years of riding in every corner of Michigan on two wheels. There are thousands of miles of wonderful motorcycling roads in Michigan, and I don't believe this fact is universally known. But to enjoy these highways and byways, one has to know where they are. In an attempt to save all of you the trouble of finding these roads for yourselves, I've written this book.

I've read various motorcycle touring books over the years that discuss the great motorcycling roads in the country, and Michigan almost always gets three mentions: M22 and M119 along the Lake Michigan coast, and US41 in the Keweenaw Peninsula. The folks who write about only these three stretches of road are simply stating the obvious. I suspect these out-of-state writers simply do a little research from California or some other sunny clime and repeat what someone else has already written. Any rider who has lived here for more than a month is aware of these roads. But there are many, many more miles of enjoyable roads for the discriminating motorcyclist in Michigan.

From the beginning, I've intended this book to be more than a typical tour guide that simply provide routes and destinations and a bit about what to do once you arrive. I want to tell you about Michigan at the same time. There are thousands of fascinating stories, places, sights, forgotten events, ghost towns, and just plain interesting things to see and do and learn while traveling across Michigan. I want to do more than just suggest some roads that you might enjoy riding or places that you might enjoy visiting. I want to tell you stories about the places you're riding through.

I want your ride to be more than a typical ride—I want to enhance the experience by allowing you to know and appreciate the history and events that shaped the places and roads you're visiting (and trying hard to not sound like your tenth grade history teacher while doing it!). And I want to tell you about the Michigan that most people don't see because they're rushing by the real stories, oblivious to all the interesting things around them.

First, I have to set the stage, so allow me to get off the subject of motorcycles for just a bit.

Michigan Geography

Being surrounded by the Great Lakes obviously gives Michigan a unique geographic fingerprint. Four features underlie who and what we are: water, farms, forests, and urban areas. We have an abundance of each. This book discusses riding opportunities that take advantage of all four of these characteristics.

Michigan isn't uniformly flat like a lot of folks assume. Though parts of it are quite flat, other areas make up for this with hills, giant sand dunes, rock outcroppings, and river valleys that provide very nice relief. To really understand Michigan roads, we have to briefly discuss two important historical events: the last Ice Age and a recommendation by Thomas Jefferson nearly twenty years before he became president. The Ice Age literally formed the Michigan we see today. You are probably assuming that I'm referring to the Great Lakes and the over 3,000 miles of coastline we enjoy, but that's only part of it. From a motorcyclist's perspective, equally important are the 11,000 inland lakes and the 36,350 miles of rivers and streams located across the length and breadth of the state that are the glacier's legacy.

These inland lakes become important because of Jefferson's recommendation that the then unsettled Northwest Territory have a more orderly survey system than what was in place in the original colonies. Instead of the tortuous winding roads and property lines found in New England and much of the east, Jefferson recommended to the early congress that a rectangular survey system based on square miles, rather than the meandering metes and bounds system, be used in the west. It was this decision that resulted in a countryside cut up in the square mile checkerboard fashion that many of us in the Midwest and west are so familiar with. It's also what gives this part of the country a bad rap from a motorcycle touring perspective—after all, who wants to ride roads that are flat and straight as far as the eye can see?

Well, you can relax because that's often not the case. Largely due to the thousands of lakes that cover Michigan, Jefferson's straight roads constantly encountered lakes or large swamps, resulting in curves, of all things! Throw in the thousands of miles of rivers and streams that crisscross the state with their beautiful carved valleys and forested floodplains, and you have even more obstacles in the way of the surveyors' straight road ambitions. Were it not for all these water hazards, our roads would be straight except for correctional jogs made at 24-mile intervals for north-south roads. (Trying to place straight lines on the surface of a spheroid planet that curves to a single point at the North Pole just doesn't work. Roads have to be corrected every so often with a jog so that they maintain straight north-south alignment).

But we have one more pleasant surprise for which we must thank Ice Age glaciers. As the huge ice sheet melted and retreated north it left behind hills! Technically they're called moraines, eskers, drumlins, and kames, but we have them all, and they give our countryside a nice rolling appearance—even downright hilly in some places.

Part of the state, including the Thumb (Lower Michigan looks amazingly like a hand, with the "Thumb" sticking out, well, like a sore thumb, into Lake Huron), the Saginaw area, and the central portion of the state from Lansing north to Clare are largely flat and fertile farmland areas. But even these locales have their charms and many miles of good motorcycling, as you'll see. The western part of the Upper Peninsula has actually been flattened a bit by the glaciers. Very old mountains have been eroding away for millions of years, but these granite mountains, made up of some of the oldest bedrock on earth, are very tenacious and exist yet today to provide beautiful hills of stone and forest.

Michigan—There's No Place Quite Like It

So we've established that Michigan's roads have the requisite curves and hills desirable for enjoyable motorcycling. But wait, there are many other reasons to get off the beaten track and discover all that this state has to offer. Because of our Great Lakes geography, weather, and geology, we have a diverse state that is unlike any other. Our microclimates give us vineyards, orchards, and truck farms that rank among the most productive in the nation. Michigan ranks first in the nation in the production of tart cherries, navy beans, blueberries, pickling cucumbers and black turtle beans. Fremont is the number one producer of canned baby foods, and at the other end of the spectrum, the state ranks first in the production of automobiles and trucks. Michigan is ranked in the top five states in the production of over thirty different types of crops and forestry resources. We are also a leader in pharmaceuticals, chemicals, salt production, limestone, iron ore, and more.[1] We are blessed with more public land than any state east of the Mississippi River, and our state and national parks provide an endless variety of attractions and scenery.

Over two hundred waterfalls grace the state with their beauty, and miles of wilderness roads provide recreational opportunities for millions. There are world-class trout streams and copper mines that have been in use for thousands of years. You'll find towering sand dunes that take your breath away, and a suspension bridge linking the two peninsulas that, even after having ridden across it dozens of times on a motorcycle, I still find to be an awe-inspiring structure and ride.

Two of the oldest permanent cities in the nation are located here, and there are three thousand miles of ocean-like shorelines where you can gaze at horizons of endless sweet water. (The early French explorers called the lakes "sweet water seas"). In fact, our very name is derived from michi-gama, loosely meaning "large lake'" or "great water" in Native American language. Only Alaska has more shoreline.

Michigan's long and fascinating heritage begs rediscovery and exploration. Our 97 state parks, scores of fascinating museums, millions of acres of public land, and more lighthouses than any state in the union are all part of the mix. Add in thousands of miles of winding back roads, and you have the recipe for fantastic motorcycle adventures.

Si Quaeris Peninsulam Amoenam, Circumspice—If You Seek a Pleasant Peninsula, Look About You—the very fitting motto for our state. This motto can actually be applied to more than just the lower and upper peninsulas. Michigan has several smaller peninsulas, ranging from the Woodtick Peninsula in the far southeast corner of the state to the magnificent Keweenaw Peninsula in the northwestern Upper Peninsula.

To make things even more interesting, Michigan is like two states in one. The Lower Peninsula, with its forests and farms, its mighty cities and tall buildings is a world unlike its northern sibling. The marvelous beauty of the coasts and inland hills, cities that put the world on wheels and that a grateful civilization called the

---

[1] Publication of the Michigan Legislature *"Getting To Know Michigan."*

Arsenal of Democracy, and productive farms that cover the countryside are all part of the patchwork that make up the Lower Peninsula.

The Upper Peninsula is Hiawatha Country. It is a land of incredible beauty and amazing history—a land of legend and song. Longfellow's *Song of Hiawatha* is a marvelous retelling of the legends, beliefs, and attitudes of Indians who lived in what are now Michigan and the northern U.S. The poem tells the story of the Indians' love of the land and their everyday closeness to nature. It also does a great job describing the majesty of Gitche Gumee—the great lake we call Superior. The following from Hiawatha's Departure says it better than I ever could:

By the shore of Gitche Gumee,
By the shining Big-Sea Water,
At the doorway of his wigwam,
In the pleasant Summer morning,
Hiawatha stood and waited.
All the air was full of freshness,
All the earth was bright and joyous,
And before him, through sunshine,
Westward toward the neighboring forest
Passing in golden swarms the Ahmo,
Passed the bees, the honey-makers,
Burning, singing in the sunshine.
Bright above him shone the heavens,
Level spread the lake before him;
From its bosom leaped the sturgeon,
Sparkling, flashing in the sunshine;
On its margin the great forest
Stood reflected in the water,
Every tree-top had its shadow,
Motionless beneath the water.
From the brow of Hiawatha
Gone was every trace of sorrow,
As the fog from off the water,
As the mist from off the meadow.
With a smile of joy and triumph,
With a look of exultation,
As of one who in a vision
Sees what is to be, but is not,
Stood and waited Hiawatha.

Of course, all isn't romance and happiness in the story of any region. Lake Superior, the lake of superlatives, is also an unforgiving place that has brought fear to the hearts of mariners over the ages. Whether natives in canoes or huge freighters made of steel, many have learned the hard and cold lessons of Gitche Gumee.

Who hasn't experienced a chill up their spine when listening to Canadian songwriter and singer Gordon Lightfoot's great ballad memorializing the 1975 sinking of the great lakes freighter *The Edmund Fitzgerald* off of Michigan's Whitefish Point?

> *The legend lives on from the Chippewa on down*
> *Of the big lake they call Gitche Gumee.*
> *The lake, it is said, never gives up her dead*
> *When the skies of November turn Gloomy.*
> …
> *In a musty old hall in Detroit they prayed,*
> *In the Maritime Sailors' Cathedral.*
> *The church bell chimed 'til it rang 29 times*
> *For each man on the Edmund Fitzgerald.*
> …

The *Edmund Fitzgerald* was for many years the largest steel-hulled ship on the Great Lakes. It was no match for the fury of a fresh water hurricane, however. Thousands of other ships, large and small, rest eternally beneath the waves of Superior and the other Great Lakes. Most lie anonymously on the bottom, the circumstances of their fate never to be known. But their stories live on in legend and tales told about this marvelous region. The modern saga of the struggle of mariners on these lakes began in 1679 with the ship *Le Griffin*. The *Griffin* was both the first true ship to sail the Great Lakes and in the same year became the first of several thousand to sink beneath the waves of these stormy inland seas.

Though a lifelong resident of Michigan, I've never lived in the Upper Peninsula. I've traveled it very extensively, however, and for years it was the destination of choice for vacations and trips. There is just so much to see and do there! I also hope that this unique part of God's Country is protected forever so that children hundreds of years from now can marvel at its beauty the way I did as a child when I first fell in love with it.

Because of our location at the crossroads of the Great Lakes navigation system, Michigan has had its share of geopolitical intrigue dating back nearly 400 years. What is now Michigan was the site of many battles involving Native American tribes and French and British forces fighting for control of this strategic region during the seventeenth and eighteenth centuries. Much of this history has been nearly forgotten. For instance, how many Michigan residents are aware that in 1712 a major battle between the French and their Indian allies against the Fox Indian tribe (who the French feared were going to ally with the British) was fought on the soil of what is now the posh Grosse Pointes, resulting in over a thousand Fox warriors and their families being killed? Only a lonely historical marker on a busy street commemorates this site near Windmill Pointe.

Indian leaders, such as Chiefs Pontiac and Tecumseh, whose intelligence and competence came to be respected by all sides, moved to the fore in the secondary fight that Native Americans were waging in an attempt to preserve their way of life. The level of political intrigue involved in those days was as sophisticated as anything in today's modern geopolitical arena. Allegiances were formed and battles fought for reasons that were far more complex than the superficial analysis we learned in elementary school.

The French and Indian War of 1754–1763 resulted in France losing much of its North American Empire and Great Britain winning large parts of the North American Continent, including half of present-day Canada. The War of 1812 resulted in the British grip on what is now the remainder of the United States west of the original colonies being largely broken. These two wars were culminations of political strategies and military battles that predate them

In 1774, in what was considered the fifth of the so-called Intolerable or Coercive Acts by the Colonists, Great Britain's parliament in London passed the Quebec Act. Among other things this Act resulted in Great Britain laying claim to what was called Upper Canada and the entire Great Lakes region west to the Mississippi River. Michigan was administered by the British as a part of the Province of Quebec. The Quebec Act of 1774 was the final straw in what our founding fathers considered intolerable grievances committed against the colonists by the King. It resulted in the Declaration of Independence, and as they say, the rest is history.

Interestingly, Great Britain retained control of Michigan and the Great Lakes for over a decade even after losing the American War of Independence. Such was the strategic value of the Great Lakes region well over 200 years ago. Stipulations of the 1783 Treaty of Paris dictated that the Great Lakes region was to be part of the new United States of America. Great Britain, however, maintained military control of the new Territory of Michigan—created by the Northwest Ordinance of 1787—by remaining in Detroit and Fort Mackinac. It wasn't until 1796 that they lowered their flag over Detroit and Colonel John Hamtramck raised the Stars and Stripes in its place. The British reoccupied key forts in Michigan during the War of 1812, but American forces regained control in 1813 and we haven't looked back since.

I find it fascinating that in 1791, when Michigan was legally part of the U.S. but still controlled by the British and administered as part of Canada, Michigan voters elected three Detroit citizens to Ontario's provincial assembly in the first election held in the state.[2]

Like the best movie dramas, Michigan has had its tragic events and major accomplishments. The state has produced people like Henry Ford, Thomas Dewey (of "Dewey Defeats Truman!" fame), Charles Lindberg, William Boeing (Boeing Aircraft Company), Sojourner Truth, General George Custer, Thomas Edison, Chiefs Pontiac and Okemos, and many more men and women who have left their indelible mark not only in this state but on the entire world. You'll please pardon my obvious pride and perhaps even a little bragging, but this is a state that needs to be seen to be appreciated. And, now I'm finally getting to the intent of this book, it has to be seen from back roads and in forgotten small towns to be really understood and enjoyed.

The tours described take you through almost every county in Michigan, missing only two of the state's eighty-three counties. This is a book about exploring the real Michigan from atop a motorcycle on back roads. I think you'll find these trips to be not only great motorcycling adventures but also learning experiences as well, while having a wonderful time motoring down thousands of miles of great biking roads.

Not just any back road, however. For roads to make it into this book as recommended for motorcycle touring, they have to meet several criteria. First, they have to be paved and in reasonably good condition so that a large touring bike or sport bike can navigate the road safely and without difficulty. Second, the road and area has to have some scenic appeal. Traffic on the roads has to be light, and the general touring area must have something to offer in the way of interesting scenery, history, land cover, geologic features, or other attractions. Third, the road has to have some character, that is, curves or hills or other qualities that make it an attractive riding route. Finally, and what may be most important, is that the routes laid out in this book rely heavily on well-maintained grey line roads—county and local roads—with state or federal highways designated only when they are either necessary for a short connector stretch or are truly worthy of a good motorcycle riding label in their own right. Some of the most interesting rides are strictly on county and local roads, staying completely away from main routes.

Over the years, motorcyclists have tried to lay out interesting routes using main highways that appear interesting (curvy) on a map. Most of us would like to avoid busy state or federal highways. I've found commercial county road atlases to

---

[2]*The US50 Encyclopedia, A Guide to the Fifty States.*

be notoriously inaccurate, so I've ridden on the back roads and have knowledge of local lore to keep you off major roads as much as feasible.

Perhaps the most difficult obstacle one encounters when riding long distances on county roads is the fact that road names change as you travel through various local jurisdictions. This makes a written description of a route sound more complicated than it really is. Usually a rider just has to follow the pavement, with an occasional jog when the road crosses township or county lines.

Flat straight stretches of roads in uninteresting areas are kept to a minimum in this book. Occasionally, one has to ride such a road to get from point A to point B, but you'll find that such roads are certainly the exception herein.

On the freeway, we're like so many anonymous strangers in our own little private world, not giving a thought to what were passing by or what's going on around us. Riding in a car with windows up, the air conditioning on, and the stereo system turned up loud heightens this feeling of separation. Motorcyclists, on the other hand, are always aware of the world around them. We can never isolate ourselves from our surroundings nor do we want to; rather, we willingly immerse ourselves in it, which is of course part of the attraction. In fact, the essence of motorcycling not only includes the mechanical aspects—the leans, the power, the acceleration, the feel and sound of the machine, and so on—it involves being part of the environment around us. Motorcyclists want to be part of the real world. We know we will get cold, wet, hot, or whatever the conditions are around us, and that's fine. We accept that because we know that when the riding is good—it's worth the occasional discomfort. And besides, the riding is always good, even when the weather is not. As the old joke goes, you can always tell a happy motorcyclist by the bugs on his or her teeth. Anything that can make one smile so much and to feel that good has to be highly recommended.

I suppose there is also a bit of Kerouac-like romantic and searcher for the meaning of life in most motorcyclists. Being on a motorcycle on this vast continent certainly puts things in perspective for a rider, and there is something about being out there in the wind on two wheels that makes the scale of things more obvious. It helps separate the important from the trivial. Because of fewer distractions, riding affords time for reflection as well as simply losing yourself in the wide-open world. There is certainly no doubt about the fact that you can see and appreciate the world around you much better on two wheels than on four. Most riders just love to be on the road searching for and thinking about life or simply enjoying the ride and discovering what's over the next hill. For some of us non-gifted folks, it's even a chance to sing our favorite songs out loud without offending anyone.

Perhaps there is even a little pride involved in knowing that we can face adversities without quitting. Rain? No problem, stop to put on raingear and keep going.

Or you stop and wait out the storm under an overpass or a pavilion at a local park, sharing stories and small talk with other bikers who have sought similar refuge. It's all part of the experience. If we didn't want to be part of the natural setting we'd drive a four-wheeled cocoon and be comfortable, and disconnected, at all times.

In our modern lives there isn't much mystery or wonderment left. It's pretty much there in our face each day, whether on the TV, radio or Internet, or in newspapers and magazines. The reality of the world assaults us, and we all try to escape in our own way.

I know that, for me, the motorcycle has been a ticket for escape and freedom for decades. I can't describe to a non-enthusiast the visceral level of enjoyment these machines and the wide-open spaces one rides through have brought me. As any citizen of this world must do, I've spent my life working and doing all the things required of a responsible person for the sake of family and community. While some may find a fishing boat, the opera, rock climbing, or the golf course as their means of escape, for me it has been motorcycles. The adventure and happiness I've experienced aboard my faithful horses of steel is immeasurable.

Not all expressways are equally distasteful. I only take urban expressways—I96, I94, and I75 south of Bay City are on my blacklist—when I'm in a hurry and not on a pleasure ride. But I must admit that, even after having ridden US127 and I75 from Clare (actually, James Hill five miles north of Clare, where the North *really* begins) to the Mackinac Bridge many dozens of times, I still find it an enjoyable ride. If you avoid summer weekend rush hour periods (northbound on Friday evenings and southbound on Sunday afternoons), you can kick back, roll on the speed on smooth blacktop, and encounter only light to moderate traffic for the most part while riding through mile after mile of gentle curves, rolling hills and mostly forested landscapes—obviously this isn't your father's urban freeway.

In this book I've also steered you away from congested urban areas whenever it's feasible to do so. Exceptions to this general rule involve historic routes that go through some medium-sized cities or Great Lakes circle tours that take you through some large lakeshore communities.

There are also certain urban areas of this state that everyone ought to go see at least once. Many of these locales have some good motorcycling if you know where to look. These places include the downriver Detroit River area, around Lake St. Clair and the St. Clair River, and Saginaw Bay. There are interesting and scenic things to see, as well as unique historical stories to be told in these locations. The Detroit and St. Clair Rivers have a long and fascinating history and are awe-inspiring to see. Watching the current eddies roiling in these massive bodies of flowing water can't help but give you the feeling that you're looking at something ageless and majestic—not unlike the Mississippi River. Watching ocean freighters plying these waters nearly a thousand miles from the ocean is mind-boggling in itself.

All motorcyclists have some favorite local riding roads they escape to when they have an opportunity to take a quick ride. I've found it more difficult to find those three- or four-hour tours close to home, and one- or two-day rides that aren't part of a longer trip to distant points. With this in mind, I've tried to identify a number of both straight line and circular tours of various lengths but mostly within that three-hour to two-day ride category. I also describe a number of motorcycle tours ranging from two-day to five-day trips for those wanting longer rides. I've laid out a number of round-trip tours so that a rider doesn't just go from point A to point B. Over the years I've noted that many of my rides are "circular" and start and end at a common point—either home, or some other base of operations such as a campsite or motel. With this fact in mind, I lay out circular trips that include scenic and enjoyable roads for the entire distance, ending up back at the beginning without doubling back on the same road.

I will no doubt expose some "secret" riding roads of long-time Michigan residents. Unlike a favorite trout fishing hole, which can in fact be ruined by over-fishing, I don't think having more motorcyclists enjoying our great riding roads will harm the experience or make these roads somehow less enjoyable for current users. It will help the sport in this state and make more folks aware of who we are and just why we love to ride. I've learned about some of my favorite roads by talking with other motorcyclists, often at a gas station or restaurant. I've observed that bikers like to talk about great riding roads that they've discovered, and they are generally more than happy to share that information with others who they know will find similar enjoyment.

In fact, one of the most fascinating side benefits of traveling on a motorcycle is the number of total strangers—people that wouldn't pay you a moment's notice if you were another car driver—who will come over to talk to you about where you're from, where you are heading, how the trip is going, and so on. It's a very interesting statement on how people view us. I'm constantly amazed that folks from young kids to great-grandmothers will go out of their way to talk to bikers at a gas pump or restaurant. I think even those who wouldn't get on a bike on a dare are still fascinated by the sense of adventure that motorcycles, and those crazy enough in their minds to ride them, represents.

I've subdivided the book into five main categories. Rides fall logically into four of these groups by geography. Michigan has unique areas—the north woods, the lakeshores, farmlands, and of course, the Great Lakes themselves. Rides are grouped according to these basic geographic breakdowns. The fifth major category is historic roads. In the same way that so many people are fascinated with

Route 66 and the sense of adventure and freedom of travel that it represented, Michigan also has historic roads that for generations represented that same kind of opportunity to satisfy the wanderlust in millions of folks in the past. These roads have been replaced by expressways and no longer represent the ticket to freedom and adventure that they once did. But they're still there, and they're part of our history both as a state and as a people. I think we ought to rediscover and celebrate them the same way we as a nation celebrate Route 66.

It wasn't easy trying to decide how to divide the various riding roads and regions into categories. A rider in Michigan can just as easily tour on the basis of Great Lakes lighthouses (with 124 of them, we have more than any other state, after all), ghost towns, ethnic lines, historical sites and forts, and so on. But I try to include information on other categories into the groups that I've decided to use so you won't miss out.

In addition, I make several recommendations about places that a resident or visitor really ought to go to and experience. Some of these are off of prime motorcycling routes, so you're not likely to get to them unless you make a special effort. Believe me, it will be worth your trouble. While I was at it, I thought I'd also lay out some great local rides in various parts of the state. These shorter rides are some that you really ought to try if you live nearby or ever happen to be in that area.

Deer and Other Hazards—Watch Out for Them!

While writing about the individual routes, I found myself making several references to safety issues—especially the reality of deer on Michigan roads. Rather than sound like I was repeating myself, I thought I'd just mention it once, so listen up! The summer population of deer in Michigan numbers about 1.7 million animals, and they are located in every county. In 2004 there were nearly 63,000 reported vehicle/deer accidents, according to the State Police. Ride accordingly, especially early in the morning or in the late afternoon. According to State Police records, eighty percent of accidents involving deer occur between dusk and dawn. I try to avoid rural roads after dark, or at least ride very cautiously if I am out. Remember, deer seldom travel alone. If you see one, there are almost certainly other animals nearby. This is especially true with does in the summer. If you see a female deer, chances are very good that there are a couple of fawns hiding within a few yards of mom.

And it's not just deer. There are other large wild critters on the loose, as well as the occasional farm tractor, cow, or other unexpected road travelers. The farming season and motorcycling weather coincide, of course, and that means that farm equipment is going to be using some of the same roads we enjoy riding. If your riding experience is primarily limited to urban areas, this reality could pose a danger if you're not cognizant of it. Also, many areas in the Lower Peninsula have large Amish populations, and they can often be seen on county roads in horse-drawn buggies. Give them a wide berth. Spooked horses are a danger to both the motorcyclist and buggy passengers.

Hmmm, it seems that basic common sense, courtesy and intelligence can make a ride safe and yet exhilarating and enjoyable at the same time. Enjoy the ride, but ride safely so that you'll still be riding many years from now.

You will find that almost all of the rides depicted in this book are great for just kicking back and relaxing. The traffic is lighter than on main roads, and the roads themselves are generally narrower and more interesting. High speed isn't what it's all about on most of these routes.

There may be some hesitancy about riding on what many consider to be back roads for safety reasons, perhaps fearing that one would be stranded should mechanical problems occur. I've found just the opposite. On main roads, many of the other motorists are either out-of-towners themselves who are unlikely to stop and help, or they're local folks going about their busy lives, and they assume that the police will be by to help you out. While there is definitely less of a law enforcement presence on county and local roads, I've found that people who live or travel these roads are much more likely to stop and lend a hand than drivers who travel main roads and expressways.

After over thirty years of hanging around with motorcyclists, I've observed that, as a group, we are far more appreciative of mechanical things than the average person. We care about how things work, about how power is created and transferred through gears and shafts. We appreciate the look of finely crafted parts and the heft of iron and steel much more than we do imagining electrons flowing through silicon computer chips. Because of this kind of mechanical aptitude and appreciation, I will point out events you're likely to be interested in, such as car shows, antique tractor and gas engine shows, railroad museums, steam locomotives, mining, lumbering, aircraft and maritime museums and so on when they are on a particular tour. Any time motorcycle shows or events are pertinent, I'll highlight them, as well.

At the beginning of each riding season, I recommend that you purchase a Michigan State Park entrance sticker for your motorcycle. Many of the most desirable destinations and unique things to see and do are located in State Parks, and therefore protected for future generations to see and appreciate. Whether it is a one-of-a-kind museum, historic villages, ghost towns, lighthouses, unique geologic formations, old forts, or just a good camping spot, during the course of the year you won't want to miss out on the many wonders and opportunities found only in State Parks. Daily or annual permits are available at State Park entry booths, or by mail. Call 517-373-9900 if you wish to conveniently order a yearly sticker by phone and credit card, or go online to the *Michigan Mall* website to order State Park permits or other recreation permits or licenses. Michigan has many dozens of parks, campgrounds and recreation areas, but state parks in particular are very popular, making reservations a must if you wish to camp. You can easily make (or cancel) reservations online at midnrreservations.com.

Every group that shares a common passion, from deer hunting to art collecting, stresses the need to get young people involved. That is no different in motorcycling. There is a bit of built in tension when it comes to our machines, however, because of the very freedom and ability to get away from life's daily issues that they represent. We usually want to escape by ourselves to find that intrinsic freedom that being on the motorcycle brings. I encourage you to make motorcycling more of a family-oriented activity when possible. It can be a wonderful way to connect.

There is one group of citizens, in particular, who I believe can benefit and find great enjoyment in this activity, and that is the handicapped. You might assume that the two are mutually exclusive, but that's just not necessarily true.

Let me relate a personal experience.

I have a son who was born with autism and extreme hyperactivity. From the time he was four or five years old, I would put him on the gas tank in front of me. I know—all the experts recommend against this, but on back roads and very slow speeds it can be safely done. No parent would knowingly expose their child to excessive danger, but taking a youngster for a ride, assuming they have the desire, is a great way to allow them to enjoy the activity and do some bonding at the same time.

My son just loved it. At home or in public, he couldn't sit still for ten seconds and his autism caused him to want to be by himself all the time. But on the motorcycle, he sat motionless for long periods of time, soaking in the world around him and enjoying all the sensations he was experiencing. He quickly graduated to the back of the bike, and to make a long story short, he has traveled many thousands of miles throughout Michigan and adjacent states. He has enjoyed every minute of it, has learned a great deal about the state, and had many memorable experiences as a result of trips we took. The alternative—sitting home and watching television or otherwise idling away his time—was just unacceptable in comparison.

If you have or know of a child who is able to ride and who is willing to give it a try, then provide the opportunity. Don't make the mistake of assuming they can't or that they don't want to—you just might be wrong on both counts.

Before hitting the road, I have just one more suggestion for you back-road wanderers. That is, experience not only the road, scenery and local lore but the other things that make up who and what we are as a state. Food, for instance, is always high on a motorcyclist's list of priorities. I appreciate the convenience of fast food establishments but do try to avoid the universalhomogenizeditalltastesthesamefastfoodhabit and enjoy real food with an ethnic or historic flavor. Whether it's a Cornish pasty in the UP, a fish sandwich in Bay Port, German food in Westphalia or Frankenmuth, Polish food in Bronson or Boyne Falls, ribs in Albion, fresh fish in Naubinway, Italian food in Iron Mountain, potatoes in Munger or Posen, maple syrup in Vermontville, or marsh beef (muskrat) in Monroe, make fun and memorable eating experiences part of your travels. Also indulge yourself with fresh fruit sold from front yard stands and at orchards and fruit farms that dot Michigan's countryside. The only way you can top off such a meal is with hand-made Mackinaw City or Mackinac Island fudge and a glass of award-winning Michigan-made wine from one of our many fine wineries. It just doesn't get any better!

Oh, one final point. I hate to admit it in this book, which after all is dedicated to motorcycle touring, but these tours make great automobile trips as well. Now if I had my way, four-wheeled vehicles would be banned from all the great riding roads identified herein any time the ground wasn't snow-covered. But if you must drive a car or truck these tours can make that burden a little more enjoyable.

Okay, time to do the pre-ride checklist and saddle up! We have some riding to do!

William M. Murphy

Lakeshore Routes

NATURE HAS SMILED bountifully on Michigan, resulting in our being surrounded on almost all sides by water. With the tremendous waterfront scenery we're blessed with, numerous water-related attractions to experience and sites to enjoy, and high quality roads that border our Great Lakes waters, lakeshore routes make for very enjoyable trips no matter what part of the state you're in. I've listed below several great rides that take in shoreline roads and deliver you to places you'll enjoy visiting almost as much as you'll love the ride that got you there.

Summer image of Lake Michigan beach near Leland. (Photo courtesy of Travel Michigan)

Sleeping Bear Dunes and the Leelanau Peninsula

ONE OF THE TRULY GREAT two-day rides in Michigan covers the northwestern portion of the state. This stretch has natural wonders that just won't quit—massive sand dunes and Great Lakes bluffs, horizons that include blue water and islands as far as the eye can see, forests, vineyards and orchards, hills and curves, and much more. The route I've laid out takes advantage of the best roads, while avoiding stretches of popular tourist roads that have become just too crowded and thus less desirable for great motorcycling. Though this route does rely on state highways to a significant degree, they are roads that in their own right deserve to be on any list of great biking roads. Much of this trip is through state and national forests, and the Sleeping Bear Dunes National Lakeshore.

Though this trip is only 210 miles, it qualifies as a two-day trip because there is so much to see and do—especially in the Sleeping Bear Dunes and Leelanau County area. You just can't do it all in one day.

Many guidebooks will recommend a trip along the northwestern coast of Michigan's Lower Peninsula on M22, and rightly so. But the trip can be made even better when one knows when to use M22 and when to avoid it.

We'll start the tour in Manistee, a port city nestled between Manistee Lake on the east and Lake Michigan to the west. The Manistee River—a well-known western Michigan river famous for fishing and canoeing—connects Manistee Lake to Lake Michigan. While you're in Manistee, go to the north end of Manistee Lake to tour the *SS City of Milwaukee,* a rail and passenger ferry that connected rail lines between Michigan and Wisconsin. The ship is a National Historic Landmark and is the last of the traditional rail car ferries, which operated across Lake Michigan from 1892 to 1981. The ship is open for tours from Memorial Day through September. Touring the engine room is especially interesting.

Upon leaving Manistee we won't take the usual US31 to M22 route. Instead, I recommend taking Lake Shore Road, aka M110, through Orchard Beach State Park and then along the Lake Michigan coast to Portage Lake, where it curves east to meet M22. Lake Shore Road is a curvy scenic road that also offers nice lake views. Following M110 around the south shoreline of Portage Lake takes you ultimately

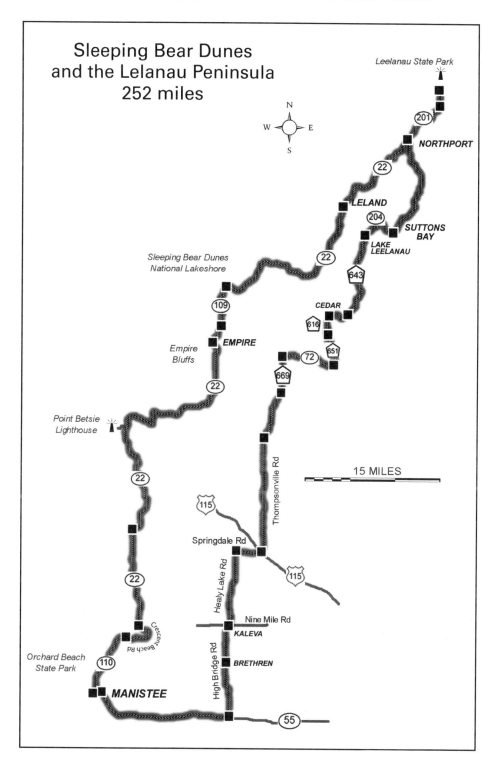

Sleeping Bear Dunes and the Lelanau Peninsula
252 miles

N
W — E
S

Leelanau State Park

201

NORTHPORT

22

LELAND

204

SUTTONS BAY

LAKE LEELANAU

Sleeping Bear Dunes National Lakeshore

22

643

CEDAR

109

616

851

EMPIRE

72

Empire Bluffs

669

22

Point Betsie Lighthouse

22

15 MILES

Thompsonville Rd

115

Springdale Rd

22

115

Healy Lake Rd

Nine Mile Rd

KALEVA

Crescent Beach Rd

Orchard Beach State Park

110

High Bridge Rd

BRETHREN

MANISTEE

55

SLEEPING BEAR DUNES/LEELANAU PENINSULA 220 MILES		
Miles	Destination	Total
0	Manistee	0
11	Onekama	11
24	Elberta	35
25	Empire	60
5	Pierce Stocking Drive	65
16	Leland	81
15	Northport	96
8	Grand Traverse Lighthouse	104
23	Suttons Bay	127
24	M-72	151
29	Thompsonville	180
14	Kaleva	194
12	M-55	206
14	Manistee	220

onto M22 and then through Onekama. The road then curves north over hills and past forests and orchards, never more than a couple of miles from Lake Michigan. Views of the lake shimmering in the distance are common. The road will take you through Elberta and Frankfort and past the Point Betsie Lighthouse, about four miles north of Frankfort. (This lighthouse has been abandoned by the Coast Guard and is currently in limbo. An organization called The Friends of Point Betsie Lighthouse is trying to save the light from further deterioration). This historic light, in service from 1858 to 1996, can be found at the end of Point Betsie Road.

The shoreline bluffs near Frankfort are a favorite gathering place for hanggliders, and throughout the summer you can watch these colorful gliders soaring high above the beach. Just a few miles beyond Point Betsie, M22 enters the marvelous Sleeping Bear Dunes National Lakeshore. Thank you, Senator Phillip Hart, for fighting to preserve this exceptional piece of landscape for all time!

Two miles south of the Leelanau County line and just west of M22 is a ghost town on Otter Creek whose existence is nearly forgotten. Only a local road retains the name of the village of Aral—named by its founders for the Aral Sea in Russia. As with many north woods lumbering towns, part of Aral's history involved violence when a local man killed two deputies trying to arrest him. A confidant was caught and hung from a still-existing pine tree until he agreed to tell local residents where the murderer could be found.[3] Aral also became the home of a religious cult in the early 1900s. The last resident turned out the lights for the final time in 1922.

Route M22 continues its sinuous way north to the town of Empire. Just south of Empire are signs pointing to the Empire Bluffs. This is a short walking trail that leads to breathtaking views of wooded dunes and unsurpassed vistas of Lake Michigan. It's a highly recommended stop and a great place to stretch your legs. At the junction of M72 and M22 in Empire is the Sleeping Bear Dunes National Lakeshore headquarters. You will be glad that you stopped in to learn about the history and geology of the area and to pick up information.

Aerial view of Sleeping Bear Dunes National Lakesore near Empire. (Photo courtesy of Traverse City Convention and Visitors Bureau)

Native Americans created the story of the sleeping bear long ago. As the story goes, a forest fire in Wisconsin caused a mother bear and two cubs to swim across Lake Michigan to safety. The mother made it but the two cubs drowned becoming North and South Manitou Islands, which can be seen in the distance. The mother waited on the beach and is now in the form of the sleeping bear dune itself.

About two miles north of Empire the road forks, with M22 heading easterly and M109 going straight north. I recommend taking M109 (Dune Highway) for a delightful trip through the Lakeshore and to access Pierce Stocking Scenic Drive—a seven-mile long narrow, one-way, paved motorized trail through the dunes. It doesn't have a straight stretch anywhere, and while you can't go fast, the tight curves and hills plus tremendous scenery make for a very pleasant ride. You can also park at several locations for short walks to view the dunes and lake. When you can begin to absorb the true scope of the sand dunes in this area and realize

---

[3]*Ghost Towns of Michigan*, Larry Wakefield, ©1994, Northmont Publishing, Inc.

Lake Michigan beach near Empire. (Photo courtesy of Travel Michigan)

that they exist up and down the east side of Lake Michigan, you begin to appreciate the fact that Michigan contains more freshwater sand dunes than anywhere else in the world.

Heading north on M109 to its northern terminus, turn right and head back to M22 and continue your shoreline journey up the west side of the beautiful Leelanau Peninsula. The Village of Leland is a great spot to stop and walk around. This old commercial fishing base has become touristy, but it's still a pleasant small town with interesting things to see and a nice ambience. It is also a good place for fresh fish meals.

The Leelanau Historical Museum in Leland is an excellent place to learn about the history of this unique area. There was a significant Native American presence on the peninsula when settlers first arrived. Two large Indian cemeteries are known to exist, though they were almost lost to time through lack of attention. One is on the Lake Michigan bluffs north of Leland at a place once called Onominee, and the other is on the east side of the peninsula near the village of Omena. The museum is supporting a project whereby these and other cemeteries are being researched and names preserved.

Continue north on scenic M22 to the town of Northport. In Northport take route 629 north to the Leelanau State Park and Lighthouse Point. The Grand Traverse Light at the tip of the peninsula is definitely worth a stop to see how the families of light keepers lived. Head south from the Point and Northport to Suttons Bay via M22. South of Suttons Bay M22 becomes congested and can be frustrating if you get caught behind slow vehicles. I recommend a better route. In Suttons Bay you'll see M204 heading west. Take this road about five miles west to the small town of Lake Leelanau, located at the north tip of this long and scenic lake of the same name. Route 643 follows the west shore south—this is the road you want. It takes you down the center of the peninsula, with less traffic and much nicer scenery than the southeast coast of Leelanau Peninsula, which is suffering from the creeping cancer of urban sprawl.

Stay on Route 643 as it winds southwest until it ends near the small town of Cedar where you pick up Route 651 that takes you south all the way to M72. Take M72 west about six miles until it makes a ninety-degree turn to the north. At this point there is a road heading straight south—CR669/Maple City Road. Take 669 south and follow it about 40 miles until it hits M55. County Road 669 changes names as it wanders south and a little southwest, becoming Thompsonville Road, Springdale Road, Healy Lake Road, and finally, High Bridge Road/Maple City Road joins US31 westbound for a quarter-mile jog before heading south on Thompson-ville Road. Just south of its intersection with M115 Thompsonville Road makes a turn to the west on Springdale Road, and goes west three miles before turn-ing south again as Healy Lake Road. When Healy Lake Road enters Kaleva you need to jog to the west a half-mile on Nine Mile Road, the main east-west road through town, and continue south again on High Bridge Road. Before leaving Kaleva, however, stop at the famous Bottle House, a house built many decades ago out of 60,000 glass bottles obtained from a local bottling factory. The building now houses the Kaleva Historical Museum, and is located at 14551 Wuoksi Street. Kaleva is an interesting small town with a very strong Finnish ethnic background. The name is derived from The Kalevala, the national epic poem of Finland.[4]

Continuing south on High Bridge Road takes you to the crossroads village of Brethren, and then over the famous Manistee River just north of M55. High Bridge Road derived its name from an 80-foot high wooden railroad bridge that once crossed the river near this point. It has since been replaced with a steel bridge. The Manistee was a famous lumbering waterway from about middle 1840 to 1920, huge rafts of logs were floated down the river, and dozens of sawmills once lined its banks. The Manistee River is fed by many springs and is less prone to freezing over in the winter than other rivers. As a result, logging could be done year-round. All that lumbering activity, forest fires, and streamside development badly damaged the river, and in the early part of the 1900s, it was only a sad shadow of its former majestic state. Largely restored, today it is a highly-prized recreational river, used by fly fishermen, canoeists, and others for outdoor recreation. Being located in the Huron-Manistee National Forest and classi-fied as a Wild and Scenic River by the federal government, the Manistee now enjoys protection from excess development and degradation. Once you reach M55, head west about fifteen miles—a very nice riding road through this stretch—back to the city of Manistee. The final couple hours of this trip are through beautiful forested and hilly countryside, making for a truly enjoyable and relaxing ride.

---

[4] *The History of Kaleva*, by Esther Haksluoto Puustinen, May 1997.

St. Clair River and the Thumb

THE THUMB AREA and that part of the state northeast of Detroit are often overlooked. Even the term "the Thumb" is a local colloquialism that brings blank stares when used in conversation with someone who doesn't live in Michigan. But Michiganders refer to "the Thumb" with the same assumptions of knowledge that people in Massachusetts refer to "the Cape" or San Franciscans talk about "the Bay." This part of Michigan, known as the Blue Water Area, has its unique charms and stories to tell, as well as nice riding roads and interesting places to explore and much greater maritime influence than what is generally attributed to it. It just isn't possible for anyone to ride along the St. Clair River and not be impressed with its power and size. Looking out over Lake Huron, which surrounds the Thumb on all sides, is awe-inspiring and makes one feel quite small. Not all attractions are along the coast either. The interior of the Thumb has country roads with very light traffic.

This corner of the state also has a great deal of history and attractions, from the world's largest freshwater delta at the mouth of the St. Clair River in the south, Indian petroglyphs near Bad Axe, to Grindstone City at the tip of the Thumb. There are stories to tell about this area that are almost forgotten in our modern lives—historic Fort Gratiot near Port Huron, manufacturing of grindstones at the tip, the impact of Great Lakes and ocean-going freighters on the area, major forest fires that swept from coast to coast in the Thumb, killing and destroying hundreds of lives in their paths—these are just a few of the historical events that should not be forgotten.

The journey begins in Algonac, the city that bills itself as the Venice of the Great Lakes, and with good reason. Located on the St. Clair River mouth, Algonac has a nautical theme. Boats of all sizes, from small fishing craft to Great Lakes freighters, are a major part of life in this town. Watching boats and ships from the half-mile-long river walk is a favorite activity. This was the home of the famous Chris Craft boat company and an annual boat parade takes place each summer. A large classic car show also occurs each August at nearby Algonac State Park. The nearby St. Clair Flats Wildlife Area is a world-renowned waterfowl nesting and staging area, and Lake St. Clair is one of the most productive fishing waters anywhere. Algonac was first settled in 1805 and derives its name from the Algonquin Indian tribe that lived in the area.

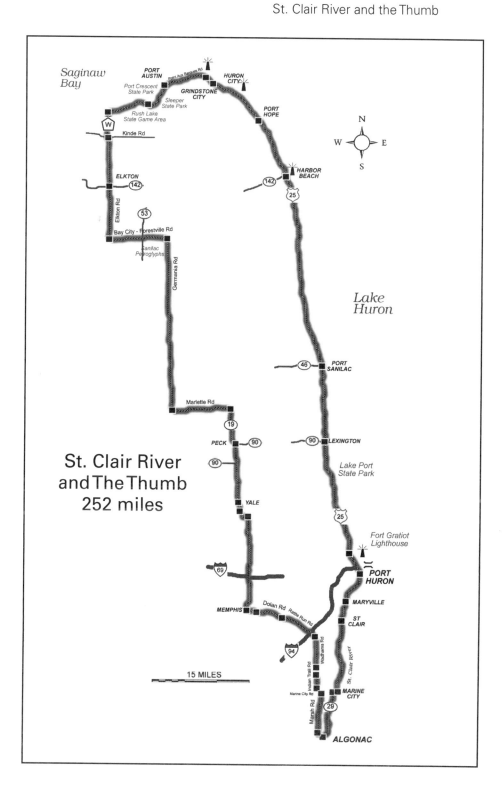

Saginaw Bay

PORT AUSTIN
Port Crescent State Park
Port Aux Barques Rd
GRINDSTONE CITY
Sleeper State Park
Rush Lake State Game Area
HURON CITY
PORT HOPE
Kinde Rd

W

ELKTON
142
Elkton Rd
53
Bay City - Forestville Rd
Sanilac Petroglyphs
Germania Rd

HARBOR BEACH
142
25

N
W E
S

Lake Huron

46 PORT SANILAC

Marlette Rd
19
PECK 90
90
90 LEXINGTON

St. Clair River and The Thumb 252 miles

YALE

Lake Port State Park

25

Fort Gratiot Lighthouse

69

MEMPHIS Dolan Rd Rattle Run Rd

PORT HURON
MARYVILLE
ST CLAIR

94

Marine City Indian Trail Rd
Wadhams Rd
St. Clair River

Marsh Rd
29
MARINE CITY

15 MILES

ALGONAC

ST. CLAIR RIVER & THE THUMB 252 MILES		
Miles	Destination	Total
0	Algonac	0
29	Port Huron	29
4	Fort Gratiot Lighthouse	33
16	Lexington	49
40	Harbor Beach	89
19	Grindstone City	108
20	State Park Road	128
31	Petroglyphs	159
64	Memphis	223
29	Algonac	252

We start our journey by going north on M29 along the St. Clair River. M29 is joined by M25 just south of Port Huron, and we'll then stay on M25 all the way to Sleeper State Park, located west of Port Austin at the tip of the Thumb. It's impossible to get lost—just keep the water on your right.

Just north of Algonac, pass through Algonac State Park with its 1,400 acres of floodplain and lake prairie. M29 passes through the towns of Marine City, St. Clair and Marysville before entering Port Huron, the largest city on the tour. All of these cities are great places to stop and enjoy the river and do some ship watching. Seeing freighters up to 1,100 feet in length plying the river just a couple hundred yards away is a tremendous sight. St. Clair boasts the world's longest freshwater boardwalk and is a great spot to relax and watch the river.

About three miles north of the town of St. Clair M29 veers inland for a three-mile stretch, and River Road cuts off to the right and follows the river shoreline. I recommend taking River Road as it's more scenic and has less traffic. River Road rejoins M29 three miles up the road, so if you miss the cutoff, no problem. Less than a mile north of the point where River Road and M29 rejoin, M25 joins in, and the road will be marked M25 from that point north.

This part of Michigan's time line extends farther back than most other parts of the state. Not counting the early fur traders and French voyageurs, the first permanent settlers came here around 1780—close to fifty years before the inland portion of the state was settled, which followed completion of the Erie Canal in

1825. The strategic importance of the Great Lakes and connecting rivers, such as the St. Clair and Detroit was recognized by French and British monarchs in Europe long before they were thought of by early Americans as American assets.

Located at the lower end of Lake Huron at the beginning of the St. Clair River, the City of Port Huron is the largest on the tour and is a strategic player in international business with the Blue Water Bridge and railroad tunnels that connect Michigan and Canada located there. Port Huron was the boyhood home of Thomas Edison and the city celebrates this fact. The Thomas Edison Depot Museum, located on the south side of the Blue Water Bridge, houses many Edison exhibits as well as being an historic railroad depot. The Port Huron to Mackinac Sailboat Race—the largest freshwater sailing event in the world—is a weeklong event held each July that's been going on for over eighty years. Sailors from around the world come to compete in this very prestigious race.

Fort Gratiot, just north of Port Huron, was built in 1814 following the War of 1812 in recognition of the strategic importance of the waterway, and to serve the increasing marine commerce on the Great Lakes. The Fort Gratiot Lighthouse, the oldest surviving lighthouse in Michigan, had its origins in 1825, making it the first lighthouse to be built in Michigan. The original lighthouse was destroyed in a storm just three years later, and the current one replaced it in 1829. The Fort Gra-

tiot Lighthouse is located off M25 on Garfield Street at the Coast Guard base just north of Port Huron. Tours can be arranged by calling 810-984-2603. A fun diversion in Port Huron and a way to really take in the nautical theme of this area is to take a cruise on the Huron Lady II, a sightseeing boat that sails lower Lake Huron and the upper St. Clair River. Call 888-873-6726 or go to huronlady.com for information and reservations.

State route M25 hugs the shoreline providing mile after mile of scenic vistas as you ride north. There are a number of local parks along the route that provide access to the lake. Three state parks on this ride also provide large blocks of public land, campsites and beach access. Lake-

View of the Fort Gratiot Lighthouse near Port Huron. (Photo by Vito Palmisano)

Enjoying the beach on Lake Huron. (Photo by Thomas A. Schneider)

port State Park is less than 10 miles north of Port Huron, and Port Crescent and Sleeper State Parks are located at the tip of the Thumb. All three are popular, so advanced camping reservations are recommended.

The village of Lexington, with its 116-year-old general store, is a picturesque small town on the lake, as is Port Sanilac, 10 miles north. Port Sanilac is a good spot to do a little walking around to view the historic lighthouse and explore the Sanilac County Museum and Historical Village.

Mile after mile, M25's smooth pavement slips under you, seldom without a view of the lake. Unlike the Lake Michigan coast, the Lake Huron coast in the Thumb is less developed and makes for a very enjoyable ride. After Port Sanilac, the next town of any size is Harbor Beach, many miles north. It seems every place has some claim to fame, and Harbor Beach's place in the record book is for the world's largest man-made freshwater harbor. There is also a nineteenth century lighthouse that is worth a stop to see.

Seven miles north of Harbor Beach is Port Hope, named in 1857 by two men who landed here after drifting in a boat. It became a lumber town shortly thereafter and the large Stafford and Haywood Sawmill was constructed in 1858. After fire destroyed the sawmill all that remained was the eighty-foot tall chimney, still in excellent condition, in Stafford Park. The chimney is now a National Historical site. Like dozens of Michigan lumber towns, the population of Port Hope grew rapidly in the late nineteenth century, only to collapse after the surrounding forests had been cut over.

Leaving Port Hope, M25 turns northwest and then west to the tip of the Thumb. The small town of Huron City is the next stop, with its museums and the Pointe Aux Barques Light. The museums and historical sites are definitely worthy of some of your time. A large portion of Huron City is a designated historical district. While the Pointe Aux Barques Lighthouse isn't normally open to the public for climbing, it is located in a county park and thus accessible for viewing. There is also a shipwreck museum in the park with artifacts, pictures, and interesting information on the shipping history of this area.

A short trip up the road from Huron City is Grindstone City, a small village that was once renowned for producing some of the finest grindstones in the world. Just prior to entering Grindstone City we leave M25 for a few miles and take the shoreline road. From M25 turn onto Old Lakeshore Road for a short distance, and then onto Bluff Road. Bluff Road will take you to Pointe Aux Barques Road, which you'll stay on as you travel west through the Grindstone City area. It rejoins M25 a short distance west in Port Austin.

Shortly after rejoining M25 in Port Austin the road starts its turn to the southwest on the west side of the Thumb. If you wanted to make this a two-day trip, the Garfield Inn Bed & Breakfast in Port Austin provides historic and luxurious accommodations. The

Fires leave mark on the Thumb

The Thumb has two stories to tell that involve forest fires that burned literally from coast to coast in 1871 and ten years later in 1881. The 1871 fire killed huge numbers of trees in the unbroken forest that still covered the Thumb, and in the ensuing decade they fell to the ground littering it with fuel for the next fire. Land clearing by early farmers added to the accumulation of forest debris and fuel for the next inevitable fire.

Try to imagine an area extending roughly from Bay City south to Flint, then east to Port Huron and almost everything north and east of those lines burning—that's what happened in 1881. In that fire well over one million acres burned and at least 282 people were killed.[5] Entire towns and villages, including many on this trip, literally disappeared off the face of the earth. People survived only by jumping into lakes or rivers, or by wading far out into Lake Huron itself. Falling cinders caused ships on the lake to catch fire and two ships collided in the zero visibility caused by the dense smoke forty miles off-shore. By the turn of the twentieth century the forests had been cut, the land cleared for agriculture, and the fire danger in the Thumb subsided.

For anyone interested in a chapter of Michigan's history that is nearly forgotten—the period from 1870 to 1920 when forest fires repeatedly raged across the state—I highly recommend reading *Michigan on Fire* by Betty Sodders, published by Thunder Bay Press. It provides a chilling yet fascinating account of disastrous major forest fires and their human toll.

---

[5] *Michigan on Fire*, Betty Sodders © 1997 Thunder Bay Press.

Sandstone formation shapes city's history

In the 1830s early explorers discovered that the Marshall Sandstone formation surfaced at the tip of the Thumb. Marshall Sandstone at this location is of an exceptionally high quality, which makes superior sharpening and grinding stones. For nearly one hundred years Grindstone City was synonymous with high quality grinding stones that were shipped around the world. The demand for the stones ended in 1929 when artificial sharpening materials were produced. During the heyday of Grindstone City, everything from small whetstones for sharpening knives to massive grinding stones weighing thousands of pounds were produced. Some remnants of these large circular grindstones still litter the ground at Grindstone City.

"Garfield" in Garfield Inn is from President Garfield, a frequent guest at this former luxurious home that dates from the 1830s.

West of Port Austin you'll go through about eight miles of mostly public lands, part of Sleeper State Park, Port Crescent State Park, and Rush Lake State Game Area. About fifteen miles southwest of Port Austin, turn south on State Park Road. After three and a half miles, the pavement ends, you will turn east (left) on Kinde Road, taking it one mile to Elkton Road. Turn south and follow Elkton Roat a total of nineteen miles to Bay City/Forestville Road. Turn east and ride for eight miles to Germania Road, then turn south again.

Very soon after turning south, you will come to Sanilac Petroglyphs Historic Site, the only known pre-Columbian Native American rock carving site in Michigan. Various pictures of animals and an Indian archer are carved into the sandstone at this site. The exact age of the petroglyphs isn't known but they are believed to be up to 1000 years old. Ironically, it was the massive 1881 forest fire, which burned off the humus and vegetation that had long hidden the petroglyphs, that enabled them to be found. There are interpreters on duty, or you can take a self-guided walking trail through the area.

Much of the second half of this trip, from Port Austin back to Algonac, is on country roads that are great places to just unwind. They are relaxing to ride, the air is clean and invigorating, and traffic is light.

Upon leaving the petroglyphs just keep heading south for twenty-two miles, at which point Germania Road will "T" at Marlette Road. Turn east on Marlette Road to M19 and turn south. Follow M19 as it goes through farm country and through the small towns of Peck, Yale, and finally Memphis, where we leave it. In Memphis turn east on Bordman Road, the main east-west road in town. Take Bordman two miles east, jog south a half mile, and then continue east on Dolan Road. Dolan Road turns into Rattle Run Road, which meanders southeast for the next nine miles to Wadhams Road. In this stretch of Rattle Run, you will cross Gratiot Avenue/M25 and I94, at which time you can consider how lucky you are

Lake Huron beach near Port Austin in Michigan's Thumb. (Photo courtesy of Travel Michigan)

compared to the people trapped in their cars on these two busy highways. About one mile beyond I94 on Rattle Run you'll intersect with Wadhams Road. Take Wadhams Road south (it becomes Indian Trail after crossing over the Belle River) about seven miles to Marine City Road. Turn east (left) on Marine City Road and take it less than one mile to Marsh Road. Turn south onto Marsh Road and follow it all the way back to Algonac.

This trip is slightly over 250 miles, more than half of which is along the waterfront. It can of course be done in one day, however, it makes a great two-day trip, with an overnight camping or motel stop near the tip of the Thumb. Two days affords time to enjoy the many things there are to see and do in this sometimes overlooked, yet very interesting and scenic, part of the state. There are many fine beaches at the tip of the Thumb that provide excellent opportunities to swim or just nap in the sun.

Whites and Reds (Wines and Tulips)

THE SOUTHWEST COAST of Michigan has many small communities that began as resort areas and due to its geographic location and has different influences and allegiances than other parts of the state. Residents gravitate toward Chicago as their large city of choice rather than Detroit. Many root for the Cubs or Sox, rather than the Tigers. There is a great influence from out-of-state folks since it is used as a resort area by vacationers from Chicago.

It is still an area of mostly small towns until you reach the Muskegon area. It is also a land of agricultural specialties—from fruit to flowers and asparagus to wine.

Fortunately it is also an area with scenic vistas—many parks, both large and small, providing access to the lake and protecting unique lands and features—and wonderful coastal roads that never roam too far from the water. This stretch of coast deserves a ride of its own.

Here's a very nice one-day trip along the southwest coast of Michigan. The two main roads used for this trip are both designated as military-recognition roads (Blue Star Highway and the Red Arrow Highway). More about that later.

We'll start this trip at the border crossing town of Michiana, in a corner of the state that bills itself as the Harbor Country, taking US12, used for hundreds of years by travelers just like you, north to New Buffalo. Michiana started life purely as a resort community for those able to afford second homes in the early twentieth century. Its most notable historic feature centered around the Old Indian Signal Oak, a tree used by surveyors long ago to mark the border of Michigan and Indiana and to use as a reference point. The tree was part of community life for many years.

Just north of Michiana is the New Buffalo Railroad Museum—a fun place to look at railroading artifacts if you're a railroad buff. Near Michiana was also the site of the country's first highway travel information center. Obviously the idea took hold.

Just beyond New Buffalo, we'll leave US12 and go north on the Red Arrow Highway. This highway is named in honor of the Army's Red Arrow Division. Just about one mile north of US12, if you wish, you can leave Red Arrow Road and follow Lake Shore Road for about three miles as it parallels Red Arrow very close to the water's edge. It rejoins Red Arrow three miles up the coast.

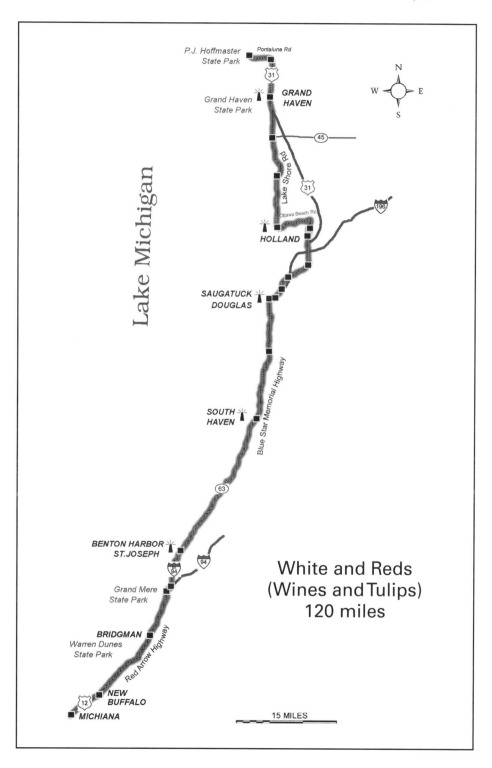

P.J. Hoffmaster State Park
Pontaluna Rd
31
GRAND HAVEN
Grand Haven State Park
45
Lake Shore Rd
31
196
Ottawa Beach Rd
HOLLAND
SAUGATUCK DOUGLAS
Blue Star Memorial Highway
SOUTH HAVEN
Lake Michigan
63
BENTON HARBOR ST.JOSEPH
94
94
Grand Mere State Park
BRIDGMAN
Warren Dunes State Park
Red Arrow Highway
NEW BUFFALO
12
MICHIANA

White and Reds
(Wines and Tulips)
120 miles

N
W E
S

15 MILES

WHITES AND REDS (WINES AND TULIPS) 120 MILES		
Miles	**Destination**	**Total**
0	Michiana	0
16	Warren Dunes State Park	16
7	Grand Mere State Park	23
33	South Haven	56
20	Saugatuck	76
12	Holland	88
25	Grand Haven	113
8	Hoffmaster State Park	121

Just south of the town of Bridgman you will encounter Warren Dunes State Park. This 2,000-acre park has a tremendous beach and is noted for its sand dunes, the highest of which rises 240 feet. This park is a favorite destination for many people in this part of the country, so if you wish to camp make a reservation utilizing Michigan's state park reservation system.

Just up the road Grand Mere State Park offers a very different opportunity to enjoy Lake Michigan and its shoreline ecology. Grand Mere is a mostly undeveloped park nearly 1,000 acres in size that is geared more toward exploration and nature study. Its relative feeling of solitude can be a nice change from the heavy concentration of users at nearby Warren Dunes Park.

Just north of Bridgman on Red Arrow Highway is the Cook Nuclear Power Plant. In saner, more normal days a tour of this plant provided a fascinating view of nuclear power generation. Unfortunately, terrorism threats have caused the plant to greatly limit access for obvious reasons.

At Bridgman, Red Arrow Highway crosses Interstate 94 and moves about a mile inland, remaining there for seven miles. On the north side of Stevensville, Red Arrow Highway crosses back to the west side of I94 and becomes BR94 leading you through the town of St. Joseph. In St. Joseph we say adieu to Red Arrow Highway and BR94 as they veer off to the northeast heading inland, while the pavement we're on continues north, unbroken now as M63, which we'll follow for roughly nine miles. At that point M63 ends and the Blue Star Highway begins. Though it's on the same alignment and no turns are necessary, the Blue Star has a distinctly different look. It is narrower and in general looks, and is, more interesting than M63. Just north of the point where Blue Star Highway begins is a small roadside park on the

Lake Michigan shore. It's a nice spot for a walk down the dune to the beach and for views of the lake.

Continue following Blue Star Highway north into the resort town of South Haven. There are many tourist-related activities in South Haven, from great beaches and parks to small shops and restaurants. If you have any interest in maritime matters visit the Michigan Maritime Museum located on the Black River in downtown South Haven. It has five buildings and several outdoor attractions, including old boats. Call 800-747-3810 or go to michiganmaritimemuseum.org for more information.

Origins of Blue Star highway designation

The designation of being a Blue Star Highway had its origins in 1944 when a New Jersey Garden Club wanted to honor the military. The idea of calling a highway a Blue Star Highway took off and now includes many roads in the nation. The National Garden Clubs, Inc. is the sponsoring organization, along with state and federal transportation agencies. During World War II, families who had members serving in the war flew a service flag that had a blue star in the center.

The Blue Star Highway goes straight north through South Haven and continues north of town for almost exactly nine miles, at which point it veers northeast. You'll see 70th Avenue heading straight north ahead of you, so leave Blue Star and continue north on 70th Avenue. Follow 70th Avenue north about eight

Tall ships in South Haven Harbor. (Photo by Vita Palmisano)

Spring at Holland's DeZwaan Windmill. (Photo courtesy of Travel Michigan)

miles to the intersection with 130th Street where a right (east) turn will take you back to Blue Star Highway, which by then has curved back to the coast in the town of Douglas. Turn north onto Blue Star Highway following it across the Kalamazoo Lake causeway into the neighboring community of Saugatuck. This is a very nice resort area with great beaches and access to the lake. Take a ride on the Star of Saugatuck paddlewheel boat. The boat operates on the Kalamazoo River and offers spectacular sunset cruises on Lake Michigan in the evening. It is located at 716 Water Street, 269-857-4261.

A tour of the *SS Keweetin,* which has been converted to a maritime museum, is a great way to see first hand the workings of the last floating Great Lakes passenger steamship. It traversed the upper lakes from 1908 to 1965 before being retired and converted to a museum. It's right alongside Blue Star Highway, so you can't miss it. Call 269-857-2464 for more information.

Continue north on the Blue Star Highway all the way to Holland. When you cross the US31 expressway BSH becomes Michigan Street, then River Street in Holland and crosses the Macatawa River.

Holland, as the name suggests, is a pocket of Dutch culture in Michigan. The town celebrates its Dutch heritage in several ways, including the Dutch Village Theme Park. The village has many attractions and gardens, including an authentic Dutch windmill brought over and reassembled in the park. The windmill, called DeZwaan, is an impressive site. It is twelve stories high, and is more than 230 years old. The park is located at US31 and James Street. Call 616-396-1475 or go to dutchvillage.com for more information. Holland is also famous for its Tulip Festival each May.

After crossing the river turn left on the second street (Douglas Street) and follow it west along the north shore of Lake Macatawa. It becomes Ottawa Beach Road, and when you get to the big lake, it swings north as Lakeshore Road. You just continue north on Lakeshore Road all the way into Grand Haven. Grand Haven is where the Grand River—Michigan's longest river and largest

Pere Marquette train engine 1223 that operated the Chicago-Grand Rapids-Detroit line during the 1940s. Located in downtown Grand Haven. For more information, contact the Tri-Cities Historical Museum at 616-842-0700

watershed—empties into Lake Michigan. There are two very nice state parks near here. Grand Haven State Park located on Lake Michigan south of the river mouth, and P.J. Hoffmaster State Park located north of town on the big lake. Hoffmaster Park in particular is a very nice place to enjoy the beach and to explore the natural beauty of the freshwater dunes environment. There are several walking trails through the 1,130 acres of forested sand dunes and an impressive visitor center with displays that tell the story of these unique dunes. Grand Haven State Park is smaller and consists primarily of lakeshore beach opportunities. Both are very popular, and if you wish to camp at either be sure to make reservations well ahead.

Downtown Grand Haven is host to what for decades was the world's largest musical fountain (apparently a new musical fountain in Las Vegas is now the world's largest). This fantastic display synchronizes music, light displays and water fountains in a beautiful spectacle that can be enjoyed at dusk each evening from Memorial Day through Labor Day. The Fourth of July show and fireworks is especially impressive. It's located downtown on the river at Harbor and Washington Avenues, west of US31.

In Grand Haven, Lakeshore Road becomes Sheldon Street. Anywhere along here you can go east a few blocks to get on US31. This is necessary in order to get across the Grand River. On the north side of the expressway, US31 becomes an expressway. Good lakeside roads that continue uninterrupted in this vicinity are rare, so it's best to take the expressway north a little less than five miles to Pontaluna Road where we'll exit and head west toward Hoffmaster State Park and the Gillette Sand Dunes Visitor Center, which marks the end of this 120-mile trip along Michigan's southwest coast.

Au Gres to the Straits

This 180-mile northeast coastal trip starts in the town of Au Gres located on the river of the same name and a couple of miles inland from Lake Huron's Saginaw Bay. As you might guess, Au Gres derived its name from early French explorers who described "gritty stones" in the area. Thus the French name of Au Gres. Today Au Gres is much more famous for fishing than the condition of its beach stones, and is billed as the Perch Capital of Michigan.

It will be impossible to get lost or even the slightest bit confused on this trip. Just stay on US23. There are no better coastal roads in northeast Michigan, so this is one instance where the state highway also happens to be the best choice.

Au Gres is a tourist town primarily. Its location provides many opportunities for recreation, including charter boats on the big water for fishing, golf courses, canoe rental on the river, and several small parks and campgrounds nearby. It has a large marina at the river mouth and is definitely a water-oriented recreational town.

East of Au Gres, US23 starts its northward journey, and the next point of interest is the village of Alabaster. A historical marker in Alabaster tells the story of

Tawas Point Lighthouse near Tawas City. (Photo courtesy of Michigan Department of Natural Resources)

what put this town on the map—gypsum. The U.S. Gypsum Company has mined gypsum here for well over a century (it was first discovered in 1837, and mining began in 1862). The large quarry located nearby is responsible for Michigan leading the nation in gypsum production, which today is used primarily in drywall.

Heading north a short distance takes us to the twin cities of Tawas City and East Tawas. This locale is also a nautically-based recreation area. Tawas Point State Park, Tawas Point Lighthouse and inviting beaches draw many vacationers to the area. Nearby inland lakes and the Huron National Forest also attract outdoor

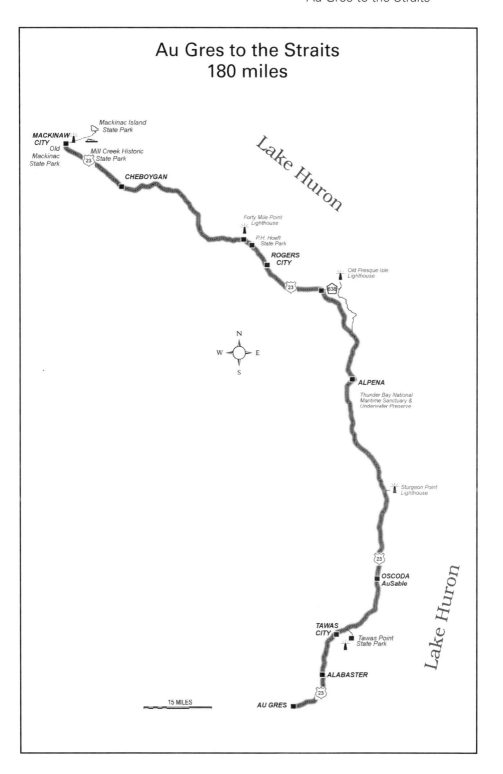

Au Gres to the Straits
180 miles

Mackinac Island
State Park

MACKINAW CITY

Old Mackinac
State Park

Mill Creek Historic
State Park

CHEBOYGAN

Forty Mile Point
Lighthouse

P.H. Hoeft
State Park

ROGERS CITY

Old Presque Isle
Lighthouse

Lake Huron

N
W   E
S

ALPENA

Thunder Bay National
Maritime Sanctuary &
Underwater Preserve

Sturgeon Point
Lighthouse

OSCODA AuSable

TAWAS CITY

Tawas Point
State Park

ALABASTER

Lake Huron

15 MILES

AU GRES

AU GRES TO THE STRAITS 180 MILES		
Miles	**Destination**	**Total**
0	Au Gres	0
14	Alabaster	14
7	Tawas City	21
33	Harrisville	54
32	Alpena	86
37	Rogers City	123
8	40 Mile Point Lighthouse	131
34	Cheboygan	165
15	Mackinaw City	180

recreationalists, ranging from snowmobilers to deer hunters. The Iosco County Historical Museum on West Bay Street in East Tawas tells the story of this area during its lumbering and railroad heydays of the last century and a half.

Fall view of Sturgeon Point Lighthouse near Harrisville during fall. (Photo by Vito Palmisano)

Heading farther north up the coast brings us to the small resort towns of Au Sable and Oscoda, located on opposite sides of the Au Sable River's mouth. Both towns have their roots in the lumbering era, as does much of northern Michigan. The Au Sable River and Lake Huron are both famous for high quality fishing opportunities. Fishing guides and charters are available on either the river or the Lake. The River Road begins in Oscoda and runs along the south shore of the Au Sable west for about 20 miles. It is a designated scenic drive that is a very worthwhile detour on this trip.

North of Oscoda, US23 becomes prettier and less developed. For the next hour you'll pass through some small towns, all pretty much dependent on tourism and Lake Huron for their source of revenue. North of Harrisville is Sturgeon Point Lighthouse.

The only large city on this tour is Alpena, a community of about 11,000 residents located on Thunder Bay, an hour north of Oscoda (see sidebar).

Heading north on US23 out of Alpena takes you through what I consider to be the prettiest stretch of the road, with its sweeping curves and forested hills. Though it is inland a couple of miles you are still treated to beautiful lake views because the road runs along the west shoreline of Grand Lake, a long narrow lake located midway between Alpena and Rogers City.

If you wish to take a different route at this point, take a county road that runs up the east shore of Grand Lake and close to the Lake Huron. Leaving US23 about twelve miles north of Alpena, Rayburn Highway goes east along the south shore of Grand Lake to Grand Lake Road, which in turn runs north on the narrow strip of land between Lake Huron and Grand Lake. The road

Alpena has much to offer tourists

Alpena is a small industrial town. It started out in lumber, but because of huge limestone deposits at the surface, it quickly became a major cement production center, continuing to this day. Several very large limestone quarries are located nearby.

In addition to the usual maritime activities that can be found up and down this coast, Alpena offers something new. It is home base for the Thunder Bay National Marine Sanctuary and Underwater Preserve, a 448-square-mile area of shipwrecks protected from being disturbed but open for viewing by divers. Alpena has at least three different companies that cater to divers and tours of the Preserve.

There are also many historic lighthouses in the northeast coastal area. Early each October, Alpena hosts the Great Lakes Lighthouse Festival. Call the Lighthouse museum at 989-595-3632 for additional information. Alpena is also home of the Jesse Besser Museum—a marvelous collection of attractions that includes a planetarium, a museum with many exhibits ranging from local history to worldwide issues, and a historic village with buildings from bygone days. It is located on Johnson Street in town, and can be reached at 989-356-2202 or bessermuseum.org for more details.

then returns to US23 on the north side of Grand Lake as Highway 638. This scenic and lightly traveled alternative also allows you to stop at the historic Presque Isle Lighthouse. Go ahead and climb the 138 spiraling steps to the top of Lake Huron's tallest lighthouse and earn the reward of a tremendous view.

Heading north from the Grand Lake area, our next stop will be Rogers City—the Nautical City. Take time to wander the waterfront and marvel at the collection of large boats moored there. Rogers City is home to the world's largest limestone quarry, which is near town.

Continuing north from Rogers City, the highway hugs the coastline. Just north of town is Hoeft State Park, which has very nice campground and beach facilities.

Summer view of Mackinac Bridge linking Lower and Upper Peninsula's of Michigan. (Photo courtesy of Travel Michigan)

Farther up the coast a bit is Forty Mile Point Lighthouse—another historic structure that can be easily accessed.

It's pretty much open road and Lake Huron vistas for many miles until we get to the city of Cheboygan, situated at the mouth of the Cheboygan River on the shore of Lake Huron. Like other cities on the northeast coast, it has a very nautical theme. In addition to Lake Huron attractions, the Cheboygan River is the eastern terminus of the Inland Waterway, a series of lakes and streams that cuts a 40-mile channel across the northern tip of Lower Michigan. A series of locks controls water levels and allows passage for pleasure boats from Lake Huron to Lake Michigan.

It's a mere fifteen miles from Cheboygan to Mackinaw City and the end of this tour. About midway between these cities is Mill Creek Historic State Park. This is a fascinating stop where you can view an operating water-powered sawmill that was first used in the 1790s. A collection of historic buildings and artifacts makes this park unique. It's a highly recommended stop.

Mackinaw City is the end of our trip. There is so much to do in this small town that I can't begin to list all the attractions here. Certainly a trip over to Mackinac Island should be high on the priority list. Mackinac Island is largely a state park, and there are no motor vehicles allowed on the island. You get around by walking, riding bicycles or by horse-dawn carriage. Historic Fort Mackinac on the island

View of Fort Mich-
ilimackinac and
Mackinac Bridge
in Mackinaw City.
(Photo by Vito
Palmisano)

is a very interesting stop, and bicycle trips around the eight-mile perimeter of the island are also popular. Arch Rock, Skull Cave and many other attractions also await in this most historic place. And perhaps, above all, there is the fudge.

In Mackinaw City the authentically reconstructed Fort Michilimackinac is an interesting way to learn about the history of the Straits area. There are dozens of stores to browse and a great shoreline on which to relax, watch the sailboats or just marvel at the sight of the Mackinac Bridge looming in the distance. You'll also want to explore Old Mackinac Point Lighthouse in Mackinaw City.

This 180-mile trip is all about the sights and places that make northeast Michigan so unique. The sunrise coast truly is an eye-opener.

The Banana Belt Coast

Yoopers (residents of Yooperland, i.e. Michigan's Upper Peninsula or the UP) are a tough crowd. They sometimes refer to those of us that are unfortunate enough in their mind to live in the Lower Peninsula as trolls (living below the bridge, i.e. the Mackinac Bridge). When they're feeling kinder, they simply refer to us as flatlanders, lopers, or fudgies. They even mock those who live in the southern portion of the UP as living in the banana belt. The southern portion of the UP does enjoy less severe winters than the Lake Superior "Snow Belt" region, though it's all relative. No one other than those people living near Lake Superior would be bold enough to refer to places like St. Ignace, Manistique and Escanaba as being in a tropical "banana belt."

But be that as it may, the southern portion of the UP has gained this title, so we'll go with it. The far southern UP may not actually be tropical, but it certainly is beautiful. And while you won't see any palm trees, its roads and byways were custom made for motorcycling, having great scenery, light traffic, and enough character to make the riding very enjoyable. By good fortune the roads on this tour that are closest to the water are state highways and thus well marked and easy to follow. Other than in small urban areas such as St. Ignace, Manistique or Escanaba, the roads are two-lane highways and are great for riding.

The banana belt ride stretches from the far eastern end of the peninsula on northern Lake Huron's North Channel, to its southernmost point on Lake Michigan's Green Bay. The two common factors as you ride will be water on one side and forests on the other.

This ride begins in Detour Village at the southeast corner of the Upper Peninsula. This strategic corner of Michigan is where the St. Mary River enters Lake Huron, and upbound shipping traffic turns west toward the Straits of Mackinac or north to go through the Soo Locks and head into Lake Superior. According to historical material published by Chippewa County, the name Detour is a French translation of the Ojibwa name *Giwideonaning*, meaning, "point where we go around in a canoe." Presumably they were referring to Detour Point that juts into Lake Huron just south of town.

Just one mile offshore from Detour across the Detour Passage is Drummond Island. A ferry operates hourly between the island and mainland. Though there isn't a lot of exploring one can do on Drummond Island on a touring or sport

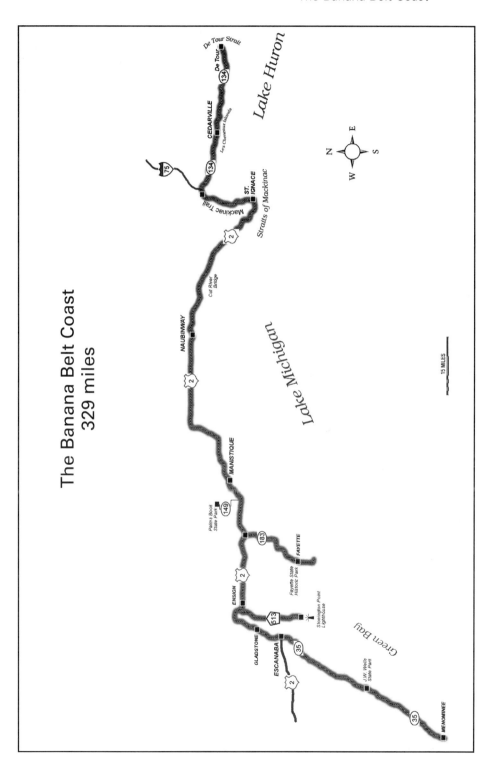

The Banana Belt Coast
329 miles

15 MILES

Miles	Destination	Total
THE BANANA BELT COAST 329 MILES		
0	De Tour	0
24	Cedarville	24
29	St. Ignace	53
42	Naubinway	95
46	Manistique	141
16	M-183/Garden Peninsula	157
14	Fayette State Park	171
7	Fairport/Land's End	178
21	Highway US 2	199
20	Stonington Peninsula	219
18	Stonington Point Lighthouse	237
18	Highway US 2	255
19	Escanaba/M-35	274
30	Wells State Park	304
25	Menominee	329

bike, it is an interesting ferry ride over and at least you can say you've been there if you take the opportunity. Drummond Island has an interesting history in that British Commander Sir Gordon Drummond built a fort on the island following the War of 1812, but it was abandoned in 1828, six years after it was discovered that the island was in American territory, not British. Oops!

We start the trip by heading west on M134 along the north shore of Lake Huron. The ride west along this stretch is very nice with cedar forest to your right and spectacular views of Lake Huron to your left. The Les Cheneaux Islands area (locally known as The Snows) is very pretty, with sailboats drifting in the quiet blue water between the many islands. The town of Cedarville, about midway between Detour and the Straits, is a boating center, and many people keep their boats at its fine harbor. It gained its name from the trade in cedar posts and rails harvested in that area.

Ultimately M134 will deliver us to Mackinac Highway, just beyond the I75 expressway. Turning south on Mackinac Highway takes us along the coast of St. Martin Bay and into the town of St. Ignace. You could take I75 the several miles south from M134 to St. Ignace, but you would miss a lot, especially riding through the town of St. Ignace itself, which is stretched out along the waterfront.

Established in 1671, St. Ignace is either the third or fourth oldest city in the country. Not all references are in agreement. Regardless, it is obviously an area with a tremendous amount of history going back well over 300 years. To appreciate this history a bit more, stop at the Father Marquette Memorial south of US2 and just west of the expressway. This museum tells the story of the early French explorers in the Upper Lakes area.

Head west out of St. Ignace on US2. It will take you all the way to the town of Escanaba. This highway is, in my mind, one of the more underrated great roads of the nation. With the exception of upstate New York, it travels across the northern tier of states from the Maine border with New Brunswick to Seattle, Washington. This highway not only gives you an up-close view of the northern USA, it is also a very enjoyable riding road across the breadth of the country. The stretch of US2 from St. Ignace west to Naubinway is certainly impressive. In many areas you're just yards away from the shoreline with continuous grand vistas of Lake Michigan. Don't be in too much of a hurry to pass up the various scenic turnouts along this stretch. Bring extra film or spare batteries for your digital camera.

About twenty miles west of St. Ignace, you will cross over the Cut River Bridge. This bridge is often referred to as the million-dollar bridge over a 10-cent stream. The Cut River isn't much as rivers go, but over the centuries it has cut a deep valley that wasn't easily bridged. The bridge is 640 feet long and is one of only two like it in the state. It has turned into quite a tourist attraction, with a parking area and trails constructed to allow travelers to enjoy the remarkable view from the bridge into the valley 150 feet below and the lake beyond.

If engineering oddities are your thing, take a gander at the siphon bridge in Manistique. The bridge is actually below the water level of the river—don't ask me to explain. Six miles west of Manistique you reach M149, a short highway going north to Palms Book State Park and the Big Spring, the largest spring in Michigan

View of the Cut River Bridge located near Epoufette in the UP. (Photo by Thomas A. Schneider)

Border lines drawn by drunken overseer

There is a fascinating story behind how the international border was drawn to the east of Drummond Island, rather than through the DeTour Strait. The 1814 Treaty of Ghent called for the international border to follow the shipping lane of the St. Mary River and through the many islands of the lower river. The trouble was that there was more than one shipping lane used at the time. The British overseer of the international border determination was an unpleasant fellow who also had a problem with excessive drinking. He argued with his peers about where the line should be all the way from the Detroit River up to Sault Ste. Marie. The pilot of the ship carrying the survey party decided to wait until after dinner one evening, when the gentleman had consumed too much grog, to sail through the channel east of Drummond Island, convincing the crown's representative that indeed that was the normal shipping channel. Even though the envoy wasn't completely satisfied, his mental state was one in which he finally conceded to the border being east of Drummond Island, rather than west of the island as he had been demanding.[6]

at 200 feet wide and 40 feet deep. You can go out on it on a glass-bottomed raft—very cool.

About 10 miles farther and about 120 miles west of St. Ignace you come upon state highway 183, going south into what's called the Garden Peninsula. This large peninsula juts south into Lake Michigan to nearly meet Wisconsin's Door Peninsula, and between the two of them forming Green Bay. The Garden is off the beaten path, but is certainly a highly recommended destination. Life goes on in this peninsula as it has for generations, not much touched by the 21st century. The primary attraction is the restored ghost town of Fayette (now a state park). From 1867 to 1891 Fayette was a company town and was one of the state's largest iron-smelting operations. Large limestone bluffs line the lake in this vicinity, and the limestone was used in the iron ore process. The town site, furnaces, and charcoal kilns have all been restored by the state. The scenic beauty is also outstanding and excellent camping opportunities are available in the park. On limestone cliffs near Fayette, known as Burnt Bluffs, the Indian cliff paintings found there are estimated to be 1,500 years old.

Resuming our westward trip along US2, about three miles past the tiny town of Ensign, CR513 heads south on the Stonington Peninsula to Stonington Point and its lighthouse. This is a pleasant side trip to take, especially if you're into lighthouses.

Stonington Peninsula separates Big and Little Bays de Noc. These bays are named after the Nokay (Noquet in French) Indian tribe that lived in the area many years ago. The bays are famous for fishing, especially walleye.

---

[6]*Drummond Island: The Story of the British Occupation* (1815–1828). A monograph by Samuel Fletcher Cook. Published by R. Smith Printing Company, Lansing, MI, 1896.

*View of the His-
toric Fayette Town-
site located near
Garden. (Photo
courtesy of Travel
Michigan.*

On the west side of Little Bay De Noc, US2 swings south along the shore through the towns of Gladstone and Escanaba (made famous by Jeff Daniels' play *Escanaba in da Moonlight*, depicting the exploits of five Yooper deer hunters). Escanaba had long been known as a major iron ore port, where ore from the nearby iron mines was shipped to various mills around the Great Lakes. It is still a major port.

US2 swings west in Escanaba, and we pick up M35, which continues the southward journey along the shore of Green Bay. M35 is a very scenic and enjoyable waterside road. Along the way south you'll have many wonderful vistas of Green Bay and drive through miles of forestland. Midway between Escanaba and Menominee is J.W. Wells State Park. This 678-acre lakeshore park is on land donated to the state for the purpose of a park in 1925 by the children of Mr. J.W. Wells—a local political leader and lumberman. In the 1930s the Civilian Conservation Corps built the infrastructure and facilities at the park. Michigan 35 ultimately delivers us to Menominee and the end of this trip. In Menominee take time to stop at the Menominee County Historical Museum near the corner of 11th Avenue and US41. The museum has a large collection of artifacts from the Indian, fur, and logging eras.

*View of limestone cliffs near Fayette.
(Photo by Don Simonelli)*

Lake St. Clair

THERE ARE ENOUGH unique things about Lake St. Clair that even though about one-third of its coast is heavily developed and the majority of its shoreline is in Canada, it really deserves to be in this book. St. Clair is really not much more than a flooded wetland. It is only ten feet deep for the most part, and channels of twenty-seven feet in depth have to be maintained for shipping. The large lake is a fisherman's paradise, full of warm- and cool-water fish, such as bass, perch, walleye, muskies, and more. It is also a haven for waterfowl and shorebirds of all types.

Lake St. Clair got its name in 1679 by early French explorers. They happened to enter the lake for the first time when exploring upstream on the Detroit River on the religious feast day in observance of St. Claire. Thus they gave the name *Lac Sainte Claire* to this newly found large body of water.

An enjoyable round trip of this lake can be easily made and there are only a few miles that could be considered tough—the stretch of Jefferson in downtown Detroit and immediately south of downtown.

Going north out of Detroit, Jefferson Avenue hugs the shoreline taking you through the Grosse Pointes and St. Clair Shores where the roadway is known as Lakeshore Drive since it follows the shoreline so closely. Detroit and the Detroit River received its name nearly 400 years ago when the earliest French explorers arrived at the northern end of the Detroit River, calling it *Le d'Etroit*, or The Narrows, separating the two land masses of current-day Michigan and Ontario in Canada.

The waterfront suburbs northeast of Detroit are reasonable to navigate on motorcycle, and there are several small parks that provide lake access and viewing. Just north of St. Clair Shores is the famous Metropolitan Beach Park and Selfridge Air National Guard Base north of the park.

Follow Jefferson right to its end just past the Metro Parkway to South River Road, which runs along the Clinton River. Go west on South River Road a mile and a quarter to Bridgeville Road, which you'll take north across the river to North River Road on the opposite shore. You'll head west for a short distance with the river on your left and the ANG base on your right. Take North River road to the I94 expressway. It is best to jump on I94 for three miles to skirt around the ANG Base. Take the first exit you come to (240a) to the east. For a mile you'll be on William Grosso Road, which will end and Jefferson will begin again and take you

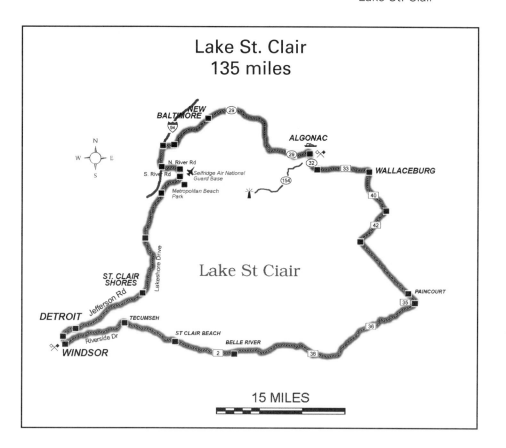

northeast along the shoreline to the town of New Baltimore, where Jefferson ends and joins M29. Take M29 along the shoreline of Anchor Bay and the north end of Lake St. Clair all the way to the town of Algonac.

The large Great Lakes connecting river of the same name flows into Lake St. Clair from the north at this point and forms a very large delta. Much of this delta has been preserved as wildlife refuge. The Harsens Island, St. Clair Flats, and Walpole Island areas are known far and wide for their waterfowl populations and are favorite destinations for duck hunters.

The Harsens Island Ferry, which runs every fifteen minutes, will transport you to the island, and M154 if you wish to explore this area further. M154 goes out to lands end in the delta and is an interesting ride through Michigan's Little Venice. There are two historic channel lights off the southern tip of Harsens Island that were built in the 1850s. Unlike most lighthouses, these lights were built on their own manmade islands, or cribs, to guide ships through the shipping channel in the delta. These lights have recently been restored by volunteers and were recently listed on the National Register of Historic Places.

Miles	Destination	Total
__	**LAKE ST. CLAIR** __ **135 MILES**	__
0	Detroit/Ambassador Bridge	0
12	Grosse Pointe	12
16	Metropolitan Beach	28
28	Algonac	56
11	Wallaceburg, Ontario	67
20	Thames River	87
48	Windsor/Ambassador Bridge	135

Once back in Algonac we'll take the *Walpole*, the Algonac Ferry, over to Ontario to continue our ride on the east and south coasts of Lake St. Clair. The ferry will deposit you on Walpole Island, a large Indian Reservation on the northeast corner of the lake. Like so much of the Great Lakes area, Walpole Island also has a fascinating history. Amazingly, the land comprising the Walpole Island "Reserve" was never ceded away under treaty by native tribes. The Walpole Island First Nation today exercises complete aboriginal title to its land and water.[7] Following the defeat of Britain in the American War of Independence and the turnover of Detroit to the Americans in 1796, and again following the War of 1812, many Indians who had been allied with the British made their way across the border to what is now Canada, with some of them settling on Walpole Island.

Many of the inhabitants live off the land as they have for millennia. The First Nation controls use of the land and issues licenses for those who wish to hunt or fish there. Tourism, especially outdoor-related activities, such as hunting and fishing, is the primary economic base of the community.

County Road 32 is the road to follow east and eventually off the island and onto the mainland shore. Once across the waterway separating Walpole Island from the mainland, you will join CR33 straight ahead to the east.

The first thing you'll notice if you look at a map of the road system in southwest Ontario is that the survey lines are laid out diagonally from southeast to northwest. There are no good roads that closely follow the east shore of the lake, so we angle inland just a bit at this point.

---

[7]Kendall Sands (www.personal.umich.edu)

Follow CR33 east and to Ontario Route 40, a main road taking you through the town of Wallaceburg. Route 40 heads south out of Wallaceburg and shortly thereafter, CR42 goes west from the main road. Take CR42 west to CR34, following this road through the tiny town of Paincourt. Just south of town, CR34 makes a ninety-degree turn west along the north side of the Thames River.

About 25 miles northeast of this point on the Thames River is the site of the War of 1812 Battle of the Thames. This decisive battle, fought on October 5, 1813, followed Commodore Perry's naval victory on Lake Erie at Put-In-Bay and was perhaps the most significant land battle of the war. The great Shawnee Indian Chief, Tecumseh, was killed during the battle, thus ending the hopes of those who saw him as the leader of an Indian confederation able to stop westward expansion by European settlers. American soldiers saw the rout as payback for the defeat and subsequent massacre suffered by the Kentucky volunteer militiamen at the River Raisin Battle near current-day Monroe in January 1813.

Follow CR34 west along the Thames River and after a little over three miles you will reach CR35, which will take you across the river to, you guessed it, CR36. Head west on CR36 as it curves along the south shore of the Thames. In the flat coastal plain that is this corner of Ontario routes 34 and 36 are favorite biking roads for local motorcyclists. CR36 in particular has many nice sweeping curves as it closely follows the meandering river west. You may even find yourself making a little detour and heading east on CR36 to Chatham just so you can follow its sinuous curves west again along its entire length. Eventually CR36 will curve southwesterly a bit and join CR2. County Road 2 will head west and take you along the Lake St. Clair shoreline once again. In the town of Belle River CR2 joins Ontario Route 2 for a short distance through town and then splits off to rejoin the shoreline just past Emeryville.

Eventually, CR2 crosses Pike Creek and enters the town of St. Clair Beach. Just after crossing the bridge over Pike Creek turn north on Brighton Road a short distance to the lakeshore, and make the ninety-degree turn west onto Riverside Drive. You'll follow Riverside Drive for the remainder of the trip, through St. Clair Beach, Tecumseh, and finally the city of Windsor and the Ambassador Bridge back to Michigan. Riverside Drive follows the shoreline closely through this stretch of Lake St. Clair and the northern portion of the Detroit River and has great views of the water. The Windsor area is, of course, fairly developed, but there are many public parks on the water that provide for additional waterside viewing and relaxing.

This total trip is only 135 miles and thus a very relaxing one-day trip with time for stops along the way.

Small Towns, Vineyards, Orchards and Farmland Tours

THESE SIX RIDES across the southern one-third of Michigan take in some of the best roads and scenery that this part of the state has to offer. Most Michigan motorcyclists live in the southern part of Lower Michigan, and except for commutes to work or short leisurely rides, they don't ride here for the most part. It seems that a rider who wants a "serious" ride heads north. That's a shame because they're really missing out on fabulous riding, good scenery and loads of interesting places and history. Let's see if we can't change some riding habits and explore all that southern Michigan has to offer.

Spring at one of Michigan's farms. (Photo courtesy of Travel Michigan)

To Hell and Back

THEY SAY THAT THE ROAD TO HELL is paved with good intentions. I know better. True, it is a paved road, but it also has nice scenery, great curves and is loads of fun to ride on. I confess that I have succumbed to temptation and have every intention to ride this road as often as possible. Hell, Michigan has become a sort of celebrity community that has taken full advantage of its unusual name. You can buy bats and pastry snowballs to take out of Hell, have your picture taken with a variety of devilish backdrops, buy postcards, T-shirts, and so on. The small town is named after Hell Creek, which flows through town, but historians aren't in agreement as to how the name was originally derived.

The tiny community is certainly well known to motorcyclists from southeast Michigan. It's a favorite gathering spot for rides on the local roads, which are probably the best motorcycling roads in that part of the state.

Hell is on a tour that starts and ends in Mason, just south of Lansing, and takes you through some of the prettiest countryside in southeast Michigan. It also takes you down three historic roads that just happen to be nice riding roads, as well.

The tour starts by taking M36 east out of Mason. After just a couple of miles, Dexter Trail angles off to the right front, heading southeast. Dexter Trail is one of Michigan's historic roads that had its origins as an Indian footpath and was used by pioneers during the 1830s, when the center part of the state was just beginning to be explored and settled. The trail originally ran from Dexter, northwest of Ann Arbor, to Ionia. Significant portions of the original trail still exist as the two-lane road by the name Dexter Trail in Livingston, Ingham and Clinton Counties. Like other territorial roads, it doesn't follow a straight line, meandering across the countryside instead—a direct result of the original trailblazers' efforts to make a trail that avoided wet areas and stayed on high ground as much as possible. The trail is named after Samuel Dexter, a New York native who moved to the Ionia area making use of this Indian path. Others soon followed. Dexter Trail is an enjoyable road, with curves and lots of trees along it. Once beyond the Mason urban influence, it is a nice riding road. We stay on the well-marked Trail as it meanders south and east until it finally "Ts" at Gregory Road in southwest Livingston County. Turn south for a half-mile on Gregory Road and take it into the small town of Gregory, where you once again join M36. Go east on M36 to

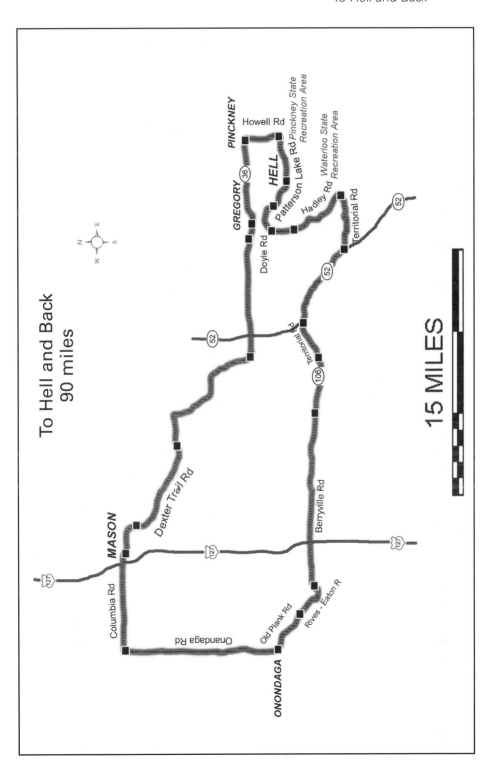

To Hell and Back
90 miles

15 MILES

Miles	Destination	Total
\multicolumn{3}{c}{**TO HELL AND BACK 90 MILES**}		
0	Mason	0
23	Gregory	23
8	Pinckney	31
3	Hell	34
4.5	Unadilla Road	38.5
5.5	Territorial Road	44
26	Berryville/Rives (Eaton Road)	70
5	Onondaga	75
15	Mason	90

Pinckney and turn south on the first main road in town—Howell Road. Take this road south to Patterson Lake Road, and turn west (right). Patterson Lake is a great road, and a few miles down, you reach Hell—not at all what I imagined. You no doubt will want to stop and take the obligatory pictures or buy souvenirs. Hell is a popular gathering place for motorcycle clubs that ride this part of the state. Northwest Washtenaw County and southwest Livingston County have some great riding roads—many more than I'm covering in this tour. Smitty's Dam Site Inn in Hell is a favorite meeting place and a great place to eat at the end of the day.

Going like a bat out of…—well, never mind—head west from Hell on Patterson Lake Road to its end at Doyle Road and turn left (west) again. Both of these roads take you through the Pinckney and Waterloo State Recreation Areas—large blocks of public land that preserve beautiful scenery and woods in a hilly setting. A little over two miles on Doyle Road takes you to Unadilla Road, heading south. If you pass a small airport and glider field, you've gone too far. Take Unadilla Road southbound and your fun resumes. This road turns into Hadley Road after you cross the Washtenaw County line, but there are no turns to make (just plenty of curves to follow). Take Hadley all the way to Territorial Road and head west. Territorial Road is an early frontier road that settlers used over 150 years ago, following its muddy ruts into the wilderness of central Michigan.

Right after turning west at this corner, you'll see a sign warning that there are many curves ahead, so drive carefully. If seeing a sign such as this doesn't bring a smile to your face, I don't know what will. Heading west on Territorial takes you through curves and over hills, and it is just a wonderful ride. As you head west on Territorial Road, it will join M52 for a short distance and then veer off again, only to repeat the same thing on M106. It is very well marked, and there is no danger of straying from Territorial Road. Ultimately, Territorial Road ends at Berryville Road, but only after you've enjoyed its ambience for about twenty miles. At Berryville Road, turn left less than a mile to Rives-Eaton Road. Follow Rives-Eaton Road northwest (to the right). When you are once again in Ingham County, it becomes Old Plank Road—another historic road. Old Plank Road will take you into the small village of Onondaga, where a right (north) turn onto Onondaga Road will take you north about ten miles through farm country to Columbia Road. Heading east on Columbia will take you back to Mason, completing an approximately 90-mile ride through beautiful countryside and on some mighty fine roads. I think you will want to make this ride a part of your regular riding routine if you live anywhere in central or southeast Michigan. I know I do.

Big Rock and the Big Bull

THIS CENTRAL MICHIGAN tour begins and ends in the southern Saginaw County town of Chesaning, which means Place of the Big Rock in Native American. The town was originally called Northampton when founded in 1839, but its name was changed a short time thereafter to the native term used for the site. I can only assume that it earned its original Indian name due to the presence of a large boulder that was scraped up hundreds of miles to the north by glaciers and left there during the last ice age. Large boulders, called erratics by geologists, can be found in many places throughout Michigan. Though Chesaning does have an elementary school called Big Rock, today's natives commonly refer to the city as the Showboat City.

Either at the beginning or at the end of your ride, I recommend that you park your bike on Chesaning's main street and take a stroll to see and enjoy this unique small town. Chesaning has been able to retain its small town charm and has a vibrant downtown with lots of events, shopping and eating opportunities. It's also a nice town in which to just walk around. On the west side of town there are many fine homes of Victorian architecture that have been well preserved. The city's main street is a beautifully landscaped boulevard and helps make Chesaning a friendly community for walking. The Shiawassee River flows through the downtown, and there is a large park along the river. The Chesaning Area Historical Museum on the main street is a great place to discover the history of the area.

On Memorial Day weekend, Chesaning hosts a large car show, and mid-July brings the famous Chesaning Showboat on the river with top name entertainers appearing each year—a must-see.

Once you've had your fill of all that Chesaning has to offer, head north on Line Street/Sharon Road, which is located four blocks west of the stop light, and follow this pleasantly meandering road as it winds through the countryside between Chesaning and the town of St. Charles. In Chesaning, Line Street is quite rough, but it becomes much smoother once you leave the city limits. Once into St. Charles, Sharon Road becomes Chesaning Street and takes you through the small downtown business district of St. Charles and to the only stop light in town. Continue straight north from the stop light, and about two blocks later, you will cross over the Bad River. One block after the bridge, look for the street sign for Ithaca Road and turn left (west) on it.

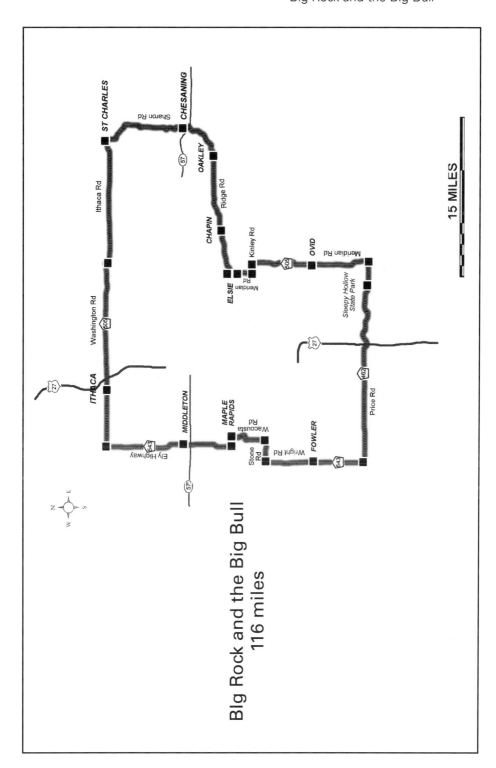

Big Rock and the Big Bull
116 miles

THE BIG ROCK AND THE BIG BULL 116 MILES		
Miles	Destination	Total
0	Chesaning	0
9	St. Charles	9
24	Ithaca	33
19	Maple Rapids	52
31	Sleepy Hollow State Park	83
8	Ovid	91
7	Elsie	98
13	Oakley	111
5	Chesaning	116

St. Charles is located at the edge of the large Shiawassee State Game Area, a wildlife area managed primarily for waterfowl. During spring and fall waterfowl migrations, a viewing area just east of here is worth the stop.

Ithaca Road will be your riding host for about the next twenty-eight miles as you wind your way through the farms and heavily wooded countryside of south-western Saginaw County and the farmlands of Gratiot County. Ten miles west of St. Charles presents a half-mile jog when you reach the county line for Gratiot County, but no problem, just follow the pavement. Once in Gratiot County the road name changes to Washington Road, where you will notice the countryside change from heavily wooded to extensively farmland. Gratiot County is fertile and productive farmland, and so it should remain for a long time.

Washington Road will take you straight west through Ithaca (Main Street when you're in town), the county seat for Gratiot County. Ithaca doesn't have a lot of glamour or fame, but the courthouse and fire station are old and unique architectural buildings worth a stop to see. These buildings are on Main Street, which goes straight west through town, so no turns are necessary.

Heading west out of Ithaca, Main Street turns once again into Washington Road. Take this about five miles west of town until you find Ely Highway. You'll encounter northbound Ely Highway first but go another hundred yards and turn left on southbound Ely Highway. Despite its highway moniker, Ely is a rural two-lane road, not a major highway. You will take this road south for twelve miles, passing through the small village of Middleton and across state highway M57. When you reach the south Gratiot County line (northern Clinton County line), the pavement will turn east one mile to a "T" at Maple Road. Turn right on Maple Road, across the Maple River, and into the town of Maple Rapids (noticing a pattern here regarding a certain tree commonly found in this area?).

Continue straight ahead to the south side of town to Hyde Road and turn right a short distance to Wacousta Road and turn left. Go south two miles on Wacousta Road and follow the pavement west onto Stone Road. Take Stone Road two miles to Wright Road and turn south again. Stay on Wright Road almost ten miles, taking it south through the town of Fowler and on to Price Road, where we'll turn back east (left). Price Road is home for the next nineteen miles as we head across Clinton County. Price Road will turn to gravel at the Shiawassee County line, just after passing Sleepy Hollow State Park and Lake Victoria. Turn left at that point onto Meridian Road, which is also the

Prime Meridian is key to land surveys

The Prime Meridian is a straight line that runs north and south the entire length of the state utilized in the surveying of land. A second survey line is the Base Line, which runs east and west across the state just north of Jackson. This imaginary line also has a road following it for much of its length, called Base Line Road. (Now called Eight Mile Road in Detroit, though some of you will recall when Eight Mile was called Base Line Road).

Except for a few old parcels surveyed by the French in southeast Michigan, all land surveys in the state are based on Jefferson's rectangular survey method (you hadn't forgotten that already, had you?) as stipulated in the Northwest Ordinance of 1787. In 1815 surveyors were hired by the federal government to establish the base line and principal meridian in Michigan. Because the only significant settlement in the territory at the time was in the far southeast corner, it is only natural that the base line is located so far south in the state, rather than the center of the state. The point north of Jackson, where the Prime Meridian crosses the Base Line, is the key to all land surveys in the state.

Clinton / Shiawassee county line road towards the village of Ovid.

Meridian Road is a nondescript road that intermittently follows an imaginary line on the surface of Michigan called the Prime Meridian. You'll make a fun double curve on your way north on Meridian Road, and after five miles you will encounter a stop light at M21. Continue north across M21 going through the village of Ovid. Two mile north of M21, the road comes to a "T" at Kinley Road. Turn to the east a short distance and then left to continue north on Meridian Road. Four miles up the road on Meridian you will pass a very large dairy farm followed shortly by a railroad track. Turn left at the first road just after you cross the tracks.

This road will take you into Elsie—the self-proclaimed dairy capital of Michigan. Proceed west about one mile to the main intersection of Elsie (the traffic light is a dead giveaway). You may want to have your picture taken with the largest

Elsie's big Holstein bull.

(concrete) Holstein bull you'll ever see, which is located in a small park at that intersection.

Ride north from the stoplight two miles to the Clinton/Gratiot County Line Road. In this vicinity you're at a geologically interesting place in Michigan—the divide between the Lake Huron and Lake Michigan watersheds. This is important because in the 1830s speculators started digging a canal just north of here with the hope of connecting the Bad River and the Maple River resulting in a cross-Michigan waterway for commerce and travel. The canal was never completed, and railroads and plank roads soon took over as the main modes of transportation.

Turn right on the Gratiot County Line Road. This puts you on an angling blacktop that will become Ridge Road about one mile east after you enter Saginaw County. Keep going east on this road, and in two miles you'll stop at the four-corner crossroad village of Chapin. Going east out of Chapin you'll see an elk farm on your right. No matter how you feel about domesticating wild animals, if you enjoy seeing large-antlered *Cervidae* up close, here's your chance! The elk are located in a field on the south side of the road. The pavement gets a little bumpy for a two-mile stretch east of Chapin, so just relax and don't try to set any land speed records here.

Seven miles east of Chapin you'll come to the small town of Oakley and M52. Take a very slight jog north (left) here and continue east on what is now Sharon Road.

If you're in the Oakley area in mid-August, be sure to attend the Mid-Michigan Old Gas Tractor Association's antique tractor show. It's been going on for over thirty years and draws 30,000 visitors. The many displays and exhibitions involving antique tractors and other old machinery are awesome. It's held just northwest of Oakley on the third weekend of the month.

Keep heading east and northeast on Sharon Road, and before long you'll find yourself heading northerly along the west shore of the Shiawassee River back to Chesaning.

This ride is 116 miles on lightly traveled roads and will take two to three hours, depending on stops. Planning it around lunch or a midafternoon ice cream break in Chesaning or St. Charles would make you look very smart to your riding partner. Both towns have pleasant parks on a river that make for an enjoyable rest stop.

Grand Roads, Al Capone, and a Tragedy in Bath

THIS IS A TWO- TO THREE-HOUR circular tour. It starts and ends at the growing town of Fowlerville, off I96 at exit 129. Fowlerville is just far enough away from larger towns to the east and west that, while it's definitely a bedroom community, its character hasn't yet been altered by large malls and big box department stores. You can still stroll about in an attractive downtown filled with restaurants, antique stores and small specialty shops.

From the expressway or downtown Fowlerville, head north on Fowlerville Road (called Grand Street in town), taking a half-mile jog to the west six miles north of town at Mohrle Road. Pick up Fowlerville Road again after the jog and continue north until the "T" at Braden Road in southern Shiawassee County. Follow the pavement east for a mile on Braden Road until it curves north again on Bancroft Road. Take Bancroft Road north for three miles to where it ends at Britten Road. Go east at this point for two miles until Britten Road ends at Grand River Road, an original territorial road with a great deal of history. Turn left onto Grand River Road. You'll stay on this grand stretch of road for almost twenty miles as it pleasantly curves westerly across Shiawassee County to the town of Laingsburg. Please note that when you hit the stop sign at Morrice Road, there is a slight left (south) jog to be made. Grand River Road is an especially pleasant ride because of the large number of mature trees along the road for much of its length.

Laingsburg began and prospered because of its location on the Looking Glass River, the old territorial road you're now riding on, and the railroad that later came through town. If you look at old maps of Michigan, you'll notice that either a river or railroad (most of which no longer exist) were very common factors in the establishment of early towns. Today Laingsburg and many towns like it prosper as bedroom communities, with the early travel and commerce routes, such as rivers and railroads, playing no role in their economic well-being, or at least a much-reduced role.

Continue west through the town of Laingsburg on Grand River Road, and upon entering Clinton County, it becomes Round Lake Road west of town. Round Lake Road is a continuation of Grand River Road and meanders west and south.

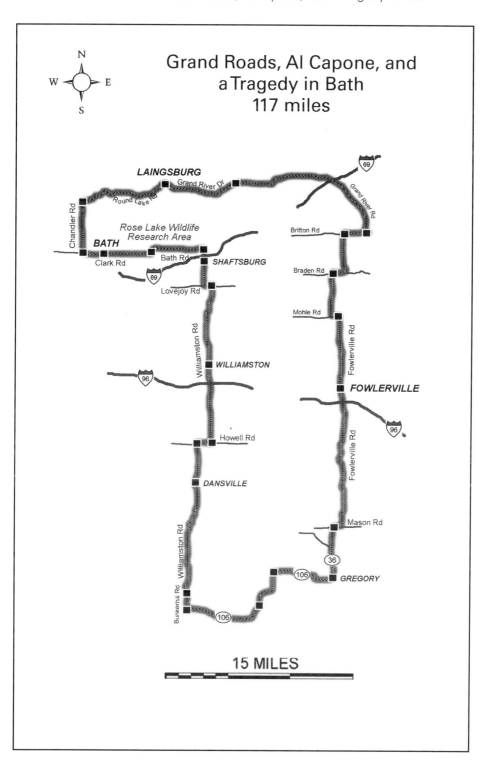

Grand Roads, Al Capone, and a Tragedy in Bath
117 miles

15 MILES

Miles	Destination	Total
	GRAND ROADS, AL CAPONE, & A TRAGEDY IN BATH 117 MILES	
0	Fowlerville	0
16	Grand River Road	16
19	Laingsburg	35
13	Bath	48
18	Williamston	66
30	Stockbridge	96
6	Gregory	102
15	Fowlerville	117

It's a favorite local riding road for motorcyclists in that vicinity, and it's common to see other motorcyclists shooting out of the many curves along this route.

Grand River and Round Lake roads generally follow the Looking Glass River as it flows from east to west just to the south of the road. They are also on essentially the same route as the early Native American footpath and the later wagon road that was used by pioneers settling the area. No attempt was made to keep these early trails straight. It was much more important to follow the high ground rather than a straight line.

About five miles west of Laingsburg on the shore of Round Lake, you'll see a large building that has served for many decades as a popular night spot and restaurant. This building has an interesting history, having been for decades a very popular resort and dance hall. For a period in the 1930s it was allegedly a hideaway for Al Capone, the infamous mobster who was seeking some quiet time and relaxation away from the hustle and bustle of his day job. More recently it has been a popular restaurant, but unfortunately it closed in 2003. Just west of the former restaurant is the base of the local Viet Nam Veterans M/C.

Continue west on Round Lake Road to southbound Chandler Road. You will pass northbound Chandler Road first—but don't turn here, because about a half-mile later you'll see the southbound road. Take Chandler south three miles to the four-way stop at Clark Road and turn left (east).

Clark Road will take you through the small village of Bath. This is a town that was best known for a tragic event that occurred on what probably started out as a beautiful day on May 18, 1927. An angry local resident and school board member, whose farm was being foreclosed on and who blamed his problems on what he

Aftermath of the Bath school explosion. (Photo courtesy of State Archives of Michigan)

felt were high taxes for the new school building, dynamited that school, killing dozens of children and teachers, and later blew himself up in a pickup truck killing even more people—44 in total, mostly children. Unfortunately, such horrors aren't new to this world.

Continue east on Clark Road through the Rose Lake Wildlife Research area, a very pretty ride with gentle hills and lots of trees. After around four miles, Clark Road will jog north for a half mile, and when the pavement resumes going east, you'll be in Shiawassee County, where the road will be called Bath Road. After five more miles you'll reach the small village of Shaftsburg and make a right (south) turn on Shaftsburg Road. Follow Shaftsburg Road south to Ingham County and follow the pavement as it jogs east on LoveJoy Road for about a half-mile. Turn south on Williamston Road (you'll stay on Williamston Road the entire length of Ingham County) and continue southbound, making a slight west jog when you get to the stop sign at Haslett Road. Continue south on Williamston through its namesake town, continuing six miles south of Williamston. At this point Williamston Road forms a "T" at Howell Road. By jogging west one mile (follow the signs), you pick up Williamston Road again as it continues southward. Take it through the Village of Dansville and continue south as Williamston Road becomes a very pleasant winding road through a mix of farms and woods. At the Jackson County line the pavement jogs a bit to the east and continues south as Bunker Hill Road. Go south one mile on Bunker Hill Road to Territorial Road, where you turn east. Stay on Territorial Road until it hits M106, and then follow 106 east and northeast as it winds its way to the small town of Gregory in southwest Livingston County. Michigan 106 is a very nice riding road through this area, with lots of curves and fairly light traffic.

The small towns of Gregory and Pinckney are favorite motorcycling haunts. On any nice day you'll see many bikers riding local roads or gathered at the local gas stations or restaurants planning their ride or talking about one they just finished. I always find the bikes at these gathering places fascinating. There is a mix of everything from full-dress Harleys and Wings to crotch rockets that you have to be a contortionist to ride. But there is one thing they all have in common—the riders are all having a blast.

About two miles north of town on M36, the road turns to the west, but you want to keep going north on Gregory Road. Follow the jog as the pavement goes to the east and then go north on Bull Run Road, another very nice, windy road that you'll enjoy. At Mason Road take a slight jog east and then continue north on what is now Fowlerville Road, taking it back to Fowlerville. The last couple of miles aren't anything to write home about, being flat and straight, but this stretch is certainly the exception on this route.

This is about 117 miles long and will take a leisurely three hours. It takes you through some very typical central Michigan farm country and small towns, as well as some enjoyable roads that even those who have lived in central Michigan for many years do not appreciate.

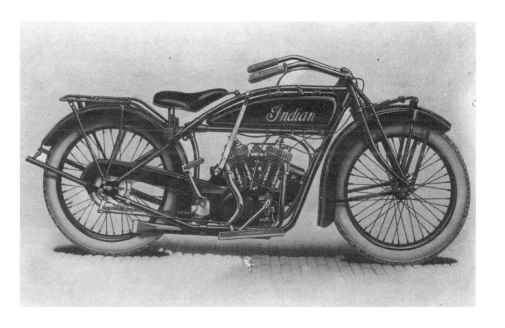

A Grand River Road
and Historic Covered Bridges

THIS THREE-HOUR RIDE winds through west-central Michigan countryside closely following the Grand River for a number of miles as it flows west toward Grand Rapids. Start the ride at the small town of Pewamo (named in 1871 in honor of a local Ottawa Indian chief), located mid-way between St. Johns and Ionia on M21. Turn south onto Hubbardston Road from M21 and take it one mile to Kimball Road, where a turn to the west will get you started on the river road. About four miles after turning onto Kimball Road you will see a small park and scenic overlook on the south side of the road. Though you've just begun the trip, this is a nice stop. The small park is named in honor of Fred Green, a former Governor of Michigan, and is located atop a high bluff overlooking the Grand River. It's an especially pretty spot in the fall. From this point west the road follows the Grand River closely for about thirty miles as it meanders in a westerly direction toward Lake Michigan.

In a short time you will enter Lyons, a small town with a very interesting history. Lyons was named in honor of Lucius Lyon, one of the earliest settlers in the Grand River valley, who later became a noted politician and judge. The site that was to become the town of Lyons was an open prairie of 1,100 acres, maintained by the local Indians. The natives referred to the site as Cocoosh, in honor of the chief who bore that name. The fascinating thing is that Chief Cocoosh was an African-American who had been captured by the Indians in the War of 1812. After reaching maturity the Indians were so impressed that they appointed him their Chief.[1]

The river road jogs south a short distance on the west side of town, and then continues west with the name Riverside Drive. After crossing M66 about five miles west of Lyons, continue west on Riverside. This stretch is very pretty, with lots of curves and wooded land as it passes through the publicly owned Ionia State Recreation Area. About eight miles past M66 you enter the town of Saranac. The river road jogs three blocks south, continuing west on Summit St., which becomes Riverside Drive again outside of town. Six miles west of Saranac the road again

[1]*Memorials of the Grand River Valley,* Franklin Everett © 1878, The Chicago Legal News Company.

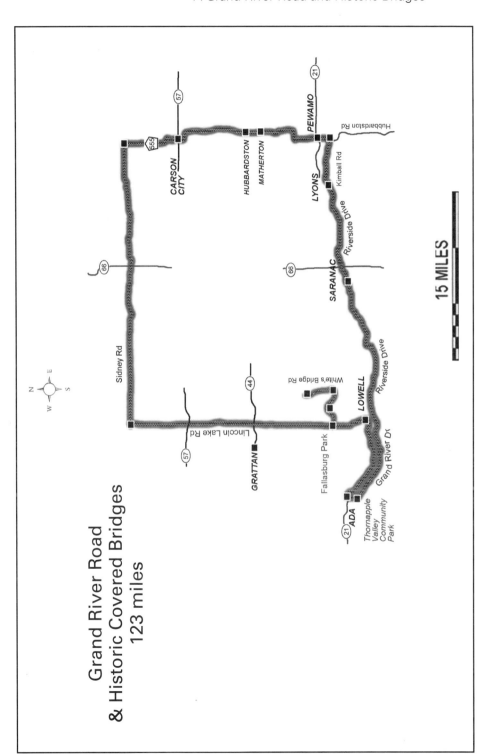

Grand River Road
& Historic Covered Bridges
123 miles

15 MILES

Miles	Destination	Total
A GRAND RIVER ROAD & HISTORIC COVERED BRIDGES 123 MILES		
0	Pewamo	0
6	Lyons	6
15	Saranac	21
15	Ada Covered Bridge	36
14	Fallasburg Covered Bridge	50
4	White's Covered Bridge	54
6	Lincoln Lake Road	60
19	Lincoln Lake/19 Mile Road	79
21	Crystal Lake/Village of Crystal	100
9	Carson City	109
14	Pewamo	123

makes a short jog to the south, and continues west now called Grand River Road. You'll stay on this road all the way to the town of Ada, home of Amway Corporation. In Ada the road ends at Buttrick Park Road, where you turn right and follow it around, as it becomes Thornapple River Road.

There is a very nice park at this juncture called Thornapple Valley Community Park. It is the location of the historic Bradfield Covered Bridge, and is a good spot to stop for pictures and to stretch your legs. Just past the park you'll see Ada Road. Turn right here and take it the very short distance to M21 where a right turn onto east M21 is needed. Follow M21 east to the town of Lowell. In the heart of town at a stoplight is Hudson Street. Turn left onto Hudson, which becomes Lincoln Lake Road outside of town. Three miles north of the stoplight you will see Fallasburg Park Road going east. Make this turn and you will soon be at the Fallasburg Covered Bridge over the Flat River. This beautifully situated bridge is one of only three covered bridges still open to traffic in Michigan.

Another functioning covered bridge is located very close by. White's Covered Bridge, named after a pioneer family that lived nearby, also spans the Flat River just a few miles northeast. Though it has seen repairs to its braces, roof, and abutments, it is essentially the same bridge as it was over a century ago. To get to White's Bridge, drive northeast on Covered Bridge Road upon leaving the Fallasburg Bridge. Turn east on McPherson Road, which becomes Potter Road after

White's Covered Bridge over the Flat River.

crossing the Ionia County line, and then north on White's Bridge Road to the bridge. Four-tenths of a mile before reaching White's Covered Bridge, the paved road turns to a hard gravel surface, which is normally easily negotiable for even large touring bikes.

To get back to Lincoln Lake Road you will have to retrace your steps as the road turns to gravel beyond White's Bridge. It's a pleasant and short ride. Seeing and riding on two historic covered bridges in one day makes it more than worth the few minutes this excursion back to another time takes.

Follow Lincoln Lake Road a total of 24 miles north of Lowell. This stretch takes you through nice countryside interspersed with orchards, lakes, farms and fields. A few hills and curves are thrown in for good order. About ten miles north of Lowell Lincoln Lake Road intersects with M44. At that point you're only about

Fallasburg Covered Bridge

three miles from the Grattan Raceway, 616-691-7221; grattanraceway.com. Grattan Raceway is located a mile west of that intersection and a couple of miles north, just north of the small town of Grattan. The raceway is very involved with motorcycle racing and track time.

Ultimately Lincoln Lake Road turns east at the lake for which the road is named. Just follow the pavement around to the east and it becomes 19 Mile Road, and in a couple of miles it becomes Sidney Road as you enter Montcalm County. You'll follow Sidney Road almost twenty-five miles east across Montcalm County countryside past Crystal Lake to CR555 (Herrick Road). This intersection is easy to find, Sidney Road turns to gravel ahead of you, so you want to turn south on Herrick Road/CR555.

The only jog that Sidney Road makes prior to Herrick Road is just west of Crystal Lake where it makes a short jog to the north. It's very easy to follow.

Once on CR-555, follow it south as it first goes straight, then makes several curves, into the town of Carson City. Once east of Crystal Lake and in the Carson City area you're in the heart of central Michigan's farm country. The wide-open fertile fields provide patchwork scenery of various crops.

In Carson City you want to turn east one-half mile and then continue south again on the County Line Road, which is located at the east city limits. Continue on this road for roughly thirteen miles as it meanders south through the tiny towns of Hubbardston (which received its name in 1865 from the Hubbardston Lumber Company and sawmill that was located there) and Matherton and over the Maple River. In this stretch the road is named Hubbardston Road. Two miles south of the river, the road takes a short jog west and then continues south again into Pewamo.

The overall length is about 123 miles, making a leisurely three hour laid-back ride through Michigan's countryside on some surprisingly nice roads, with stops at not one, not two, but three covered bridges!

A Trail through Orchards, Vineyards and Pawpaw Trees

SOUTHWEST MICHIGAN has a great deal going for it: miles of beautiful shoreline, beaches that seem to go on forever, sand dunes, winding country roads, well-tended orchards, fruit farms and vineyards, and enough lakes and hills to make things interesting.

The trip starts in Paw Paw, easily accessible just off I94. Paw Paw has some wineries that one should stop at to sample their wares, but for safety's sake let's save the wine sampling for the end of the trip. Going south out of Paw Paw, take Kalamazoo Avenue / M40 over I94. Just past the interchange you'll see CR665 going west off of M40. Take 665 as it turns south, about two miles south, it makes a quarter-mile jog to the east then continues south again, and about two miles later, the road comes to a "T" at CR669, where you turn right. CR669 is a very nice riding road with curves, small hills, well-kept farms and fields, vineyards and orchards, and lots of trees as it angles through the countryside about ten miles, finally intersecting with Dewey Lake Road. Just prior to Dewey Lake Road, CR669 turns into Valley Road and then Roth Road, as it angles toward the southwest and then south.

After turning right on Dewey Lake Road, go straight west for about eight miles, then curve northwest, then north as it travels between a chain of lakes. The west half of this stretch is actually M152. Why the state DOT has taken over this short stretch of road is beyond me—it looks just like the county road before and after the state-maintained stretch. As it winds between the lakes it is also called 66th Street. After going north two miles on M152/66th Street, you will hit 92nd Avenue. Turn west at this point and travel into Berrien County where the road becomes Napier Road. It is very easy to follow—just stay on the main pavement. At this point you're deep into orchard and fruit farm country. You will see lots of roadside stands all along this tour where you can buy fresh fruit or berries, depending on the season, to enjoy at your next stop.

Continuing west on 92nd / Napier Road for about seven miles you find Park Road where a turn to the north for less than two miles will take you to Territorial Road. Traveling west on Territorial for roughly seven miles will take you to the northeast corner of Benton Harbor. Territorial Road will join with Red Arrow

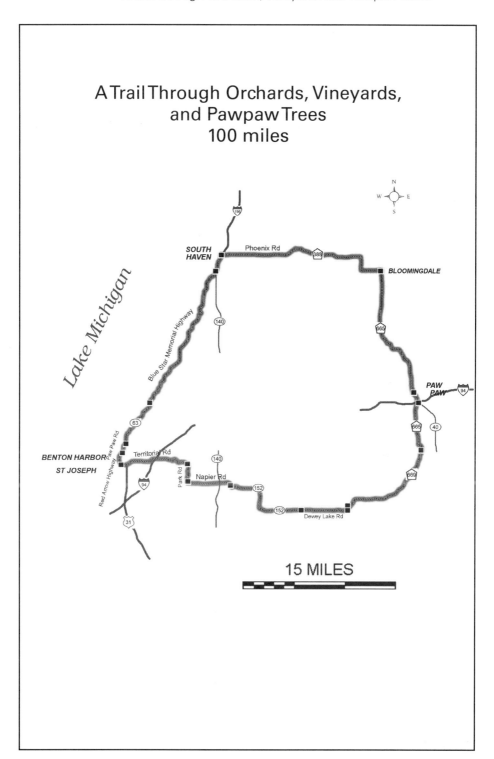

A Trail Through Orchards, Vineyards, and Pawpaw Trees
100 miles

15 MILES

A TRAIL OF VINEYARDS, ORCHARDS, AND PAWPAW 100 MILES		
Miles	Destination	Total
0	Paw Paw	0
26	Dewey Lake	26
17	Benton Harbor	43
25	South Haven	68
18	Bloomingdale	86
14	Paw Paw	100

Highway for a short distance, and shortly after passing the airport you find Paw Paw Road. It's real easy to find—just after the airport is an elementary school, then a downhill stretch, and at the bottom is Paw Paw Road. There is even a building on the northwest corner with the street name on it in large letters.

If you're interested in the history of religious groups, there is a museum in Benton Harbor just a mile or so off this route that may satisfy your curiosity. Benton Harbor has been home to a religious sect called the Israelite House of David for the last century. In the early part of the twentieth century their population was quite large. They had traveling bands and their own semiprofessional baseball team. The group has an interesting history, with their roots traced back to seventeenth century England. They were reorganized in 1930 and have opened a museum called Mary's City of David Museum. To get there, take Crystal Avenue, located at the east end of the airport, south several blocks to Britain Avenue, then go west a few blocks to the corner of Eastman Avenue. You can't miss it. There are even persistent rumors of a mermaid occasionally seen at the natural spring on the grounds. Who knows, you just might happen to spot her.

Back on the trip—take Territorial Road past the airport to Paw Paw Road and turn north to its juncture with M63—the shoreline road. Almost exactly two miles north of Territorial Road Paw Paw Road comes to a fork with Riverside going straight ahead and Paw Paw Road quartering to the left / north. Follow the well-marked signing and take the left fork and very soon you will hit M63. Go north on M63 for six miles where the Blue Star Memorial Highway begins, and keep following this beautiful winding coastal road north about fourteen miles into the resort town of South Haven. Blue Star Highway is one of those well-kept secrets unless you're familiar with the area. It's a lightly traveled winding road that twists between forested dunes, with Lake Michigan often visible to the left. There

Warner Vineyard located near Paw Paw. (Photo courtesy of Travel Michigan)

are a couple of great local parks on this stretch where you can stop and enjoy the view or take a walk down the dune to the beach.

At the south end of South Haven Blue Star Highway will intersect with M140/LaGrange Street. Turn left/north onto LaGrange to go into town. South Haven is a resort town where you'll want to spend some time to sightsee, relax, and stretch your legs.

There are several public parks on the beach and lots of places to walk around and enjoy the sights. If you have any interest in maritime issues and artifacts, don't miss the Michigan Maritime Museum. It is located downtown on the Black River at 260 Dyckman Avenue. Call 800-747-3810 for more information. The museum and surrounding wharfs offer much for the boating enthusiast.

For antique engine and tractor aficionados, the Michigan Flywheelers Museum, located on 68th Street two miles east of South Haven, may be your cup of tea. They have a large tractor and engine show each September. Call 269-639-2010 for more information.

Of special interest to motor sports enthusiasts is GingerMan Raceway, located on Phoenix Road five miles east of town. They host a variety of motor sports racing, including motorcycles races. They also have open track time Tuesday—Thursday after 5:30 p.m. Their phone number is 269-253-4445. If for some mysterious and totally illogical reason you don't want to go into downtown South Haven or the beach area, just continue northeast on the Blue Star Highway until it intersects with Phoenix Road—the main east/west road.

Leave South Haven by taking Phoenix Road/CR388 east of town and follow it for almost twenty miles as it curves easterly and a bit south past orchards, farms and fields to the charming small crossroads town of Bloomingdale. Take 42nd Street/CR665 south out of Bloomingdale and follow it all the way south and east fifteen miles back to Paw Paw. The last half of this stretch has a number of fun curves and jogs, but remains CR665 all the way. Just about the time your brakes begin overheating from all the high-speed deceleration you'll be back in Paw Paw.

This route is almost exactly 100 miles in length, but with the many attractions, especially in the South Haven area, it makes for a great daylong trip. Plan an overnight stay in Paw Paw at the end of the trip to enjoy dinner and wine tasting and tours at local wineries in town. It's a very enjoyable way to spend the evening following a great ride.

A Trail Through Orchards, Vineyards and Pawpaw Trees

Tall ship entering the harbor at South Haven. (Photo by Vito Palmisano)

The Southern Frontier

A VISITOR FROM ANOTHER PLANET might assume that Michigan was tilted to the north, resulting in a weekly migration of people traveling from south to north. "Going up North" is a phrase that has become part of Michigander's language and one that needs no explanation.

While the southern part of the state can't compete with the north when it comes to scenery and wide-open spaces, it does have plenty of charms and attractions. It also has history and historic places and events that rival any in the region.

Motorcyclists generally ride roads in the far southern part of Michigan for short rides or commutes, but don't often plan extensive tours. I wanted to remedy this situation and define a two-day trip across far southern Michigan that would be not only an enjoyable ride on good roads through nice scenery, but also one that immerses the rider in some very interesting and important history. This tour starts in one of the most historic places in Michigan—Monroe County (see sidebar).

As decreed in 1805 the western boundary of the Michigan Territory was originally a line running due north from the southernmost point of Lake Michigan to the Canadian border. This line would have been near the city of Munising. The southern border of the new Michigan Territory was also established by Congress in 1805, and was to be a line running from the southernmost point of Lake Michigan straight east to Lake Erie. Ohio and Indiana were both admitted into the Union prior to Michigan, and used that advantage to gain prime waterfront property. Acts of Congress in 1816 and 1836 respectively moved Indiana's and Ohio's borders northward conveying access to Lake Michigan, and control of the important Maumee River all the way to Lake Erie.

We'll start this southern border odyssey by heading west on Dumbar Road, picking it up at its intersection with Telegraph Road (M24) one

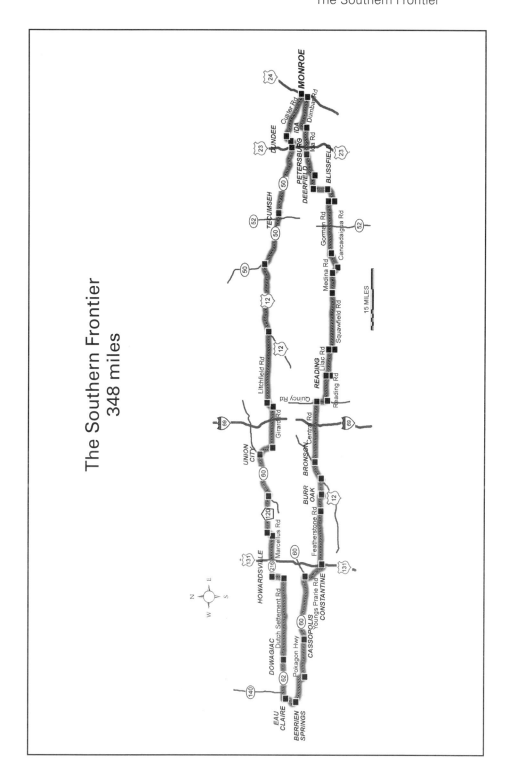

The Southern Frontier
348 miles

Miles	Destination	Total
	**THE SOUTHERN FRONTIER** **348 MILES**	
0	Monroe	0
29	Blissfield	29
30	US127/Hudson	59
22	Reading	81
27	Bronson	108
9	Burr Oak	117
12	Klinger Lake Road	129
24	Vandalia	153
15	Hopewell Indian Mounds	168
10	Berrien Springs	178
14	Dowagiac	192
56	Union City	248
23	Litchfield	271
30	Cambridge Junction	301
16	Tecumseh	317
16	Dundee	333
15	Monroe	348

mile south of the City of Monroe. Dumbar Road comes to a "T" after almost eight miles and takes a mile jog to the south to the small village of Ida, where you continue slightly over six miles farther west on Ida Road. Take Ida Road all the way into the town of Petersburg, and continue west out of that town on its main east/west road—Deerfield Road. Westbound Deerfield Road will take you through the small town of the same name and around a couple of small jogs just outside of Deerfield.

Stay on Deerfield Road almost five miles past the town, to the north/south road of Blissfield, which you take south into the town bearing that name. In Blissfield you have to go east on M223 about a half-mile to cross over the River Raisin, followed by a right turn onto Lane Street at the stop light. A small historical museum is located at this intersection along the railroad tracks. Lane Street will take you through town and will curve southwest and turn into Beamer Road. Follow Beamer westerly along the River Raisin to Crockett Road, go north one mile and turn west again onto Gorman Road. After thirteen miles Gorman Road curves to the southwest as Cancadaigua Road, and then finally Medina Road—the same pavement that meanders westerly.

Once you cross into Hillsdale County, Medina Road becomes Squawfield Road—and continues west fourteen more miles until it Ts at Hillsdale Road. At this T, jog north a mile then go west again on Lilac Road, through the tiny town of Cambria, continuing west to the stop sign at M49. Going less than a mile north on M49 takes you to the south edge of the small town of Reading, and Reading Road going to the west. Follow this road, with a jog west of town, west about seven miles to Quincy Road, and then turn right/north 2.5 miles to Central Road. Follow Central Road west fifteen miles to its juncture with US12 and the town of Bronson—a town that celebrates its Polish heritage with dancing, food and lots of fun at the annual Polish

Monroe County steeped in history

This area's history goes back nearly four hundred years, with the arrival of French missionaries and explorers. The city of Monroe was called Frenchtown until 1817 when its name was changed to honor President James Monroe. French place names are still very common in the area, including La Plaisance Bay and the River Raisin (River Aux Raisin) so named by the early French because of the many wild grapes that grew in the area.

Monroe County was the site of a major battle in the War of 1812, and of course was the site of the bloodless Michigan-Ohio war of 1835, when the state of Ohio used its political advantage to claim the city of Toledo and the mouth of the Maumee River, rather than allow this strip of land to go to the Territory of Michigan as was the initial plan. Congress interceded and allowed Ohio to keep the Toledo Strip, but in compensation gave Michigan what is essentially the west half of the Upper Peninsula. Hmmm, sorry, Ohio, but I think we got the better of that deal! The "worthless wilderness" of the western UP of course proved to be extremely valuable with its iron, copper and forest resources.

Today in addition to its continued natural resource-based economic contributions, it is the destination of hundreds of thousands of people each year who enjoy its natural beauty for travel and vacation purposes.

Festival Days. Head west on US12 five miles to Deer Park Road where the westward trip continues.

Follow Deer Park Road into the small town of Burr Oak, dropping south a couple of blocks to follow the railroad tracks west through town on Front St. While riding in the Burr Oak area you may notice a sweet smell in the air. Burr Oak bills itself as the Gladiolus Capital of the Nation due to the number of commercially grown Gladiolus and other flowers on farms near town. They appear to have some competition regarding this claim, however, as promotional material for Bronson also claims the title of gladiolus capital for that neighboring town. I just don't think this War of the Glads will ever go down in history as did the War of the Roses.

Take Front Street to its dead end at Highland Road (you'll find a classic car museum at this 'T' intersection (call 269-489-5058 for more information), and follow Highland less than a mile north for a west turn onto Maystead Road. Maystead Road is very easy to find—it's just north of the city park and ball fields.

Follow Maystead Road four-and-a-half miles west to M66, where a very slight jog is made to continue west on what is then called Featherstone Road/CR130. Follow Featherstone Road about thirteen miles as it takes you through the heart of rural St. Joseph County. Take it all the way into the town of Constantine and highway US131.

Follow US131 just a few blocks north and when it veers off to the east. Youngs Prairie Road will continue straight ahead. Turn left onto Youngs Prairie Road and follow it as it meanders northwesterly five-and-a-half miles to M60. M60 is a very nice riding road through this area so we'll follow it about sixteen miles, all the way to the historic town of Cassopolis.

M60 happens to follow the Underground Railway in this area. Both Vandalia and Cassapolis played a major role in the Underground Railway prior to the Civil War. Cass County was a recognized safe area for slaves escaping to the north or Canada, and many people and churches in this area provided refuge and relief to escaped slaves.

In Cassapolis M60 makes a ninety-degree turn south, but State Street continues straight west, and this is the road we want. Continue west on State St. and outside of town it becomes Pokagon Highway, which will deliver you almost nine miles west to the crossroads of Pokagon, and highway M51, which at this point is aligned east and west. Follow M51 west about a mile to the point where it turns south and Pokagon Highway continues straight west.

Take Pokagon Highway into the Village of Sumnerville for two wonderful attractions: On the east edge of town in a small park you'll find Hopewellian Indian mounds that are well over 1,000 years old. The far southern portion of Michigan had many such mounds when settlers first arrived. Unfortunately most have been destroyed during clearing, farming and other land development that has occurred over the last 150 years. Just down the street is the Old Tavern Inn, built in 1835. The Inn is still serving great food to hungry travelers. It is the oldest operating business of its type in the state.

At the tavern turn north onto Indian Lake Road taking it one mile north to Crystal Springs / Pokagon Road and proceed west again. Continue following Pokagon Road as it goes west, then northwest about seven miles to Deans

Hill Road just east of the St. Joseph River and the town of Berrien Springs (the Christmas Pickle Capital of the World). In Berrien Springs the 1839 Courthouse Square and Museum provide an interesting historical overview of the history of this area. Berrien Springs was the original county seat of Berrien County, and the very unique original courthouse built in 1839 is still there.

Follow Deans Hill Road and then Hochberger Road as this pavement winds its way to the small town of Eau Claire (the Cherry Pit Spitting Capital of the World. You think I make this stuff up?) In fact, if you fancy yourself a pit spitting contender, show up at the annual international cherry pit spit championship held in Eau Claire each July. Hochberger Road intersects with Pipestone Road on the west edge of this village.

This marks the west apex of our trip and we'll start back east on Pipestone Road, which becomes M140 and then picking up M62 as our road continues straight east and M140 heads north. We'll continue east for nine miles on M62 through the town of Dowagiac. On the east side of town M62 angles southeast and Dutch Settlement Road goes straight east—turn onto Dutch Settlement Road and follow it almost twenty miles across Cass County and two miles into St. Joseph County to Bent Road. Turning north on Bent Road and following it three miles takes you to M216 and the tiny village of Howardsville. Bent Road goes only north off of Dutch Settlement Road, and is five miles east of M40, which you cross. At the point where Bent Road meets Dutch Settlement Road a large gray farmhouse, with a wooden fence, is located. If you go too far Dutch Settlement Road turns to gravel a half mile past Bent Road—a clear signal that you need to turn around.

The entire trip east across northern Cass and St. Joseph County is very nice. The roads are lightly traveled and pleasantly hilly, with enough curves to make them fun. This is what most of southern Michigan looked like just a generation or two ago. The countryside is made up of well-kept farms that proudly grow cattle and crops, not houses and strip malls, with picturesque fields and woods that roll into the distance.

M216 is also called Marcellus Road, and it certainly doesn't have the look or feel of a state highway. It is lightly traveled and nice for riding. The state highway designation ends at US131. Follow Marcellus Road straight east for eleven miles. Just before ending it will jog north and 'T' at Michigan Avenue at the south end of Portage Lake. Turn right on Michigan Avenue, following it east ten miles to 44th Street, with a half-mile jog south to M60. Follow M60 a little over nine miles east to Union City.

On the west side of Union City M60 will curve northeast around town and Division Street will continue straight ahead. Take Division east into town, turning south one block on Ann Street when Division Street ends. At the stop light

Iron mining gave Union City its start

Union City may seem like any other small southern Michigan town, but it has some interesting history that is nearly forgotten, save for a state historical marker and a stack of stones. In 1847 a company built iron furnaces producing iron from locally mined iron ore. This ore was in the form of bog iron and kidney iron stones, present in the native soils and rocks. The ore concentration was too low to make such a venture profitable, however, and the furnaces were shut down after several years. Emphasis was shifted from the production of pig iron to the manufacture of farm equipment for the rapidly growing agricultural market. The historic marker at the site is all that's remains of this small part of Michigan history. I'm not aware of any other instances of iron mining activity in Lower Michigan. According to the historical marker, this may have been the first iron ore smelting in Michigan, predating even the Upper Peninsula mines by a short period.

go through downtown, over the headwaters of the St. Joseph River, and then left onto Coldwater Street. The historical marker commemorating the iron furnaces is on Coldwater Street on the east edge of town. A stack of the original bricks from the furnaces are next to the sign. In trying to find out a bit of local lore about Union City and the furnaces, I talked to three people in town at random asking them if they knew anything of the location of the furnaces and the history of iron ore smelting in their town. All three local folks knew nothing of that piece of their town's history—not even realizing that mining had ever occurred there.

Follow Coldwater Road east to where it turns into Union City Road after crossing the Coldwater River just east of Union City. It then runs southeast for three miles to Girard Road. Go east on Girard Road ten miles to Quincy Grange Road, following the pavement as it jogs north and then east two times, finally ending up eastbound on Litchfield Road. Stay on Litchfield Road almost eighteen miles, through the town of Litchfield, and east to its juncture with US12.

Stay on US12 about seventeen miles, riding it along its nicest stretch as it winds through the Irish Hills area. US12 is a historic road, as is M50, the road we'll turn onto when we reach the Walker Tavern at Cambridge Junction. M50 follows the route of the La Plaisance Bay Pike—a trail completed in 1835 connecting Monroe with the tiny town of Jacksonburg—now the city of Jackson. The La Plaisance Bay Pike crossed the Chicago Pike (now US12) at Cambridge Junction making this crossroads one of the most important out state locations at the time.

The La Plaisance Pike, also known as the Monroe Pike, allowed thousands of early settlers to more easily reach the interior of the state. After completion of the Erie Canal, creating a water highway stretching from the east coast of the country to the Great Lakes, many people started their inland journey upon arrival at the ports of Monroe and Detroit utilizing these very early trail roads.

Follow M50 southeast all the way into Monroe County and the town of Dundee. Along the way you will pass the Hidden Lake Gardens, a Michigan State University facility definitely worth an hour of your time. Tecumseh is the next town you will pass through. Tecumseh is a very pleasant town, and each year they host an antique car, motorcycle and airplane show. Call Ididit, Inc. at (517) 456-4133 for event information.

In downtown Dundee you will notice that M50 turns southward crossing the River Raisin, and Main Street goes straight east ahead of you. Stay on Main Street and take it east about a mile to Stowell Road, which will curve northeasterly, becoming Bigelow Road as it winds along the river. Take Bigelow to its juncture with Plank Road and follow Plank Road south to where the pavement turns east becoming Custer Road. Follow Custer Road along the north side of the river all the way back to Monroe. Abandoning M50 for the stretch east of Dundee results in a much more enjoyable and scenic ride back to Monroe.

It only seems fitting that the area around a river named for its grapes should develop into a wine growing area. Southeast Michigan has a developing wine industry, with several new vineyards and wineries located in Monroe, Lenawee, Jackson, and Washtenaw counties. Wineries are located in Dundee, Tecumseh and Somerset Center—towns that you ride through on this tour.

While this ride of 348 miles can be done in one day it's highly preferable to make it a two-day ride and take the opportunity to relax and explore a bit.

Historic Roads

ALMOST EVERYONE has heard of Route 66--the famous federal highway that linked Chicago to California. The story of Route 66 has become part of our culture and demonstrates the level of passion Americans have for great roads to drive on. While Michigan doesn't have any roads that have been the subject of movies, TV shows, and songs, (other than Woodward and 8-Mile in Detroit, great roads in their own right, just not great motorcycling roads) we do have long stretches of road whose history and stories date back far longer than Route 66. Like Route 66 our historic roads also connect distant points, and were the primary routes of travel for many years—in our case for much longer than Route 66's fabled history. The historic roads I've chosen to describe here were selected because they covered long distances connecting important distant points, and were not just local roads. These roads are:

- Old Territorial Road / The Potawatomi Trail / Michigan Avenue (also called the Northern Route)
- The Chicago Pike / Old Sauk Trail / Old U.S. 112, now U.S.12;
- Grand River Indian Trail / Old U.S. 16
- Old U.S. 27, which ran from the Indiana Border to Cheboygan

By the way, making a two-day circular trip using Michigan Avenue and the Chicago Pike is an enjoyable way of exploring these two roads.

The number of motorcyclists who can remember a pre-expressway Michigan is getting very small, but there are still folks alive who can recall when these historic roads were the main routes for east—west and north—

south travel in Michigan. Long before station wagons filled with families plied these roads in the 1940s and 1950s, however, pioneer families on foot or in horse-drawn carts followed the very same routes when Michigan was being settled more than 150 years ago. The first stagecoach from Detroit to Chicago had a very rough ride on the Chicago Pike in 1833.[1] For hundreds of years before that Native American families walked these paths on their travels. Given our typically myopic view of the world, this history is often unknown or unappreciated by modern day observers.

---

[1] *The Old Northwest;* Vol. I. Carlyle Buley, © 1951 Indiana University Press

Like all old roads they follow original footpaths fairly closely, which means they followed the high ground, and tend to meander a lot. Making these roads even more enjoyable is the fact that the majority of traffic utilizes the nearby parallel expressways, making for relatively light traffic on many stretches.

While these roads may not be your cup of tea for riding over and over again, it's a worthwhile accomplishment being able to say you've ridden all four of Michigan's own versions of Route 66 from beginning to end. As these roads get more developed and urbanization spreads they will be harder to find and ride in the future. Now is the time to do it. Most of the towns along the original territorial roads were founded 150 or more years ago because of these roads.

There are other roads with significant historic importance in Michigan beyond these four. I try to weave in those roads, or stretches of them, in the other tour categories. One that is highly deserving of note is the Dixie Highway—the famous road that linked Sault Ste. Marie with Florida. The problem is—this road had many different variations depending on the locale in the state and the time period.

With that, let's get started.

Canoeing on the AuSable River near Grayling. (Photo by Terry W. Phipps)

Old Territorial Road / Original US12 Michigan Avenue

THOUSANDS OF PEOPLE drive or live along this route but may be unaware of its unique history. It was instrumental in settling the second tier of counties in Michigan, and for the formation of several cities along it. For generations it served as a Potawatomi Indian trail long before the first European explorers arrived.

This road originally started just north of downtown Detroit according to the earliest available Michigan state maps. The 1931 and 1932 Michigan highway maps show that US12 followed the current Plymouth Road from Grand River Avenue in Detroit west through the City of Plymouth, then angling to the northeast corner of Ann Arbor. The current M14 expressway follows the same general route today.

In keeping with my promise to keep you off heavily traveled urban roads, we'll start this route at the intersection of Zeeb Road and Michigan Avenue (called

Jackson Road in that vicinity) on the west edge of Ann Arbor. If you want to take the original US12 from its very beginning in downtown Detroit, it is still possible to do for the most part. Many miles of stop and go traffic, however!

The area west of Ann Arbor Jackson Road / Old US12 is fairly built up until Chelsea, but not bad riding. It runs parallel to I94 and just to the south. It crosses I94 east of Chelsea and again just west of Chelsea where the name changes to Michigan Avenue and some signs showing Old US12. Chelsea is one of those revitalized towns that try hard to not be just another bedroom community

Old Territorial Road / Potawatomi Trail / Michigan Avenue

170 miles

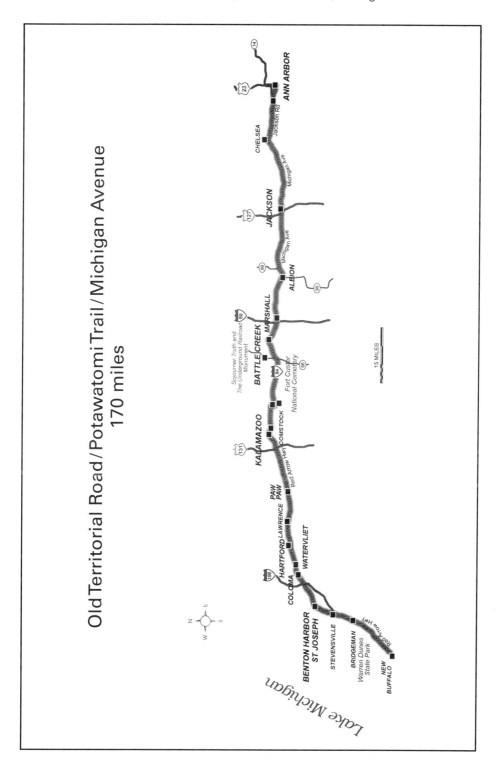

OLD TERRITORIAL ROAD / POTAWATOMI TRAIL / MICHIGAN AVENUE 170 MILES		
Miles	Destination	Total
0	Ann Arbor	0
10	Chelsea	10
21	Jackson	31
19	Albion	50
11	Marshall	61
7	I94 / Battle Creek	68
19	Exit 85	87
9	Kalamazoo	96
16	Paw Paw	112
15	Hartford	127
16	Benton Harbor	143
27	New Buffalo	170

for nearby large cities. It has a nice hometown, if toney, flavor with lots of antique shops, restaurants, and boutiques. Between Chelsea and Jackson there are some nice stretches and traffic lightens up quite a bit. The fact that I94 is on the same corridor means that mostly local traffic is all you'll encounter—few large trucks.

Michigan Avenue is quite easy to follow straight through Jackson (becoming Louis Glick Hwy. for a stretch). Besides being the home of Jackson State Prison, the city's main claim to fame is being the place where the Republican Party was formed. Though an informal meeting regarding forming a third party that was to become the Republican Party was held earlier in Ripon, Wisconsin, it was in July 1854 that a meeting was held in Jackson officially forming the party and nominating candidates on an anti-slavery platform. Interestingly, according to a 1904 version of the *Albion Recorder* newspaper, the Republican Party's name was agreed upon in a meeting earlier that year held in a livery stable in the nearby town of Albion. One Ebenezer Grosvenor supposedly recommended the new party be named "The Republican Party" at that Albion meeting, and it was approved by the twelve delegates present.

It is definitely worth a trip to Jackson in the evening to witness the Cascades— illuminated multi-colored water cascading from pool to pool down a large man-made hill—all set to music. It's an amazing sight after dark. Jackson also hosts a large three-day hot air balloon event every July that has grown into a major spectacle. See hotairjubilee.com for more information and dates. Each August Jackson also hosts what is billed as Michigan's largest civil war muster and battle enactment. Call 517-788-4320 for more information. If you feel like getting spaced out, stop at the Michigan Space Museum 517-787-4425 to see a wide variety of space artifacts and rockets, as well as moon rocks. It's a blast.

Of the two early east-west routes, US112 and US12, the more northerly old US12 goes through more large cities. This pattern of light traffic and then a city to pass through continues all along Old US12 from beginning to end. Between Jackson and Albion there are some very nice stretches of quiet winding road, and once again west of Albion. In far western Jackson County, just east of M99, a marker placed by the Daughters of the American Revolution in 1915 on a large boulder marks this road as the "Old Territorial Road," and one of two such trails over which immigration came into Michigan.

When you do hit M99, a jog a half-mile to the south over the I94 overpass is necessary, though not well marked. Once you cross over the expressway the road curves west and continues on toward Albion.

Albion is a nice quiet hometown sort of place that is worthy of some of your time. It is built on the forks of the Kalamazoo River and has a nice river walk to stroll along to see various historic places. The downtown main street is paved in brick giving the town a unique old-time flavor. Albion is famous for several things, including being the birthplace of Mother's Day and home of Albion College—a private four-year liberal arts college known for academic excellence.

Following Michigan Avenue into Albion, the pavement shares old US12 with M99 and BR94, with M99 eventually turning off to the south and BR94 heading north. Stay on BR94 / M99 to Superior Street where a right (north) turn is necessary. Take Superior Street north about five blocks to Austin Street which angles northwesterly. Follow Austin west. BR94 will veer off to the north but you want to stay on Austin Street, which eventually reverts back to Michigan Avenue / Old 12 just west of town. The stretch between Albion and Marshall is short but quite nice with farms and good scenery along a nicely winding road.

The next city you'll pass through is Marshall. If you stop to explore only one city on this tour, it should be Marshall. This is one of those small towns that Norman Rockwell would have loved. Steeped in history, vibrant, and fighting hard to maintain its true character. You won't find a vacated downtown surrounded by big box cutthroat, I mean cut-rate, discount stores and malls around the edges of this town. Despite its precarious location adjacent to two major expressways, it still maintains a healthy small town pre-expressway and pre-urban sprawl existence. It is also filled with history. Take time to read the various historical markers and view the old buildings. All of Michigan Avenue through town has been designated as a National Historic Landmark District. I believe at last count there are fifteen historical markers in Marshall. Even the City Hall has a great story—originally built as a stone barn in 1857 and used as a livery stable for decades. It later served as a stagecoach stop. It was renovated and since 1930 has been serving as city hall. Now here's a town that values its history!

After being made a state by Congress in 1837, Michigan leaders were given ten years to come up with a permanent capital. In the 1840s Marshall had grand dreams of being designated state capital. It was already a well-established town, while Lansing to the north was barely more than a collection of log cabins in the wilderness. An early investor even built a house that was to serve as the governor's mansion. It can still be seen at 612 South Marshall Street. It is currently a museum maintained by the Daughters of the American Revolution. The National House Inn, located at the Town Square and fountain, is the oldest operating inn in the state. It served as a stagecoach stop in its early days. Marshall is famous for its many unique and stately old homes, and has a tour of these old houses each year. Over 800 buildings in Marshall are listed on the National Register of Historic Places.

The Brooks Memorial Fountain is a beautiful Greek revival structure that features color light and water shows in the evenings. It's situated in a roundabout at the intersection of Michigan Avenue and Old US27. Finally, if you're interested in magic, the American Museum of Magic is a must-see for you. This museum offers tours by appointment so call ahead 269-781-7674. They have thousands of magic memorabilia from around the world.

Early Marshall was a stronghold of anti-slavery sentiment and many residents were active in the Underground Railroad. In one well-known incident Francis Troutman, a slave hunter, arrived at the home of the Crosswhite family—former slaves who had escaped to Marshall. When Troutman and his associates tried to take the Crosswhites back to Kentucky angry mobs confronted them and prevented it. The threat of being tarred and feathered convinced the Kentuckians to consider alternatives. This action allowed the Crosswhites to escape to Canada.

Michigan Avenue is easy to follow out of Marshall. Just keep going west on the main street of Marshall and cross over the I69 expressway. After a few miles of countryside you will cross over I94 and Old 12 becomes BL94 into Battle Creek. The I94 expressway and other construction in the Battle Creek area caused the elimination of much of the original US12 alignment, resulting in its intermittent stretches. I've always found Battle Creek to be a confusing city to navigate through, so given the fact that one isn't accurately retracing the original old highway, and the realities of urban congestion and confusing streets, an option is to bypass the Cereal City. If you don't want to have breakfast with Tony The Tiger get on

Kellogg's Cereal City in Battle Creek is rated the second best factory four in the U.S. (Photo courtesy of Kellogg's Cereal City USA)

westbound I94 when Michigan Avenue / Old 12 intersects with it about five miles west of Marshall (which is about three miles east of Battle Creek). Maps do show a Michigan Avenue running immediately adjacent to I94 for several miles west of Battle Creek, but this is not the original US12 route. The expressways, airport, and Fort Custer National Guard base have disrupted the original route.

Once on I94, stay on the expressway for about fifteen miles to the Galesburg exit (35th Street / Exit 85) where you can pick up Michigan Avenue / Old 12 again by going a mile north and turning left on what will be Michigan Avenue and M96.

Battle Creek does have a lot going for it and if you're interested in riding through town, it's easy to do—as long as you're not in a hurry, just stay on BL-94 through town. On the west side of the city BL-94 will turn south to rejoin the expressway and M96 will continue straight west. Stay on M96, which in a few miles once again becomes the old Michigan Avenue.

You may want to save further exploration of the home of ready to eat breakfast cereals for a trip in the car with the whole family. A tour of the cereal production facilities is quite fascinating (you might even say it has lots of snap, crackle and pop). Because the tour is so popular, Kellogg Company has created a facility called Cereal City with various events and attractions for the whole family. A factory tour is also included. The Cereal City attraction has been called the second

Hot air balloons during Battle Creek's Balloon Festival. (Photo courtesy of Travel Michigan)

best factory tour in the U.S. by The Discovery Channel. For a fascinating history of the Kellogg family and their revolutionary approach to health and nutrition, read *The Road to Wellville* by T. C. Doyle (Signet Press, 1994).

Other attractions nearby include Fort Custer and the Fort Custer National Cemetery just west of town, and the Sojourner Truth and Underground Railroad monuments in downtown BC. In early July each year you'll also find the fabulous hot air balloon festival. This several day event includes huge colorful balloons, a car, and a motorcycle show and lots of other events. It is held at the W.C. Kellogg Airport. See bcballoons.com for more information.

In Comstock, just east of Kalamazoo, Michigan Avenue splits off from M96 and runs just north of and parallel to M96 / King Highway - the main east / west road into Kalamazoo. When the road divides take the smaller right fork to leave M96 and stay on Michigan Avenue. (Like Yogi Berra said—when you come to a fork in the road, take it).

Michigan Avenue / Old US12 can be followed through Kalamazoo without a lot of effort (though the name of the old highway changes in town). In the downtown section Michigan Avenue joins M43 for several blocks heading west through town. On the west side of downtown Stadium Drive angles off to the southwest and M43 will continue west. Take Stadium Drive several miles and it will change to Red Arrow Highway at the Van Buren County Line. Red Arrow Highway is the highway designation given to honor the Red Arrow Division (32nd Infantry Division) from Wisconsin and Michigan, which played significant roles in both World Wars I and II.

Old 12 / Red Arrow Highway is very easy to follow once you're past Kalamazoo. It goes straight through Paw Paw, Detroit Tigers slugger Charlie Maxwell's home town of course, but you knew that, and named after the Pawpaw tree which can be found in southwest Michigan. The small towns of Lawrence and Hartford are on the old road west of Paw Paw. The Van Buren County Museum and Historical

Society located two miles west of Lawrence is an interesting stop. It's housed in the old county poor-house and the building itself has a very interesting history. Shortly after Hartford you enter Berrien County and the towns of Watervliet and Coloma.

The land west of Kalamazoo is wine and fruit country, and you will see many vineyards and orchards on the hillsides as you ride through this unique area. Any time from early June to mid-October you will find delicious berries and fruits of every description available at large and small roadside stands. You owe it to yourself to buy some fresh strawberries, apples, blueberries or whatever happens to be in season and stop under a shade tree for a most delicious snack.

About six miles after Coloma you'll hit the outskirts of Benton Harbor and Old 12 / Red Arrow Highway join Territorial Road / BL 94 and then M63 for several miles through both Benton Harbor and the adjacent town of St. Joseph. In St. Joseph a very interesting stop is at the Fort Miami Heritage Center (708 Market Street). This museum preserves the history of the area dating back to 1679 when French explorer Rene de La Salle built Fort Miami at the mouth of the St. Joseph River. This fort was eventually abandoned and Fort St. Joseph was built upriver at current-day Niles.

The Red Arrow Hwy picks up again south of St. Joseph (the road is now running north and south close to the Lake Michigan shoreline). When BL 94 rejoins the I94 expressway, continue just past I94 and you'll see Red Arrow on your right heading south. There are several local municipal parks on this stretch, plus the

large and very popular Warren Dunes State Park, which is a great place to enjoy the beach and see the massive sand dunes that line Lake Michigan's eastern shore.

The highway will take you through Stevensville and Bridgman, and then travel through dunes and nice countryside until it terminates when it hits the new US12 (the former US112) on the north side of New Buffalo.

Congratulations, you've retraced the steps of Indians and pioneers, and while you didn't have to worry about wolves and bears, you had to brave conditions and traffic they never dreamed of! On the other hand, you just traveled over 170 miles in the time it would have taken them to go a couple of miles on a mud trail.

St. Joseph Harbor at Sunset.
(Photo by Vito Palmisano)

The Sauk Trail / Chicago Pike / Old US112 / Current US12

THIS ROAD FROM DETROIT to Chicago, going through the southern tier of Michigan counties, is most commonly referred to as the Chicago Road. Native Americans traveled paths linking the southern end of Lake Michigan and the Lake Erie and Detroit River area for centuries. The British tried to upgrade the paths as a military trail connecting Fort Dearborn at what is now Chicago, Fort St. Joseph in Niles and Fort Detroit. Following the war of 1812, after experiencing great difficulty moving troops into this region, the American government took steps to upgrade the road further and by 1830 it was a rough but identifiable trail for horses and wagons. With the completion of the Erie Canal, settlers by the thousands began streaming into Michigan from the Toledo and Detroit ports. They used this road to enter the unsettled interior portion of the state. By 1835 two stagecoaches per week made the trip from Detroit to Fort Dearborn. At that time it was called the Chicago Military Road. It was described as "practically an extension of the Erie Canal and….a great axis of settlement in southern Michigan.[2]

Prior to the Civil War this road was a major route on the Underground Railroad, with many escaped slaves finding freedom via this muddy track through the villages and farms of southern Michigan. There are still buildings in the towns along this road whose cellars and attics at one time provided refuge for escaping slaves while they were following that drinking gourd in the sky to freedom in Michigan or Canada.

My favorite description of this road is that it: "...stretches itself by devious and irregular windings east and west like a huge serpent lazily pursuing its onward course utterly unconcerned as to its destination."[3] Now if that doesn't sound like the description of a great motorcycling road, what does? Unfortunately, of course, highway engineers have significantly straightened the road since its earliest days, but it still has lots of redeeming qualities.

---

[2] G. N. Fuller, *Economic and Social Beginnings of Michigan p. 76*
[3] *Michigan Pioneer and Historical Collections.* I 1876, pg. 231. Quoted by C. E. Pray.

The Sauk Trail/Chicago Pike/Old US112/Current US12
185 miles

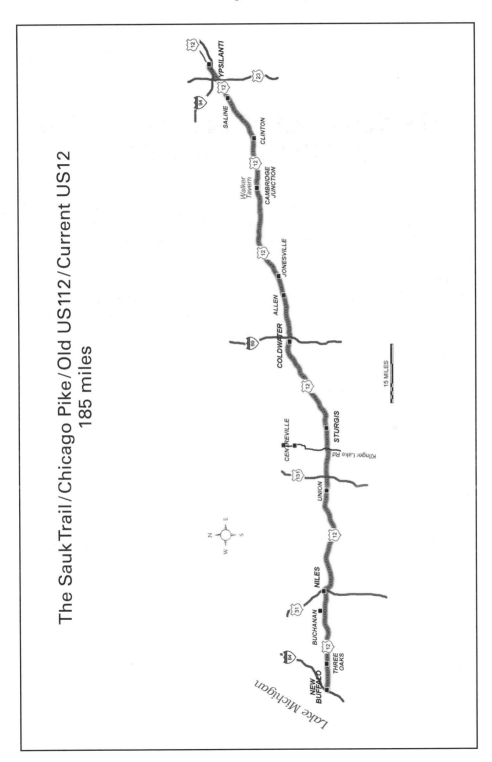

SAUK TRAIL / CHICAGO PIKE / OLD US212 / CURRENT US12 185 MILES		
Miles	**Destination**	**Total**
0	Ypsilanti	0
10	Saline	10
13	Clinton	23
11	Irish Hills	34
29	Jonesville	63
19	Coldwater	82
13	Bronson	95
14	Sturgis	109
13	White Pigeon	122
25	Edwardsburg	147
11	Niles	158
21	Three Oaks	179
6	New Buffalo	185

Following a fire in 1805 that essentially leveled Detroit, territorial judge Augustus Woodward devised a plan for the new city that initiated the familiar spoke of a wheel design that is still evident today.[5] One of the spokes emanating from the hub was the old Sauk Trail, today's US12. This road is still located today where it was then. It is possible to follow US12 from its starting point in downtown Detroit, then through Dearborn, Inkster, Wayne, Canton Township and Ypsilanti. Your clutch would be in need of replacement after all the stop and go traffic on that heavily urbanized stretch of highway, however. Expressway construction and bypasses have also altered the original route somewhat.

Because this book is all about motorcycle riding, not stop and go exercises in heavy urban traffic, I suggest picking up US12 in Ypsilanti, and forego the road east of town. Besides, the stretch east of Ypsilanti actually started out as route 17, and was only later designated as part of the US112/12 corridor.

Starting the day with coffee and breakfast at Haab's Restaurant on Michigan Avenue in downtown Ypsilanti, just west of the river, will guarantee your day gets off to a good start. I can vouch for the quality of the food and service.

---

[5] *Michigan: A History of the Wolverine State.* Dunbar. © 1970 Eerdmans Publishing Co.

Ypsilanti has a healthy downtown and a lot of history. It also has one of the most recognizable water towers to be found anywhere. The limestone structure was built in 1890 and certainly has a one-of-a-kind shape. Founded in 1825 and named after Greek General Demetrius Ypsilanti—a leader in the Greek War of Independence that had just concluded—it's a good place to start this tour of history.

A tradition started in 2000 in Ypsilanti is the Elvis Fest. Held each July, this event draws Elvis impersonators and Elvis fans by the thousands to Riverside Park. Call 734-480-3974 or go to mielvisfest.org for dates and more information. The Ypsilanti Automotive Heritage Museum and Miller Motors Hudson dealership (Miller Motors was the world's last dealer selling the Hudson brand of automobile) is open year-round and is devoted to Ypsilanti's many contributions to the automotive industry.

At the west end of downtown Ypsilanti, BR12 splits off to the south towards I94—you don't want to take it. Stay on Michigan Avenue / US12 and keep heading west out of town. Unfortunately, sprawling development has left its large footprint on the land between Ypsilanti and Saline, about twelve miles to the southwest. The fact that most of this was farmland just ten years ago is still evident, but it's being gobbled up fast.

The many incarnations of a Michigan road

In 1926 the Federal government designated the road, now known as US12, as a federal highway, paved it through the 1920s, and assigned it route number 112. The numbering system was just beginning at that time at the federal level, though Michigan had been numbering roads for identification for a few years already. The highway was the major route from Detroit to Chicago, while the more northerly Old US12 was the main road from Detroit to cities like Jackson, Battle Creek and Kalamazoo. In 1961 the Old US12 was decommissioned, and at that time US112 was also decommissioned and renamed US12. The state of Michigan named this road as Pulaski Memorial Highway in honor of American War of Independence hero Count Casimir Pulaski. In 2004 the State of Michigan designated all 209 miles of US12 as a United States Heritage Trail in recognition of its great historic and cultural significance.

So that's the story behind US12. As you ride down this historic road you'll be in the company of ghosts that recall a very different time and place. A press release from the Michigan Department of Transportation says it best: "US12 is among the oldest road corridors east of the Mississippi River and accesses some of the most extensive and significant historic, cultural, scenic and recreational resources in Michigan."[4] And unlike the now-unmarked Old US12 just north of here, this road is clearly signed and very easy to follow. So all you have to do is kick back and relax as you ride through history on this famous road.

---

[4] MDOT Press Release, May 4, 2004.

Saline, as the name suggests, was built near a large salt spring. This important source of salt had been used by Native Americans for generations, and is one of the reasons the Sauk Trail traversed this locale. In Saline, take a few minutes to see the historic Schuyler gristmill. Originally built in 1843, it was later purchased and refurbished by Henry Ford in 1935 to help power small factories. West of Saline the countryside opens up and there is nice farmland to ride through. All along this road there are signs that its history is being kept alive. Words like "Sauk," "Pike," "Chicago Road," and so on are used to describe streets, developments, malls, and so on.

Riding through the Irish Hills area in northwest Lenawee County takes you back forty or fifty years when all tourist areas looked like this. Small-time tourist attractions line the road, including two observation towers built in the 1920s. Those old enough to remember a better form of roadside advertising wouldn't be at all surprised to see Burma-Shave signs with their poetic advice and analysis of life's major issues along this stretch of road.

While the Irish Hills area today look quite small-scale and tame, one hundred and fifty years ago they were a pocket of unsettled woodlands where highwaymen and renegade Indians reportedly hid out. The land was also of poorer quality than surrounding lands and was thus not desirable for settlers who were intent on clearing land for farming.

Not long after you ride through the pleasant town of Clinton, you will see signs for the Hidden Lake Gardens. This beautiful but little known Michigan State University facility is a wonderful place to visit any time from May through October. Besides gardens and display buildings, there is a nice scenic ride through the park. It's a short diversion from US12 but well worth the detour.

At the intersection of the Chicago Pike and the Monroe Pike in Cambridge Junction is Walker Tavern. This original structure was a tavern built in 1836 and known as Snell's Tavern. Sylvester Walker bought the tavern and operated it from 1843 to 1855. It served as a stagecoach stop for stages bouncing along the rough road between Detroit and Chicago. The original house and farm buildings have been saved and now serve as the Walker Tavern Historical Complex, interpreting the early settlement period of Michigan.

What I find very ironic is that immediately west of the Walker Tavern is the gigantic Michigan International Speedway racecourse. What a juxtaposition of then and now! Could the early travelers stopping at the Walker Tavern for a meal and a bed after a freezing (or very hot) and very rough daylong ride through the wilderness on the Pike ever have imagined the demonic scream of an Indy car as it races around the track at speeds of over two hundred miles an hour—all just outside the windows of the Tavern? I think not!

After leaving Cambridge Junction and the Irish Hills area the road is mostly quiet for the next twenty-five miles or so. You'll pass through Jonesville and Allen (which bills itself as the antique capital of Michigan. Given the number of really nice old houses and buildings this small town has, they just might be right in their claim).

Unlike Old US12 just to the north, there are no really large towns on this road. Coldwater is probably the largest once you leave Ypsilanti. Coldwater is an interesting and historic city that would be a good place to stretch your legs and walk around. The city has five designated historic areas. The city of Coldwater today is a pleasant city surrounded by an attractive rural area with lakes, farms and woods. It exists because of the Sauk Trail having passed through that location.

When the first settlers came to this area they found a beautiful natural prairie of some six square miles (natural prairie openings were very common in southernmost Michigan in presettlement times). The area was inhabited by the Pottawatomie Indians, a tribe which was not happy to see the coming of the Europeans. Their presence deterred settlement of south-central Michigan. Chief Topinabee "sold" a large tract of land to the government in 1821, but natives continued to live and freely roam the area, living off the land as they had for generations. It wasn't until they were unfortunately relocated to a reservation in Kansas in 1840 that settlement really took off.

The entire issue of settlers versus Native Americans is of course a major theme throughout the settlement of what was to become the United States. I think it can be said that during the settlement of Michigan there was in general a more legal and moralistic approach in dealing with aboriginal peoples. There doesn't seem to be the kind of duplicitous dealings that unfortunately were more common later in the nineteenth century in the West.

In one of its first Acts, when passing legislation for governance of the Northwest Territory in July 1787, Congress stipulated the following:

"The utmost good faith shall always be observed towards the Indians; their lands and property shall never be taken from them without their consent, and in their property, rights, and liberty, they never shall be invaded or disturbed, unless in just and lawful wars, authorized by congress; but laws, founded in justice and humanity, shall, from time to time, be made, for preventing wrongs being done to them, and for preserving peace and friendship with them." Noble words and intentions that unfortunately didn't always survive human failings.

Coldwater derives its name from an Indian word for the area which literally meant "cold water."

The I69 expressway is just east of Coldwater, running north and south, and intersecting with I80/90 just a few miles south. There seems to be noticeably fewer large trucks on the road west of Coldwater. I suspect that given the very close proximity of the I80/90 toll road west of Coldwater truckers find it easier to take that highway rather than two-lane US12.

The Pike is an interesting, if not spectacular ride the rest of the way to Lake Michigan. Gentle hills and gentle curves is the best way to describe it. All along the road reminders of its heyday are present. Old buildings that were obviously the service stations, motels and restaurants of 1955 are still present; though used for different purposes today. Those families in the station wagons of fifty years ago certainly didn't stay in air-conditioned Holiday Inns from the looks of the old motels! Many buildings along the road date back to a period long before 1955.

In St. Joseph County, about five miles west of Sturgis, scenic Klinger Lake Road takes you north to Centreville, and an impressive covered bridge which spans the St. Joseph River three miles north of town. It's only about a twenty-five mile round trip diversion to see the bridge, and it's worth the detour. Covered bridges are a rapidly disappearing part of our American landscape, and one should take advantage of any opportunity to cross rivers the same way our great grandparents did.

West of the small town of Union in Cass County the original US112 of the 1920s and 1930s turned south and went to Elkhart, Indiana, according to state road maps of that era. A few years later US112 was extended through Michigan to New Buffalo. In the Niles vicinity the original road has been disrupted by a divided highway, which now takes you around town, rather than through it. Business US12 goes through Niles and is quite easy to navigate.

One should take the short loop into Niles for a stop at the Fort St. Joseph Historical Museum (269-683-4702). It is located on Business 12 right behind Niles City Hall—a very historic building in its own right. The museum has fur trade displays and military artifacts from the time the fort was used two hundred years ago and Indian art and articles of every day life. Admission is free and the two floors of displays make for a pleasant place to explore. This corner of Michigan is the only part of the state to be ruled by four different countries during its nearly 320-year history (France, Great Britain, Spain and of course the U.S.).

Fort St. Joseph was one of the very early outposts in Michigan. It was built by the French in 1691 at a strategic point where the Sauk Trail crossed the St. Joseph River. The river was originally named The River of the Miami's, after the Maumee Indians that the first explorers found living in the area. Shortly thereafter a mission named St. Joseph was built there and eventually the river and location became known simply as St. Joseph and the original name of the river was lost in time. St. Joseph was the Patron Saint of Travelers and early missionaries used the name more than once in hopes of enjoying safety and success in their endeavors. A large boulder now marks the location of the original fort about a mile southwest of downtown Niles on the east bank of the river.

The French occupied the fort for the next seventy years, enjoying very good relations with the Indians, and of course doing very well financially with the fur trade. In the French and Indian War the British captured Fort St. Joseph in 1761 and held it for the next twenty years. Their relation with the natives was markedly different than the French, and they came to be despised. The bad treatment and general disrespect shown the Indians by the English were in part responsible for Chief Pontiac's bloody rebellion of 1763. The Indians successfully attacked the fort, killing all the soldiers except three who they took to Detroit for exchange of Indian warriors being held by the British.

The Spanish captured Fort St. Joseph for a very brief period in 1781 but they did not maintain a military presence there. At the urging of two Indian chiefs, the Spanish commander in St. Louis supported a joint Indian and Spanish raid on the fort. They were successful, capturing the English soldiers and raising their own flag over the fort. The Spanish flag flew for only a very short period before the English briefly reoccupied the fort prior to its final abandonment following the American War of Independence.

A short distance west of Niles, just north of US12 is the town of Buchanan. A fascinating, and really quite unknown fact about Buchanan is Bear Cave - a large natural cave on the bank of the St. Joseph River. In fact, it is the only natural cave in Michigan. Supposedly the cave received its name from Native Americans years ago due to the use of the cave by Black Bears.

Prior to the Civil War the cave served as a hiding spot for slaves on the Underground Railroad. Today the cavern has electric lighting to illuminate the sanctuary where runaway slaves were hid. The cave is located off Red Bud Trail about three miles north of Buchanan. Visiting this cave is an interesting glance at a little-known piece of our history. The cave is now privately owned and is located at the Bear Cave Resort. Tours are provided by the resort owners.

West of Buchanan is the village of Three Oaks. If you're into bicycles be sure to stop at the Three Oaks Spokes Bicycle Museum, with its interesting display of antique bicycles and artifacts.

US12 goes all the way to the State of Washington, but after 185 miles on the odometer we'll end our tour at New Buffalo sipping locally produced wine on the beaches of Lake Michigan. This is definitely a two-day round trip, so call ahead for reservations and enjoy a well-earned break on Michigan's beautiful west coast.

Grand River Avenue / Old US16

ANOTHER OF THE ORIGINAL Indian trails that turned into a major highway is the Grand River Trail. The early trail version of what was to become Grand River Avenue is amazingly close to the actual route of Grand River Avenue today.

When Lansing was made the state capital in 1847 an effort was made to connect the state's capital city, which was surrounded by almost unbroken wilderness, with its largest and most important city—Detroit. Plank and corduroy roads (literally cut trees laid across the road to form a solid, albeit very rough, surface) were thus built on or along the old Grand River Indian trail in 1848. As with other territorial roads, Grand River was gradually improved, and in 1926, it was designated as US16—part of a longer national road that went all the way to Yellowstone National Park. US16 still exists in its western portion, connecting Rapid City, South Dakota, with Yellowstone National Park. Historically, a ferry at Muskegon linked US16 in Michigan and Wisconsin. Over the years changes were made to the road in large cities to ease traffic flow but what we ended up with was a two-lane highway that was the main artery connecting major cities along a line from Detroit to near Muskegon until the construction of I96 in the late 1950s. Following completion of the parallel I96 expressway, U.S. 16 was decommissioned in 1962 with the majority of the road turned over to local control.

With the exception of only a few stretches near its western terminus it is still possible to follow this road as it was known to millions of drivers since before World War II. It also helps that along much of the road it shares the common name of Grand River. Like Old US12 and US112, this route was one that took drivers through small towns and large cities. It wasn't meant for speed, but rather as the means of connecting distant cities.

Grand River Avenue starts in downtown Detroit as one of the spokes on Judge Woodward's wheel. It turns into State Route 5 and travels through some of the densest urban geography in Michigan from Cadillac Square northwest through Novi; not a motorcycle-friendly stretch of pavement! With that in mind, let's start our ride on Old US16 / Grand River Avenue at Novi Road and the town of Novi where you'll find Grand River Avenue running just south of I96 and parallel to it. There are several restaurants at this locale for a good breakfast and cup of coffee prior to starting off.

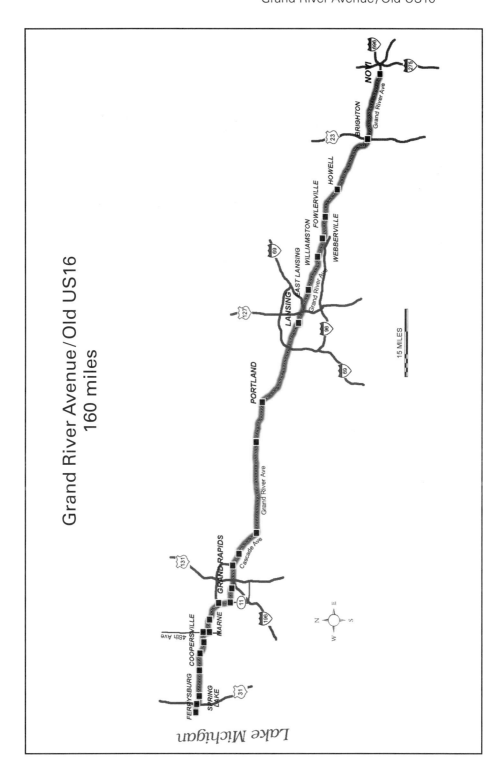

Grand River Avenue/Old US16
160 miles

GRAND RIVER AVENUE / OLD US16 160 MILES		
Miles	Destination	Total
0	Novi	0
16	Brighton	16
11	Howell	27
31	East Lansing	58
26	Portland	84
29	Cascade	113
30	Coopersville	143
17	Ferrysburg	160

Grand River Avenue runs along the south side of I96 until Brighton where it turns north for a stretch and crosses to the north side of I96 until just west of Lansing. Grand River serves as the main street in every town it passes through, including Brighton, Howell, Fowlerville, Webberville, Williamston, and East Lansing. Just west of Williamston is a Michigan Historic Site marker about the Grand River Trail. From Webberville through East Lansing Grand River Avenue is also State Route 43. In East Lansing, Grand River runs along the north edge of Michigan State University. On the west edge of East Lansing Grand River, M43 and Saginaw Road coexist for a few miles, then Grand River veers off again to the right on Lansing's east side.

Following Grand River through the greater Lansing area is not difficult. It's well marked and traffic isn't too heavy. Once Lansing is left behind, in fact, it is mostly a rural, lightly traveled road all the way to Grand Rapids. Portland is the only town of any size that one encounters between Lansing and Grand Rapids. As you travel through the peaceful and productive farmland of Ionia County, you'll be surprised just how far removed from the outside world you feel. You can sometimes see I96 just a short distance away, but it seems like you're many miles removed from its hustle and bustle.

Once Kent County is reached Grand River Avenue turns into Cascade Avenue. Upon reaching Grand Rapids and the I96 expressway you have a choice. It is fairly easy to follow the original road through Grand Rapids, but of course it means several miles of urban traffic. If you want to take the challenge, follow Cascade over I96 until it hits Fulton Street. Go west on Fulton all the way through town and at John Ball Park and I196 it turns into State Route 45. Continue west on M45 and you'll eventually intersect with M11—turn north when you do. Michigan 11 will begin to angle northwest and the street name will change to Ironwood Drive. Ironwood Drive will eventually take you alongside I96, and at this point the original road disappears under the expressway. You will turn onto Hayes Road and continue heading west for a mile where you'll follow State Street into the small town of Marne. Follow State Street west out of town to where its name changes to Berlin Fair Drive. Berlin Fair will follow along I96 until it too turns to the west on Garfield Road, because the original road once again is under the concrete of the expressway.

Michigan Historical Museum located in Lansing. (Photo courtesy of Michigan Historical Museum)

In just a few miles Garfield will intersect with 48th. Street. Take 48th north across the expressway. Just beyond I96 you will once again see Ironwood Street, turn left onto it, follow it as it becomes Randall Street and take it through Coopersville to the west. I96 will turn north and Randall Street will end when it hits the expressway but State Road will be a fork to the right. Take State Road, if you take the left fork it will put you on the expressway. Once on State Road you're back on the original road. Follow State Road just over a mile to Cleveland Road and turn west. You will stay on Cleveland Road as it crosses I96 at which point it becomes M104 and will take you into Spring Lake. Cleveland Road / 104 becomes Savidge Street in Spring Lake. Savidge Street crosses the river and leads onto Pine Street for a block, then 3rd Street and finally Shore Street, which takes you to the Lake Michigan shore at North Beach Park—a public park where you can enjoy the beach and Lake Michigan scenery.

This is the route of the original road in the 1920s and 1930s. The alignment was changed in 1940 with the highway terminus moved from Ferrysburg to Muskegon, followed by other route changes made in ensuing years and then construction of various Muskegon-area expressways, all of which have made the revised routes difficult to retrace.

From Novi to Lake Michigan is just less than 160 miles, making it an easy one-day trip, or a good first day of a two-day round trip from the Detroit area.

Oh, the choice you have to make back on the east side of Grand Rapids? Well, if you don't want to ride through the city, jump on I96 where Cascade Dr. intersects it, and stay on 96 until exit 23—the Marne exit. If you take this bypass, drop south across the expressway after exiting at Marne and pick up State Street in Marne, then head west as described above. That's all there is to it!

Old US27 / Mackinac Highway

FOR UNTOLD THOUSANDS of people over several generations "27" was the road up north. It was the route running up through the center of the state, past lakes, rivers, and vacation resorts, to go on vacation in northern Michigan. Places like Clare, Houghton Lake, Grayling and Gaylord became part of our common language because of this road. Fishermen used it in spring; boaters, campers and cabin dwellers traveled it in the summer, and deer hunters clogged its two lanes every November.

Old 27 originally went at one time from Florida to the Straits of Mackinac before being replaced by various expressways. In Michigan these new highways are I69, U.S-127, and I75. From Indiana all the way to Cheboygan, old 27 runs adjacent to and parallel to these expressways. South of Cheboygan it veers northeast for its last few miles.

Since every straight line has to have start and end points, we'll begin our tour of Old US27 near its southern-most point in Michigan, three miles north of the Indiana state line. Assuming you take I69 to get to this point, get off at exit 3 (Copeland Road) and take it west one-half mile where it intersects with Angola Road/Old 27. In Branch County Old 27 is very easy to follow. It runs next to I69, but unlike the expressway Old 27 goes through the town of Coldwater rather than bypassing it. Old 27 is easy to follow through town. In the southern part of Coldwater it angles southwest to northeast and is called Division Street. Once it resumes going north again it is called Marshall Road. It remains Marshall Road the rest of it journey through Branch County.

Just south of the small town of Tekonsha in southern Calhoun County, Old 27 and I69 cross over one another and Old 27 runs on the east side of I69 from that point north. It runs through the town of Tekonsha and straight north for five miles, then angling to join 17 Mile Road, then joining M227 as it continues its journey north through Marshall. You stay on the same road, only the names change, not the roadway itself. In Marshall, Old 27 takes you through the town's roundabout, and continues straight north out of town. As I've discussed in greater detail about the Old US12 tour, Marshall is a great town to stop and do some exploring. There are lots of historical sites and buildings, and a great downtown for walking, shopping, or eating. This route will take you by the famous Honolulu House on Marshall's north side.

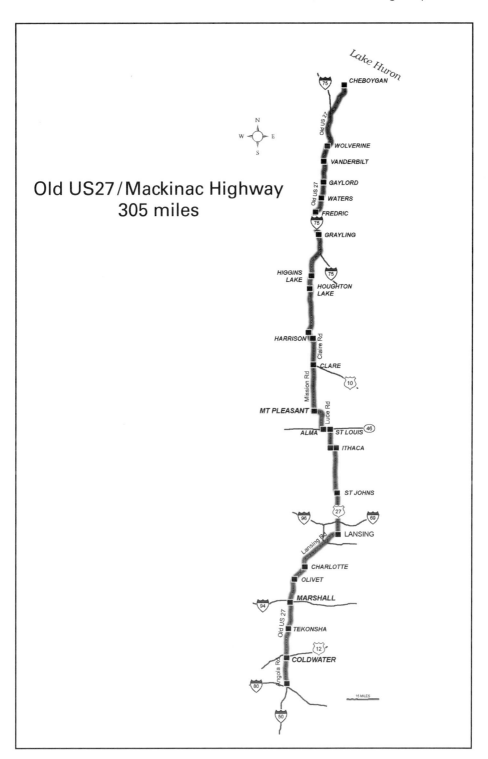

Old US27/Mackinac Highway
305 miles

Miles	Destination	Total
	**OLD US27 / MACKINAC HIGHWAY 305 MILES**	
0	Indiana Border	0
13	Coldwater	13
11	Tekonsha	24
13	Marshall	37
12	Olivet	49
10	Charlotte	59
20	Lansing	79
43	Ithaca	122
29	Mt. Pleasant	151
30	Harrison	181
23	Houghton Lake	204
19	I75	223
5	Grayling	228
28	Gaylord	256
19	Wolverine	275
9	Indian River	284
21	Cheboygan	305

Old 27 is easy to follow as it meanders north out of Marshall to Olivet. It is a very nice road with light traffic due to I69 being only about one mile away. Old 27 is known as Marshall Road both south and north of Olivet, and is Main Street in Olivet, taking you past historic Olivet College. The road turns to the northeast once out of Olivet, and several miles northeast of town it swings north, becoming Cochran Road, and crosses I69 once again. Cochran continues north into Charlotte, where at the main intersection in town it intersects with Lawrence Street. Turn right on Lawrence and after a few blocks it turn northeasterly and becomes Lansing Road and once again crosses I69. From this point northeastward it follows along I69 into Lansing, crossing over to the north side about midway to Lansing.

With all the expressway construction in and around Lansing, it becomes a bit challenging, but certainly not too difficult to follow Old 27 all the way through

Historic Honolulu House located in Marshall. (Photo by Robert J. Smith)

Lansing and north again. You simply stay on Lansing Road as it angles into town, until it hits Main Street at which point you take a quarter turn to the east, following Main Street to Cedar Street/Larch Street signs and go north. Cedar Street splits shortly after you turn onto it with one-way traffic on each street. The northbound street becomes Larch Street. You will take Larch Street north out of town with no turns. The stretch of road from Charlotte through the north side of Lansing is by far the most urbanized and non-scenic stretch of the entire route. But riding it reminds us of the days when one drove through towns, instead of skirting around them. Old 27 continues north all the way to St. Johns as a divided four-lane highway. It is very easy to follow through St. Johns and continues as a four-lane highway all the way to just south of Ithaca.

At the point where Old 27 turns northwesterly and becomes an expressway just south of Ithaca, you'll see Bagley Road that splits off straight north. This is the old route of Old 27 so take that fork. Bagley goes north a short distance to Washington Road. Turn west onto Washington and take it into Ithaca. Follow the signs as Old 27 turns to the north in Ithaca and continues north out of town toward Alma. Going north from Ithaca Old 27 is called State Road. Take State Road north all the way to M46 in St. Louis where you will turn left (west) on M46/Old 27 and go four miles to Luce Road/Old 27 where a right (north) turn is necessary. When you cross over the U.S. 127 expressway Luce Road is just a short distance west. Luce Road/Old 27 goes straight north, becoming Shepherd Road in Isabella County. Just outside of Shepherd the road curves around to the west side of town and then turns west for a short distance becoming Blanchard Road, which in turn swings back north on Mission Road. The turns are very obvious—being curves, not ninety-degree corners. Just follow the pavement.

Once northbound on Mission Road to Mt. Pleasant the old highway is easy to follow all the way north to Grayling. The only somewhat tricky spot is at the north end of Mt. Pleasant where you want to be sure to take the Mission Road fork to the left, and not curve right as that is the access road onto the U.S.-127 expressway. From here it's basically just follow the road as it goes through Clare and Harrison, then just west of Houghton Lake and Higgins Lake, all the way north to Four Mile Road south of Grayling. The stretch of Old 27 in southern Crawford County is a bit rough with expansion bumps having cropped up every hundred yards or so. You'll need to slow down for about five miles.

Beyond Four Mile Road the expressway has obliterated the old road, so you have to jump on I75 and take it north a couple of miles to the south Grayling exit. Once you exit here you'll be back on Old 27. It's very easy to follow it as it goes basically north through Grayling.

Grayling is a good place to explore a bit. The town derived its name from a now-extinct fish that frequented the Au Sable River prior to the lumbering era. Destruction of habitat through logging, floating logs down the river, warming the water through removal of streamside brush, and covering vital bottom habitat with sand and dirt washed into the river all doomed the cold and clean water loving Grayling. There were so many sawmills in the Grayling area in the late 1800s that the town was then called Milltown—a name that is still used today. It's interesting to note that as this book is going to press the dam that formed the old mill pond in Grayling in support of those very sawmills is in the initial phase of being finally removed. Removal of this dam will once again allow the Au Sable River to run clean and cold, as it did for millennia.

In downtown Grayling visit the Crawford County Historical Museum in the old railroad depot for a fascinating look at the area's history. If you're a fisherman, visit the old Grayling Fish Hatchery. Once a functioning state-run hatchery for trout, the local parks department now runs the facility as a tourist attraction. Some mighty huge trout prowl its eleven ponds.

Grayling is also the headquarters for Camp Grayling, a 147,000-acre military reservation utilized by National Guard units from Michigan, Illinois, Indiana and Ohio. The area just north of Grayling forms the watershed divide between Lake Huron and Lake Michigan. The Au Sable and Manistee Rivers begin within one mile of each other north of Grayling, but the Manistee flows west to Lake Michigan, and the Au Sable flows east into Lake Huron.

Just north of Grayling, M93 splits off to the right, and Old 27 requires a quarter turn to the left to continue north to the villages of Frederic and Waters, past Lake Otsego and finally into Gaylord. When you hit the stop sign at M32/Main Street in Gaylord Old 27 makes a two-block jog to the east before continuing north.

Gaylord is a good case study in the modern evolution of towns in this day of urban sprawl and big box stores. Thirty years ago Gaylord was a small town with lots of natural character. Mom and Pop businesses thrived, and it was a desirable destination because of attractions that took advantage of the natural beauty of the area. It existed in harmony with the rolling farm and forest lands surrounding it. Today it is a city with a contrived character (the Alpine City), surrounded by suburbs, fast food restaurants, chain hotels and chain department stores, with most sporting *faux* Swiss facades. The local flavor that was so much a part of the community has been trampled. Ah well, another example of the Chamber of Commerce "bigger is better" philosophy. This isn't to say it isn't a nice place to visit, just don't expect to find a typical northern Michigan small town.

The Gaylord area, situated on the 45th parallel, has transformed from a destination largely for outdoors men and women engaged in hunting, canoeing, hiking, and so on, to a golf Mecca with several large golf resorts having been built nearby. Each July the city hosts a week-long Alpenfest celebration. Call (800) 345-8621 for festival information.

Continuing north, just beyond Vanderbilt the road curves west crossing I75 before taking you to the village of Wolverine. In this vicinity the road is called Straits Highway as well as Old 27. Once in Indian River the road curves northeasterly and follows the west shore of beautiful Mullet Lake and on into Cheboygan.

In the 1940s US27 followed the same corridor as US23 and went from Cheboygan to Mackinaw City where it ended. In more recent years Old 27 ended at Cheboygan, as it does today.

For about 305 miles from Indiana to Cheboygan Old 27 makes it way through peaceful countryside and small towns. Except for the stretch near Lansing, Old 27 is a charming road that hearkens back to a simpler and slower time. There is something about going through small towns such as Tekonsha, Olivet, Ithaca, Clare, Vanderbilt, and so on that causes one to forget about schedules and high speed and to just relax and really notice the world around them. Life still goes on in these interesting small towns—life that you completely miss when you rush by them on the Interstates.

The Great North Woods

WITH THE EXCEPTION of the Great Lakes themselves, when folks think of Michigan, they imagine all that is summed up in the words "Up North." Northern Michigan evokes thoughts of forests filled with wildlife, sparkling rivers hiding elusive trout, hills ablaze with color in the autumn, lakes for boating or swimming, and clean air and blue skies.

Michigan is blessed with millions of acres of public lands that provide a wonderful balance between development and conservation in the northern two-thirds of the state. These public lands, primarily state and national forests, guarantee natural resources for future generations, and they provide beauty and open spaces for today. Much of northern Michigan depends on these lands for their economic well-being through tourism and forestry related industries.

Like so many paradoxes in this strange world, our priceless and irreplaceable state and national forests came about as a result of natural and human tragedies. The period of approximately 1870 to 1900 saw the literal stripping of northern Michigan, changing it almost overnight from an immense virgin forest to a barren wasteland. Much of the soil in the northern part of the state is quite unproductive and makes poor farmland. However, eager farmers who followed the loggers didn't realize this. They thought that the newly cleared land would make wonderful farmland. Unfortunately, it didn't work out that way. During the ensuing years, farmers tried to make a living out of this poor land and lost the fight. The Depression years of the 1930s were the final straw, with thousands of farmers losing their land, which then reverted to the state.

Michigan's government, as well as Congress and President Roosevelt at the federal level, saw value in preserving this land as forest rather than trying to keep it in struggling farms that were hopelessly doomed to fail. During the 1930s, at the height of the Great Depression and Roosevelt's New Deal programs, young men in the Civilian Conservation Corps (CCC) planted millions of trees to reforest the land. Much of it wisely remained in public ownership for forest and recreational land for future generations—the public forests and parks that millions of people enjoy today.

Motorcyclists today can take advantage of these prudent land use policies and the beauty of northern Michigan thanks to the many two-lane paved roads that crisscross this part of the state. These roads curve around frequent obstacles, such as lakes, swamps, rivers, and over the many glacial hills that cover northern Michigan, resulting in very enjoyable and scenic rides.

There are many superb riding roads in the north and I discuss seven trips, taking in some of my favorite roads and attractions below. Get ready for some great riding.

Tip of the Mitt

THIS RIDE STARTS and ends at Mackinaw City—a destination for thousands of motorcyclists from around the country every year. The route I've laid out here will take you along the most beautiful sections of both Lake Huron and Lake Michigan coastlines, as well as through miles of hills, curves, and forests.

Mackinaw City could take a chapter of its own, but I think once a person is there the things you can do are obvious. I talk about the area in detail in other tours, so I won't repeat myself. Just park your bike, walk around, and take it all in. Historic Fort Michilimackinac and the Old Mackinaw Point Lighthouse are interesting places to see, and of course if you're there for more than a day, include a trip over to Mackinac Island. Mackinaw City is still small enough so that you can cover everything without having to drive from place to place. It is a misdemeanor for a person to leave Mackinaw City without at least one-quarter pound of locally made fudge in their possession—be sure to buy some. You'll be glad you did!

To start the trip, head west on Central Avenue - the main east-west street in town. This will become Emmet County Road C81 outside of town. Follow the curves west of town along the shoreline, staying on C81 as it heads south at the general store and gas station. Follow C81 (Cecil Bay Road) south about two-and-a-half miles to the junction of Elder Road, turn west (right). Follow the pavement around to the south and soon you'll reach Gill Road. Turn west (right) again. Follow this curving pavement, which becomes Lakeview Road without any fanfare with a curve to the right. Ultimately Lakeview Road heads south along the shore and becomes Sturgeon Bay Road. There is only one somewhat tricky point when you will come around a curve and Sturgeon Bay Road will go straight ahead to the east, but there will be a sign just past the curve that points south to Emmet County Scenic Route 1. Take this right turn onto Scenic Route 1 and soon you'll be on the Lake Michigan coast on Lakeshore Road. Follow this great stretch of road south along the coast and you'll eventually encounter Cross Village.

If you like Eastern European foods, and lots of it, plan on Leg's Inn in Cross Village for dinner some evening. They serve great food in an out of the ordinary building, with unique ambience and a wonderful view of the lake thrown in for free.

Continue south on this coastal road to M119, one of the most scenic roads in Lower Michigan. M119 is also called the Tunnel of Trees. Designated as a State

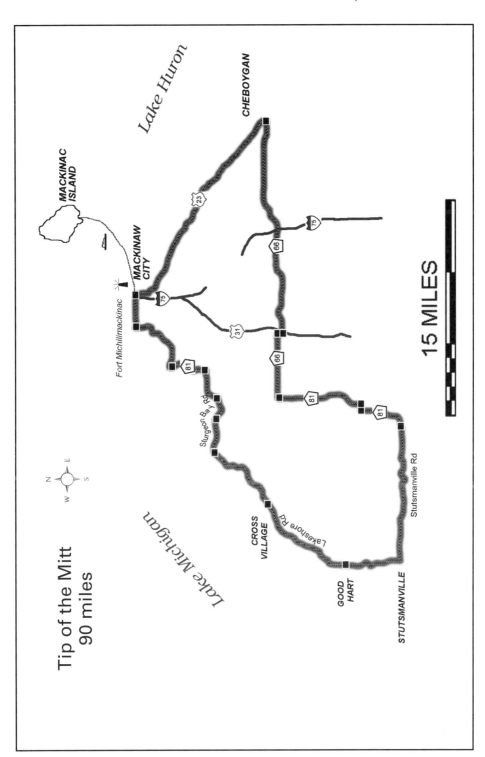

Tip of the Mitt
90 miles

15 MILES

Lake Huron

Lake Michigan

MACKINAC
ISLAND

MACKINAW
CITY

Fort Michilimackinac

CHEBOYGAN

CROSS
VILLAGE

GOOD
HART

STUTSMANVILLE

Sturgeon Bay Rd

Lakeshore Rd

Stutsmanville Rd

23

75

66

75

31

66

81

81

81

TIP OF THE MITT 90 MILES		
Miles	**Destination**	**Total**
0	Mackinaw City	0
7	Cecil Bay Corners	7
16	Cross Village	23
13	Stutsmanville Road	36
24	Levering	60
15	Cheyboygan	75
15	Mackinaw City	90

Scenic Heritage Route, M119 is the one state highway for which an exception has been made for shoulders and tree trimming—there is none of either. What it does have are occasional glimpses of the lake from high on the shoreline bluff, and many, many curves. Use caution, as the road has its share of gawkers and it really is narrow with no shoulders and trees at the very edge. Signs along the road tell the Native American and early explorer history of the area but unfortunately there isn't always room to pull off to read them.

As you ride south along M119 you will go through two tiny corner villages, Good Hart and Middle Village. About three miles beyond Middle Village you will see Stutsmanville Road. Turn east here. At this point you will have ridden what is by far the best part of the Tunnel of Trees. Unfortunately, from that point south the road becomes more developed, busier, and straighter.

Stutsmanville Road is a lightly traveled two-lane pavement that is wonderfully hilly for the first few miles. You will be tempted to put your arms up in the air as if on a roller-coaster ride! Keep going east on Stutsmanville Road for about nine miles at which point you will hit C81 once again. Turn north (left) at this intersection and follow C-81 north almost ten miles, turning right when it intersects with C66, also called Levering Road. Stay on Levering Road—C66—noting that there is a slight jog to the south at US31—for about eighteen miles, following it all the way east to the intersection with US23 in Cheboygan. East of the I75 expressway C66 is called Cheboygan Road and continues into Cheboygan. The road angles to the southeast on State Street for four blocks just before hitting US23. Turn left onto US23 and follow it north the approximately fifteen miles back to Mackinaw City along the beautiful Lake Huron shoreline.

Summer image of the lighthouse located in Mackinaw city. (Photo by Vito Palmisano)

This loop is ninety miles long, but be sure to add at least an hour for stops along the way. A person certainly wants to stop and enjoy the shoreline views and beach opportunities on both coasts. Average speeds on the M119 stretch will only be thirty miles per hour or thereabouts.

County Road 612 and the Famous River of Sand

THIS IS A GRAND full-day ride on some of the best back roads in northern Lower Michigan. The trip starts in Grayling. Go north on Old US27—Business Loop 75 to M93 and turn right. Go over the I75 expressway and continue northeast into Hartwick Pines State Park. This fantastic park has almost 10,000 acres of forestland, including 45 acres of virgin Pine forests that allows a glimpse of what lumbermen saw across northern Michigan 150 years ago. The park has an interesting display of authentic logging equipment from the lumbering era, and two log buildings (built by the CCC), which house a museum with more exhibits and a theater. In the park you can stand in awe under the largest remaining white pine of them all, a magnificent 300-year old tree called Monarch. This specimen stands 155 feet tall! Try to imagine the entire northland covered in trees like this. Between 1870 and 1900, Michigan was the leading lumber producer in the nation. Michigan lumber built the great cities of the Midwest.

When you are ready to leave the park, head north on M93 (called White Road at that point) and turn right (east) on County Road 612. This is one of the longest continuous county primary roads in the northern Lower Peninsula, and is a pleasure to ride. You will take 612 east through Lovells and Lewiston, all the way to M33.

If you enjoy fly-fishing or want to learn a bit about the history of this area, stop at the Lovells Township Historical Museum. It is located on County Road F97 just north of CR612 in the small village of Lovells, located nine miles east of White Road. The museum is based in a log cabin and includes many fly-fishing antiques and artifacts as well as other interesting northern Michigan exhibits.

CR612, through this entire stretch, is a newer blacktop pavement with many nice sweeping curves and hills and light traffic. It meanders mostly through forested countryside with lakes and farms interspersed along its length. It also takes you through the Kirtland's Warbler habitat area where Jack Pine forests are maintained for this rare bird. The Kirtland's Warbler nests only in these Jack Pine forests, and they winter in the Bahamas.

When you hit the M33 junction, turn south (right). The first few miles on M33 are especially enjoyable with nice roller-coaster hills. Take M33 south all the

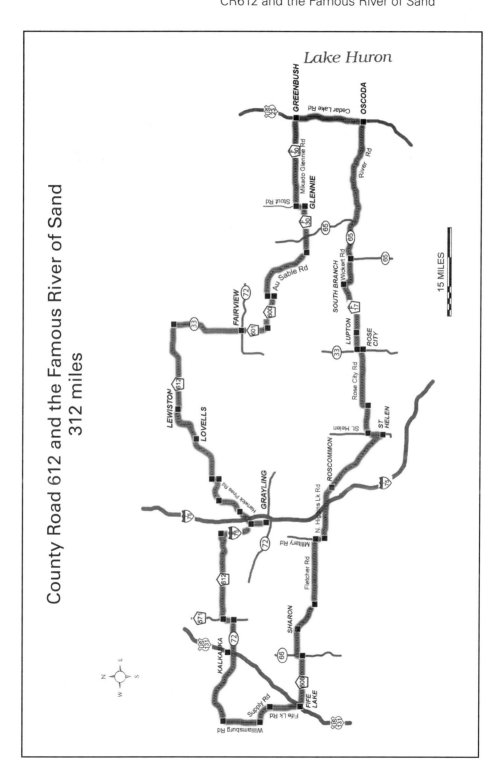

County Road 612 and the Famous River of Sand
312 miles

Lake Huron

CR612 & THE FAMOUS RIVER OF SAND 312 MILES		
Miles	Destination	Total
0	Grayling	0
8	Hartwick Pines State Park	8
13	Lovells	21
28	M33	49
13	M72	62
50	Greenbush	112
14	Oscoda	126
32	South Branch	158
14	Rose City	172
33	Roscommon	205
9	CCC Museum	214
20	Sharon	234
16	Fife Lake/US131	278
28	Kalkaska/CR612	303
25	Frederic	303
9	Grayling	312

way to M72, where you'll encounter a stop sign in the village of Fairview. M33 turns right at this point, but you want to continue south straight across M72 on Abbe Road—County Road 601. Continue on 601 five more miles until it "Ts" at County Road 600—F32 (also known as McKinley Road). Turn left (east). Follow this winding blacktop as it meanders eastward through forested countryside. About three miles east of the Village of McKinley you'll "T" at what is Au Sable Road—F32. Turn right. Two miles later F32 splits off, but you want to stay on Au Sable Road and continue south as this winding road follows its namesake river— the *Riviere Aux Sable* (River of Sand). Au Sable Road eventually "Ts" at Bamfield Road—F30. Turn left (east) at this intersection going into the Village of Glennie. East of Glennie the road is called Glennie Road—County Road F30. Go east on F30 about twenty-two miles all the way to the small town of Greenbush at US23 on the shore of Lake Huron.

The Au Sable River in the Huron-Manistee Natinoal Forest. (Photo courtesy of Huron-Manistee National Forets)

Going south on US23 about ten miles you'll come to the town of Oscoda where the famous Au Sable River enters Lake Huron. If you prefer an alternative route to US23, very shortly before you reach 23 on Glennie Road you will notice Cedar Lake Road heading south. Going south on Cedar Lake Road will take you parallel to 23, but with less traffic. It rejoins US23 about eight miles to the south, just north of Oscoda.

Once you are in Oscoda, turn west on River Road. Just outside of town this road becomes a designated National Forest Scenic Byway. There are many things to see and do along this very scenic twenty-two mile stretch of winding two-lane road. Just beyond the Oscoda city limits at the beginning of the Byway there is a welcome center with some walking trails. About twelve miles along, visit the Lumberman's Monument. There is a museum and visitor center. This monument and the interpretive displays tell the story of Michigan's fabled lumber glory days of the late nineteenth century. Just a mile further west is the Iargo Springs. A wooden stairway of 294 steps takes you down the bluff to the river and the large springs. If

View of the Lumberman's Monument over-looking the Au Sable River near Oscoda. (Photo courtesy of Travel Michigan)

you don't feel up to the walk down to the river, an overlook at the top provides a wonderful panoramic view of the river valley. In fact, there are several great scenic overlooks along the Byway that are well worth the stop.

The Au Sable River has been dramatically changed from its natural state due to the construction of six hydroelectric dams between 1911 and 1924. These dams create six impoundments flooding the valleys behind them. The Au Sable is world-renowned for trout fishing. A stretch of the river downstream from Grayling is reverently called "The Holy Water" by purists who try to entice trout with dry flies. For the Trout fisherman the impoundments harm the fishery by warming the water and causing siltation. For the warm water sports person the impoundments create large lake-like bodies of water that provide a home to fish such as Bass and Bluegill. Thirty-seven miles of the mainstream's 129 miles of stream are impounded. Eighty percent of the river's watershed is forested resulting in an environment conducive to the clean high-quality water for which the Au Sable is famous.[1]

The Au Sable is also a very popular river for canoeing. Each weekend hundreds of novice canoeists float their aluminum rental crafts down the river, with more than a few careening off the various natural obstacles in the river. For the very serious canoeist, the grueling Grayling to Oscoda canoe marathon is an annual event, drawing the best canoeists in the world to compete in this 120-mile, sixteen hour non-stop race.

If you want to experience the river but don't canoe or have your own boat, you can take a ride on the River Queen paddlewheel riverboat. (1775 East River Road, Oscoda, 989-739-7351. Make reservations if you want to take a boat ride on weekends or during the fall color period.

---

[1] Au Sable River Natural River Plan, Michigan Department of Natural Resources. July 1987.

Before heading farther west I'd be terribly amiss if I didn't write a few sentences on a devastating forest fire that destroyed the Village of Oscoda and the Village of Au Sable, just south of Oscoda. At the time the Village of Au Sable had about 10,000 residents and was a bustling port city. On July 11, 1911 a forest fire pushed by high winds, and made worse by drought conditions in the area, raced from the west and destroyed virtually all in its path, including houses, stores, churches, saw mills and other structures in these two towns. Because of the ready supply of lumber, everything had of course been built of wood. Both towns were essentially obliterated.[2] Au Sable never recovered and to this day is smaller than it was a century ago. The number of people who perished could never be accurately confirmed. Some artifacts salvaged from the fire are still on display at the Iosco County Museum in Tawas City, about ten miles further south on US23.

Catastrophic forest fires were a major factor in Michigan's history from 1870 through about 1920. Widespread logging, with the resulting huge piles of slash lying across the countryside, resulted in fuel for forest fires that literally swept from coast to coast. Forest fires during that time period were a major part of the state's formative history, helping shape our economy, laws, and the way we manage our natural resources.

The name of River Road changes to Iargo Road as you travel west, but the name change affects nothing. The Scenic Byway ends when it hits M65 but this great ride doesn't end there. At this point M65 is aligned east and west, continuing along the south shore of the river and impoundments. Go west on M65 about five miles at which point M65 curves south—but you want to just keep going straight west on what becomes Wickert Road. Stay on Wickert for about four miles and you'll hit East County Line Road (also called Branch Road) at the Ogemaw County line. Wickert ends at this point and you'll turn north one mile to the small village of South Branch. Heath Road — F17 will go west out of South Branch (at the Post Office). You want to take this road, following it west and somewhat south as it curves around many lakes in that area eventually taking you through the village of Lupton and then south on M33 about a mile into Rose City.

At the main intersection in Rose City turn west on what will be Main Street in town. This road becomes Rose City Road — F28 outside of town. You will continue on F28 about fourteen more miles going generally west but winding a little south also, until it "Ts" at F97 (St. Helens Road). Turn left on F97 and go a little less than two miles south and you will intersect with Old M76 just north of the town of St. Helen. Turning right on Old M76 will take you northwesterly the roughly thirteen miles into Roscommon.

---

[2] *Michigan On Fire*. Copyright 1997. By Betty Sodders.

After logging left much of the previously forested land looking like this, young men of the Civilian Conservation Corps not only reseeded the barren landscape, they also helped build many of the roads that are still being enjoyed today.

Continue going northwest on this same road through Roscommon, which becomes Federal Road, and then Higgins Lake Road as you travel along it. In Roscommon it also becomes Business Loop 75. Once in Roscommon you might wish to take a two-mile detour south on M18 and visit the Fire Fighters Monument. It is two miles south of town on Robinson Lake Road about one mile east of M18.

Back on the tour—just west of Roscommon the road curves and then begins going straight west. After you go over the I75 expressway BL-75 ends and you'll find yourself on North Higgins Lake Road—continue going west and in a few miles you'll curve around the north end of Higgins Lake. Here you will find North Higgins Lake State Park, and the CCC Museum. The Civilian Conservation Corps programs of the 1930s still benefit us today. Young men of the CCC played a major role in the reforestation of Michigan after the wholesale logging of the state and devastating fires of the previous decades. Many of the depression-era projects they (and the WPA) built are enjoyed today by millions, including some of our favorite motorcycling roads such as the Blue Ridge Parkway, the Going to the Sun Highway in Glacier National Park, lodges in Yellowstone Park, state and national park campgrounds and facilities, and much, much more. A stop at the CCC museum is recommended. I've long found it ironic that many of the roads and recreational facilities we enjoy today are a direct result of the worst economic depression in our country's history. These roads and parks were also built by the same young men who then went on to fight and win World War II.

Very shortly after leaving North Higgins Lake State Park you will stop at Old US27 and then go over the I75 expressway. Just beyond the overpass the road will "T" at Military Road. Turn right, go north a little less than two miles and then turn left (west) onto Fletcher Road. Follow Fletcher Road as it meanders westerly about seventeen miles to the Village of Sharon.

Every town in Michigan, whether a large city, a crossroads village, or a ghost town, has a story to tell. Some of these histories are well known, some are arcane, and some are just bizarre. Sharon was a boomtown that grew rapidly during the

CR612 and the Famous River of Sand

1870–1900 lumber heydays and especially after the arrival of railroads that crossed there. Sharon applied to the state legislature for incorporation under the name Jam One—the reason being that in the 1870s it was the site of one of the largest log-jams that the state ever saw. Located at the juncture of three waterways that floated logs, so many logs were released into the streams one spring that it resulted in a jam of such proportions that it took lumberjacks weeks to clear it out. The legislature rejected the request for the name of Jam One, recommending Sharon instead. After the surrounding countryside had been reduced to a barren plain. Its post office closed in 1921.[3]

CCC camps housed German POWs

An interesting side-note about the CCC is that six of the then-abandoned CCC camps in Michigan were used during World War II to hold German Prisoners of War. One camp was in Allegan County and the remaining five were in the Upper Peninsula. According to a documentary called "The Enemy in Our Midst" by WNMU of Northern Michigan University, the five camps in the UP were Camps Evelyn and Au Train in Alger County, Camps Sidnaw and Pori in Houghton County, and Camp Raco in Chippewa County. About 1,100 German POWs were held in the UP. Those who were able to were paid eighty-cents per day to cut pulpwood for the war effort according to research by WNMU. A significant number of German soldiers, joined by their families, stayed on after the war.

In Sharon, turn west on West Sharon Road and take it five miles to M66. Jog south on M66 for a mile and turn west again on Ingersoll Road, which you'll follow for about eight miles west around Fife Lake, and into the Village of Fife Lake where you will find CR605 (Fife Lake Road). Go right on US131 for one-half mile to pick up Fife Lake Road. Go north on CR605 and it will wind north and northwest for about fifteen miles—all the way to M72. In this fifteen-mile stretch the pavement changes name from Fife Lake Road, to Supply Road, and finally heads straight north on Williamsburg Road. Take M72 east and it will take you the approximately thirteen miles to M66—US131 on the north side of Kalkaska. You want to continue straight across 131/66 on what is now Nash Road—CR612 again. Six miles east of Kalkaska 612 takes a two-mile north jog on Darragh Road, and then heads east again. County Road 612 travels east twenty-five miles from Kalkaska to the Village of Frederic and Old US27. Turn south here and it will take you back to Grayling and a tour of Michigan's northern heartland will be completed.

This trip is 312 miles in length, but with all the things to do it will be a good full day's worth of riding. I recommend making it a two-day trip with an overnight stop midway, allowing time for all the attractions along the way.

---

[3] *Ghost Towns of Michigan,* Larry Wakefield, © 1994, Northmont Publishing, Inc.

The Sunrise Tour

THE NORTHEAST QUARTER of the state has some of the nicest touring and sport-riding roads in the state. With less traffic density than much of the rest of the Lower Peninsula, and some very nice scenery, hills and winding roads thrown in, there are many great byways in the sunrise side of Michigan to make for fabulous riding. This 370-mile ride makes a great two-day trip if you stop to visit sites along the way, and camp or motel at the Cheboygan area, which is mid-way.

We start this ride at the town of Standish—a traditional kicking off point for travel to the northeast corner of Michigan. At the main intersection in Standish (M61 heading west, US23 going north and south, and Pine River Road going east) go east on Pine River Road a little over five miles, past some great curves along the Pine River, to Main Street Road (somebody got a little redundant in naming this road). Take Main Street Road north to Arenac State Road and continue north on it to the town of Omer. Omer is billed as the Sucker fishing capital of Michigan. It's hard to believe the amount of excitement and partying that can occur every April when these unattractive fish are running in the Rifle River! Of course it doesn't take much of an excuse to get the average Michigander to party—especially at the end of another long winter!

Turn right onto US23 for two miles to M65 and head north. Almost all of this trip from Omer to near Rogers City will be on the original route of US23 from the period of the 1920s and 1930s. Back then of course it was a dirt road but I can easily imagine adventurous Harley, Henderson, or Indian riders during that period making the same trek that we are today.

Take M65 about sixteen miles north to M55 and turn east, riding fourteen miles to the west edge of Tawas City, and Wilber Road—Old US23. Going north on Wilber Road, follow the main pavement as it makes a total of five jogs to the east, finally ending up on Old US23—Au Sable Road, heading east toward the town of Au Sable on the Lake Huron shore. Heading north on Wilber Road the pavement becomes Sherman, Curtis, Brooks, Hart and finally just Old US23. It sounds complicated but just stay on the main road as it curves north and east and there is no chance of getting lost.

Once on the current US23 and the towns of Au Sable and Oscoda, take 23 north less than two miles to County Road F41—once again the route of the old

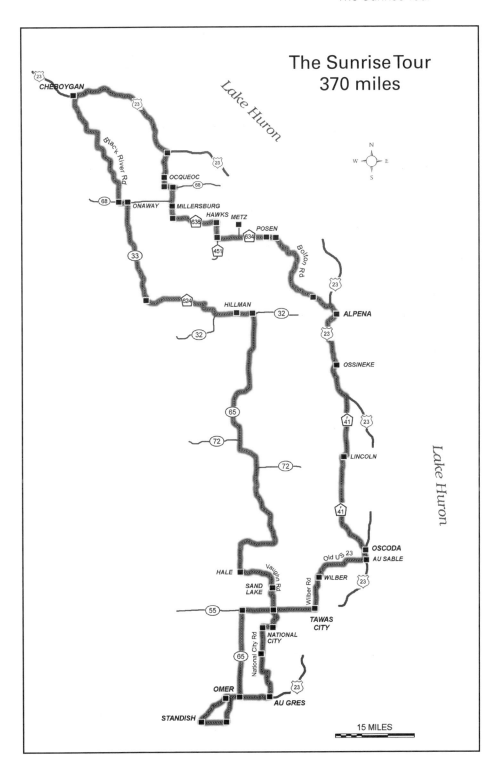

THE SUNRISE TOUR 370 MILES		
Miles	Destination	Total
0	Standish	0
10	Omer	10
32	Old US23/Tawas City	42
18	Oscoda	60
22	Lincoln	82
27	Alpena	109
25	Posen	134
23	Millersburg	157
37	Cheboygan	194
27	M33/Onaway	221
33	Hillman	254
56	Au Sable River	310
21	Sand Lake	331
24	Au Gres	355
15	Standish	370

US23. CRF41 angles northwest past the former Wurtsmith Air Force Base and eventually turns straight north taking you all the way through Alcona County. In Alcona County the road also carried the designation of Route 171—a vestige of road designation changes that occurred seventy years ago when this was the alignment of US23. When the new roadway for US23 was built along the coast the numerical designation was moved from this alignment to its modern route, and the old highway was temporarily renamed as M171. It doesn't matter what you call it though. What is important is that you simply follow this road north through the town of Lincoln, where it jogs east one mile, and then all the way north to its juncture with current US23 near the town of Ossineke. This entire stretch is a very pleasant riding road through Alcona County forests and farms.

Follow US23 about thirteen miles as it curves around Thunder Bay and through the town of Alpena. On the north side of town, shortly after crossing the Thunder Bay River, turn left (west) onto Long Rapids Road. This is a very nice riding road that winds northwesterly along the river, and then curves north as Bolton Road into

Presque Isle County. One mile into Presque Isle County turn left onto Long Lake Highway—when Bolton Road turns to gravel. Follow the pavement for five miles as it winds west and north to County Road 634, where you turn west into the town of Posen. The town of Posen was settled by Polish immigrants in the 1870s and still has an eastern European flavor to it. If you like potato pancakes, Posen is the place to be. It is a potato-growing area and has a large potato festival each September (the weekend following Labor Day) with lots of potato dishes, polka dances, and just plain fun.

Continue heading west on CR634 and five miles west of Posen you'll see CR441 which goes north two miles to the small town of Metz. While this small detour isn't necessarily part of this trip, it's worth noting the presence of Metz, and recalling a terrible day in October 1908 when a forest fire destroyed the town and killed almost all the people in a train—mostly women and children attempting to escape the flames. The train was trying to make it to Posen but became derailed due to rails that had been warped by the fire two miles east of Metz. A state historical marker near the site commemorates the tragedy. This was one of the last truly devastating forest fires that swept across Michigan after the lumbering boom, and if there is a bright side to this tragedy it is that it helped awaken a conservation movement that was instrumental in reviving Michigan's natural environment and giving us what we have today in the way of state and national forests and parks.

Forest fires continue to plague Michigan and the rest of the nation, of course, but current technology and manpower employed by the Department of Natural Resources means fires today are seldom over one hundred acres. One hundred years ago forest fires were allowed to burn as there was simply no way to extinguish them. The huge amount of slash (tree branches and other dead material) that covered the forest floor following removal of the mature trees by loggers and farmers resulted in fuel for the devastating fires of a century ago.

Nine miles west of Posen is CR451 that we'll take north three miles to the small village of Hawks. Once in Hawks turn west on CR638 and follow it west, then north, into the town of Millersburg. Millersburg is typical of almost all small northern Michigan towns. The first settler arrived in 1898, but just three years later, due to the logging boom, there were over 1200 residents. Today the population has leveled off at a reasonable 300 or so. This boom and bust process occurred repeatedly across the northland.

Small towns like Millersburg, Lincoln, Posen, Metz, and Hawks are places that are seldom visited by the majority of tourists because they're not on main highways. They are proof, however, that self-sufficient and self-sustaining small-town America still exists—you just have to get off the main roads bit to find it.

Going north out of Millersburg you will follow M68 for two miles, but when it turns east you want to go west at that corner onto Ocqueoc Falls Highway. The

Ocqueoc Falls on the Ocqueoc River are the only true waterfall in the Lower Peninsula. Some folks would smirk a bit that the classification of waterfall has been given them. They're really just tumbling rapids that wouldn't get a second notice in the Upper Peninsula. But though a Yooper might scoff, they are very scenic nonetheless. Two miles after turning west onto this highway, the pavement turns north, and you will follow Ocqueoc Road north all the way to the end at its juncture with US23. Turn north onto US23 and take it a little over twenty-five miles as it follows closely along the Lake Huron shoreline.

This stretch of US23 is perhaps the nicest of its entire length. It is lightly developed with mile after mile of grand scenery and lake vistas. Just prior to entering Cheboygan turn left (south) onto Butler Road, and take it to Black River Road, which you will continue to follow as it meanders south along the Black River and then along the west shore of beautiful Black Lake.

The Black River and Black Lake are one of the few inland waters in the state where the Sturgeon exists. The Sturgeon is a fish like no other. They are a relic from the age of the dinosaurs, and look every bit like they came here in some sort of weird time warp. Living up to one-hundred years, reaching eight feet in length and weighing well over a hundred pounds if they live long enough, these fish are quite a sight as they spawn in the shallow waters of the Black River south of Cheboygan. If you happen to ride this route in April or May take time to check them out. Any local gas station or restaurant in the area can direct you to likely spots where you might see some.

Just south of Black Lake, where the road swings due east, you want to turn south on Maxon Road, and take it south four miles to M33—M68 where you'll turn east and take it into the town of Onaway (reportedly named after a young Indian woman of the same name) It is now officially the Sturgeon Capital of Michigan. Take a look at the unique building on the west side of town locally called the Onaway courthouse. In 1909 this building was built for the purpose of serving as a courthouse, hoping to entice the seat of county government to be in Onaway, but the effort failed. Today this much-photographed building houses the local historical society. In Onaway, turn south on M33 and follow this very scenic road through Michigan's Elk country about twenty miles to Montmorency County Road 624 where you'll turn east. CR624 will meander through more forests and beautiful countryside all the way to Hillman, Montmorency County's largest town, about fourteen miles east.

CR624 joins with CR451 just north of Hillman, so you need to take it south a mile to M32 where you go left—east about seven miles to Flanders Corner and M65. Turn south on M65 and follow it for a little over sixty miles as it winds south through some gorgeous countryside. M65 is one of those state highways that deserve to be on a list of motorcycling roads. It has hills, curves, and great

View of Thunder Bay Island Lighthouse near Alpena. (Photo by Terry W. Phipps)

scenery, especially through Alcona County and in the vicinity of the Au Sable River in northern Iosco County.

In Iosco County M65 takes an east-west turn right after crossing the Au Sable River. After roughly six miles it turns to the south again. Five miles after it turns to the south you will enter the small town of Hale at its intersection with Esmond Road. Go east on Esmond road, following the pavement as it curves to the south, becoming Vaughn Road. After about five miles on Vaughn Road, turn south on Lake Road (the first pavement you'll come to on your right) and follow Lake Road around Sand Lake to the south side of the lake and the burg of Sand Lake, where Sand Lake Road is encountered. Turn south onto Sand Lake Road and take this south just about six miles to Whittemore Road. Jog west on Whittemore Road two miles to the crossroads village of National City, turning south there onto National City Road. Riding south on National City Road for a tad over eight miles will get you to Twining Road where a one-mile jog to the east is necessary. After making the jog, continue south by following the pavement all the way into the town of Au Gres. In Au Gres, turn right (west) onto US23 and follow it the approximately fifteen miles back to Standish.

On this route you will have ridden through the best of northeast Michigan's beautiful countryside, experiencing unsurpassed roads, great scenery, historic places and some mighty fine motorcycling.

The Emerald Isle Nostalgia Tour

IN CASE YOU HADN'T noticed, Michigan has quite a strong connection to Ireland with many Irish immigrants having made this their home. These settlers brought more than just personal belongings with them. Like other immigrants the Irish also brought place names that reminded them of home. County names like Clare, Wexford, Antrim, and Roscommon. Cities, towns and rivers such as Boyne, Dublin, Waterford, Darragh, and Boardman are a few examples. And of course, Irish surnames are so common you can't throw a stone without hitting someone of Irish descent.

I call this the Emerald Isle tour because it not only starts and ends in the City of Clare, and the County of Clare, but also goes through Wexford, Antrim and Roscommon Counties, as well as several towns of Irish extraction and over the Boardman River.

Clare has an Irish Festival in conjunction with St. Patrick's Day each March, but it's often a little too cold to make this event a motorcycle-based trip. Clare also celebrates a Halfway-To-St. Patrick's Day celebration in September as part of their Septemberfest activities.

If you arrive at Clare from a distance and want to spend the night at the beginning or end of this trip, a great place to stay in this nice small town is at the Doherty Hotel located downtown. It's a local institution with reasonable rates, a pool and very good food. For a special treat enjoy some Irish beer and Irish Potato Skins appetizers in the hotel's Leprechaun Lounge.

We'll start by heading west out of Clare on Old US10, also known as Ludington Road, through the town of Farwell and continuing northwest on M115 once past the US10 expressway. About three miles after crossing the Muskegon River, (almost fifteen miles beyond the US10 Expressway) turn left onto 15 Mile Road, taking it west about sixteen miles to the village of Leroy, making a half-mile jog to the north just east of Leroy. Take Mackinaw Trail southwest out of Leroy a little over two miles to Luther Road, also known as Old M63. Take Luther Road over the US131 expressway, and continue west about ten miles as the road curves its way through a very nice rolling countryside with about a 50—50 mix of forest and fields to the town of Luther. Once in Luther you will be heading straight north, so just keep going north on State Road for about ten more miles to Hox-

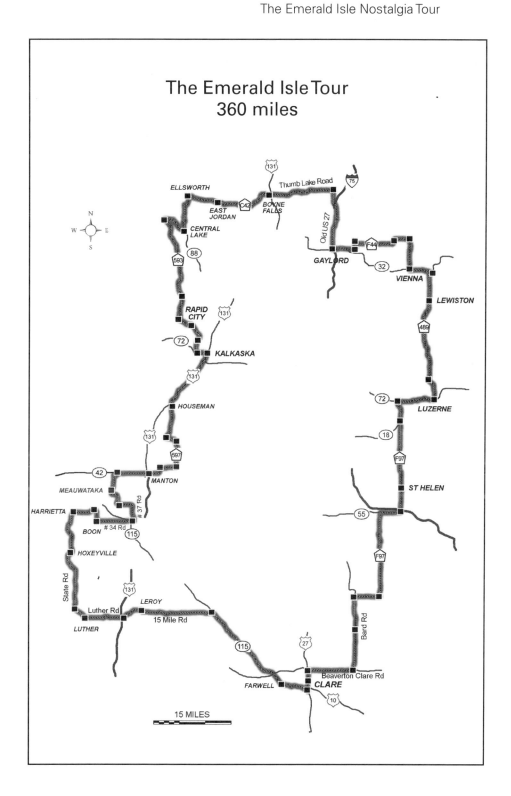

The Emerald Isle Tour
360 miles

THE EMERALD ISLE NOSTALGIA TOUR 360 MILES		
Miles	**Destination**	**Total**
0	Clare	0
41	Leroy	41
14	Luther	55
21	Harrietta	76
20	Meauwataka	96
44	Kalkaska	140
14	Torch Lake	154
30	Ellsworth	184
19	Boyne Falls	203
16	Vanderbilt	219
31	Vienna/M32	250
31	Luzerne/M72	281
24	St. Helen	305
25	M18	330
30	Clare	360

eyville. One mile north of Hoxeyville jog east a half-mile then continue north to M55. At M55 a slight jog to the west is necessary, and then continue north over the hills and around the curves on the very scenic Caberfae Road six miles to the town of Harrietta. This is ski country and home of the large Caberfae Ski Area—a great place for alpine or Nordic skiing when your motorcycle is resting during the winter season.

On the south edge of Harrietta, three blocks south of the railroad tracks you will see Gossman Road—County Road 30¼ heading east. Turn here and follow the pavement and the adjacent railroad tracks east, then south through the tiny village of Boon, and then east again all the way to and across M115. Go one mile east beyond M115 to No. 37 Road and turn left, taking this north three miles to No. 28 Road, following the pavement as it goes west three miles, then north again. Follow the pavement in this stretch as it meanders generally north to M42. Midway you will pass through the tiny crossroads village of Meauwataka—which quite coincidentally means "half-way point" in Native American tongue. Meauwataka, like so many other small burgs in the north, was at one time a bustling lumber town. Now it has a small general store and a few houses. Taking Road 29 north out of Meauwataka will eventually get you to M42 where an east (right) turn will take you to Manton.

In the center of Manton, M42 jogs south on the same alignment as US131, but you want to go straight across US131 on what is Main Street in town and No. 16 Road outside of the city limits. East of town a couple of miles the road meanders north and northeast before heading straight east again on No. 14 Road that soon becomes Rhoby Road when you cross into Missaukee County. Two and a half miles into Missaukee County you will reach the junction with Lucas Road—CR597. Head north on this nice blacktop and follow it as it winds north and northwest into Kalkaska County, with a slight east jog at the county line, and then follow the pavement north all the way to US131 and the village of Houseman. Head north on 131 and take it through Kalkaska, turning west on M72 on the north side of town. Two miles west of Kalkaska on M72 Valley Road angles off to the northwest. Turn onto this great riding road and follow it as it traverses the Rapid River valley wandering through wonderful scenery northwest almost ten miles to the town of Rapid City.

Upon arrival at the main crossroads in the small town of Rapid City, turn north onto Rapid City Road and take it across the Antrim County line where it becomes East Torch Lake Road. The great ride continues as you follow the east shore of magnificent Torch Lake north (bear left at "Y" intersections) almost twenty miles to the road's end at M88. At 18,770 acres Torch Lake is Michigan's second largest inland lake and at 285 feet deep it is the deepest inland lake in Michigan.

Turn right (east) on M88—appropriately named Scenic Highway—and follow its meanderings southeast toward the town of Central Lake. Just prior to reaching the town of Central Lake you'll see Ellsworth Road—CR65 going north to the town of Ellsworth—take this road to downtown Ellsworth. In town Ellsworth Road turns east and continues east about five miles to the town of East Jordan. In East Jordan the road becomes Water Street. Follow it across the bridge at the south end of Lake Charlevoix, where you'll pick up M32 for a very short distance. After about a mile M32 turns south, but you want to stay on the east—west East Jordan Boyne City Road that curves its way eastward to the town of Boyne Falls. On the west side of Boyne Falls the East Jordan Boyne City Road becomes Deer Lake Road, and ends at M75. Turn right on M75 taking it less than a mile into Boyne Falls to US131. Turn left (north) on 131 taking it a half-mile to Thumb Lake Road, where we continue our easterly travels over hills and around curves twelve miles to Old US27. Follow Old 27 another twelve miles to M32 and the city of Gaylord. Go east on M32 a little over a mile to where Wilkinson Road—F44 veers off head-

Elk in the Pigeon River State Forest area near Vanderbilt. (Photo by Charles Cook)

ing straight east. Take F44 as it jogs east and northeast about sixteen miles to the county line and turn south on Meridian Road—F01 which heads south six miles to the town of Vienna and M32 once again.

Take M32 just under five miles east to County Road 491, which runs south to Lewiston. Continue south on this pavement across CR612, along the east side of East Twin Lake and into Oscoda County, where the pavement becomes Red Oak Road - CR489. As in many other instances, this is the same pavement alignment, just different names as it crosses jurisdictions.

Follow CR489 south through state and national forestland all the way to M72 and the village of Luzerne. Go west seven miles on M72 to the junction of M18, which you'll follow south for about four miles where you pick up St. Helen Road - CRF97. Follow F97 southward for seventeen miles, through the town of St. Helen and over the I75 expressway. Just after crossing I75 the road curves to the west on Old M55 - West Branch Road. Take this west four miles and F97 turns south again. F97 will be your riding host for about seventeen more miles as you follow it south to M18 in northwest Gladwin County.

Go west on M18 and just shy of five miles the state road makes a ninety-degree turn north but at this corner you want to turn south onto Bard Road. Follow Bard Road south for fourteen miles to the Beaverton-Clare Road. Turn west on the BC Road and take it all the way west to Old US27, then following 27 south three miles back to the city of Clare and the completion of this 375-mile tour. If you're not likely to ever ride in Ireland or on the Isle of Man, maybe this little bit of the ol' sod will satisfy your yearnings for the taste of potatoes, stout Irish beer, and the smell of peat smoke.

The Sunset Tour

THIS TOUR, AS THE NAME suggests, is the west side version of the Sunrise Tour described above. It takes you through the northwestern part of the state from south to north, covering 450 miles worth of marvelous roads, countryside, people and places in the process. This tour takes the rider through a variety of land uses ranging from vegetable farms in the southwest to cherry orchards and vineyards in the north, with a good mix of forests, hills, and trout streams thrown in for good measure. It is truly a wonderfully unique area.

I start this tour in the small town of White Cloud, located in Newaygo County about an hour's drive north of Grand Rapids. It is very easy to get to with the US131 expressway located not far east of town.

Start the trip by heading north on M37 a couple miles to westbound M20. Go west almost twenty miles into Oceana County—with its wonderful mix of forests, truck farms, and fabulous sandy beaches on Lake Michigan—to 154th Avenue. Take 154th north just under a mile and follow the pavement as it jogs west then north again on what will then be 148th Avenue. 148th jogs west again and you end up on 144th Avenue which you follow north ten and one-half miles to Madison Road.

About midway between M20 and Madison Road you will pass nearby a monument to a famous Indian leader from the earliest days of Michigan's history. Cobmoosa was the son of a French voyageur and the daughter of an Indian Chief who grew to be a great leader and signed several treaties with the government. He is buried nearby and the D.A.R. erected a plaque nearly one hundred years ago in his honor.

Once you reach Madison Road you will jog west to 126th Avenue, then follow the pavement north with two more jogs west, ending up on Scottville Road, which you follow straight north to the town of Scottville and US10. Turn west onto US10 following it three miles to Stiles Road where you turn north. Follow Stiles Road and after several miles it makes a slight east jog then north again on what is now called Quarterline Road.

Three and one-half miles north of the jog on Quarterline Road you will see a paved forest trail leading west. This is a delightful winding road through the Nordhouse Dunes Wilderness Area that leads you to the Lake Michigan shore. The road makes this a very nice side trip all by itself, but in addition the beach is

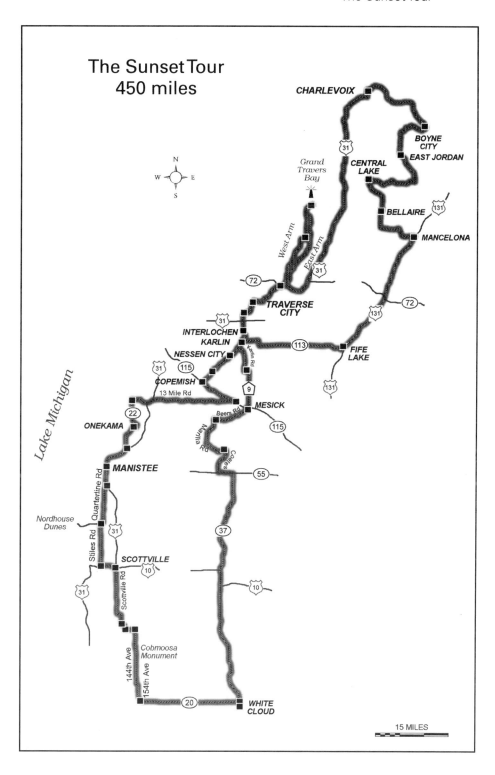

The Sunset Tour
450 miles

Miles	Destination	Total
	THE SUNSET TOUR **450 MILES**	
0	White Cloud	0
15	Hesperia	15
37	Scottville	52
25	Manistee	77
22	Bear Lake	99
25	Copemish	124
14	Interlochen State Park	138
16	Traverse City/M37	154
20	Old Mission Lighthouse	174
19	US31/Traverse City	193
16	Elk Rapids	209
32	Charlevoix	241
18	Boyne City	259
10	East Jordan	269
28	Bellaire	297
25	Kalkaska	322
15	Fife Lake/M186	337
38	M115/Mesick	375
23	M55	398
26	Baldwin	424
26	White Cloud	450

a great place to take a break and enjoy the lake and you can stretch your legs on nearby trails and sand dunes.

Continuing north on Quarterline Road will eventually get you to the junction with US31 at the south side of Manistee. Follow this road through Manistee and a few miles northeast of town you'll see M22 veer off to the north. Take scenic M22 north a little over thirteen miles, around Portage Lake and through the village of Onekoma to Thirteen Mile Road. Turn east on Thirteen Mile and follow it around the south shore of Bear Lake to US131, which you have to follow for about a mile northeast before heading east on Thirteen Mile Road once again. Keep going east on Thirteen Mile Road about sixteen miles—until you reach M115, where a left turn is called for. Follow M115 northwest all the way to the town of Copemish. As you enter Copemish from the south you'll see 2nd Street angling straight north. Take this street north to Railroad Street and turn right. Railroad Street will turn into Nessen City Road, which you follow northeasterly into Benzie County and the village of Nessen City. The pavement takes a slight east and then north jog in Nessen City, continuing northeast again as Karlin Road, still angling northeast. Follow Karlin Road as it eventually takes you to the city of Interlochen and through Interlochen State Park.

Interlochen is home for the world-renowned Interlochen Center for the Arts, a boarding school where the most promising musicians, artists, dancers and writers can attend a college prep high school, while focusing on an arts-based education. Some of the country's best musicians, artists, dancers and writers attended this academy.

In Interlochen, Karlin Road turns into M137 and will take you north to US31 (which seems to keep angling across our path). Go straight across US31 on what now becomes Long Lake Road, following this to Long Lake itself, taking the right fork which becomes East Long Lake Road when you reach the lake. Follow East Long Lake Road north to Secor Road, taking this east to Silver Lake Road, and following Silver Lake to US31—which we want to turn onto this time, following it into Traverse City.

Head east on US31 once it makes the turn in Traverse City, and after a couple of miles you will notice M37 heading north into the Mission Peninsula. The traffic and congestion of Traverse City is a necessary evil to get you to this point. But getting through TC does get you to the Mission Peninsula and that will make it worth your troubles.

The Mission Peninsula is a beautiful finger of land dividing the east and west arms of Grand Traverse Bay. It is covered with cherry orchards, vineyards, and farms, and local residents are fighting hard to keep development from destroying its unique charms.

Though it's a narrow peninsula, it is possible to make a loop by taking advantage of coastal roads for the most part.

Take M37 onto the peninsula and after several miles you'll see Bluff Road angling northeast. Turn onto Bluff Road and it will take you along coastal bluffs overlooking the water to the east and beautiful hills and orchards on your left. Bluff Road rejoins M37 near the northern tip of the peninsula. If you wish, continue north on M37 to the tip and Old Mission Lighthouse. The lighthouse has long been inactive and is currently a private residence, though the land around it is public. The northern tip of Mission Peninsula is almost exactly on the 45th Parallel.

Leaving the peninsula, head south on M37 until you see Bowers Harbor Road going west. Take Bowers Harbor Road to Peninsula Road, and follow this coastal road down the west side of the peninsula until it once again rejoins M37 just north of Traverse City.

Take M37 the short distance to US31 and turn left (east) onto US31. This coastal road will be your companion for many miles as you wander up the east shore of Grand Traverse Bay and Lake Michigan all the way to Charlevoix. This is a beautiful stretch of real estate and though the road isn't spectacular it is certainly very nice and deserving of the fun motorcycling stamp of approval.

Once you reach Charlevoix cross over the waterway connecting Lake Charlevoix and Lake Michigan and continue northeast on US31 about two miles to Boyne City Road. Follow Boyne City Road southeasterly along the shore of Lake Charlevoix to the town of Boyne City, located at the opposite end of Lake Charlevoix. Continue following the lakeshore road through Boyne City and around the opposite side of the lake. The road changes from Boyne City Road to Front Street to Lakeshore Road on the southwest side of Lake Charlevoix.

Follow Lakeshore Road west until you see Advance-East Jordan Road heading south. Turn onto this road and follow it into East Jordan. In town Advance-East Jordan Road becomes 7th Street, jogging west on Nichols Street, then south again on 3rd Street. From 3rd Street go southeast on M32, taking M32 south until it turns ninety degrees to the east, at which point you keep going straight south on Mt. Bliss Road. Mt. Bliss Road is a great riding road that winds southeast to Old State Road, where it 'T's. Turn west on Old State Road ten miles to the town of Central Lake. Old State Road is also CR624.

On the east side of the town of Central Lake, prior to going around Intermediate Lake, you'll see Intermediate Lake Drive heading south—turn onto this road. Take Intermediate Lake Drive south along the east shore of Intermediate Lake until you see Derenzy Road take off straight south from ILD. Derenzy Road continues going south along the east shore of Intermediate Lake, taking you to the town of Bellaire. Take M88 south out of Bellaire, following it as it turns east heading to the town of Mancelona and US131. Turn south (right) onto US131. Follow US131 southwest many miles, through Kalkaska County and to Fife Lake in the southeast corner of Grand Traverse County. Out of Fife Lake take M186 west for three miles where it ends against M113. Turn north onto M113 and it very shortly turns to head straight west taking you twelve miles across southern Grand Traverse County to M37. When you reach M37 continue straight across on what is Miller Road. Two miles west of M37 the pavement curves north one mile onto Youker Road, on which you continue westward to Karlin Road. Take Karlin Road south two miles and then turn east in the crossroad town of Karlin, taking Karlin Road east then south again. At the Wexford County line Karlin Road turns to gravel so you have to jog east one mile and continue south on County Road No. 9. Take CR9 straight south to its terminus at M115 just west of Mesick.

Go west on M115 for about a half-mile then turn south onto scenic Hodenpyl Dam Road. Hodenpyl Dam Road angles southwesterly along the Hodenpyl Dam Pond, an impoundment on the Manistee River, entering Manistee County as Beers Road. Take Beers Road west to its 'T' at Marilla Road, and follow Marilla south as it meanders to its own T at Coates Highway. Takes Coates Highway east, crossing the Manistee River midway, and when the pavement Ts, turn right (south), ending up at M55.

Go east on M55 to M37 and turn south. Though it's a state highway, you'll enjoy M37 as it takes you on a wonderful ride through forests and around curves all the way back to White Cloud.

Thus ends a 450-mile trip through some of the best roads and sites that west Michigan has to offer.

The Eastern Yoop Loop

LET ME START OUT by stating that there are no bad riding roads in the Upper Peninsula. None. Some are better than others; some are fantastic, some are great, some are really good, and the rest are good. But there aren't any bad ones that you need to stay off. Any paved road in the UP is a good motorcycling road, period.

Therefore one can't go wrong in heading to the UP and just riding wherever you happen to end up. But there are roads and places that one should definitely ride, either because of the road itself, or the destination. If a person had an entire month they could crisscross the entire peninsula and never run out of good roads and worthy destinations. But for those without the luxury of unlimited time, or who are strangers to the UP, I've selected two good loops that will take you on some of the best roads and most desirable sights and places. These two loops cover some of the same roads as the Lake Superior Circle Tour, but many folks may well not have the luxury of time to make that grand circle trip, and one sure doesn't want to miss out on these attractions and roads.

I should also explain some of the native language spoken in the UP so that those not familiar with it aren't confused while traveling there, or worse, unwittingly insult the locals. In Yooper language "Da" means the; "Eh?" ends each sentence or question; "Ya" means yes; "Fudgie" is a tourist; "gaas" = gas (as in gasoline); "Holy Man!" = the ultimate Yooper exclamation; "Kromer" = an old fashioned, but very warm, cap with flannel and ear flaps; "Troll"—a Lower Peninsula resident; "chuke" = stocking cap; "Pasty" (pronounced with a short a, please!) = Cornish or Finnish meat pie, originally made for taking into the mines for lunch; "swampers" = muddy season boots; "Eino and Toivo = names used in about 99% of Yooper jokes; "no-see-ums" = small vicious biting flies; and "Wha!" = Wow!

So there you have it—a very basic dictionary for Yooperese. Memorize these prior to your trip so that you don't look like just another stupid fudgie troll. It is also a very good idea to not brag about teams such as the Detroit Lions or Chicago Bears (especially not the Bears), and never, ever, say anything disparaging about the Packers, Lambeau Field, or Vince Lombardi.

The first of these two basically circular tours I call the Eastern Yoop Loop because, duh, it's a circular tour in the eastern UP. With the many sights to see and things to do along the way this is a great two-day trip at 360 miles.

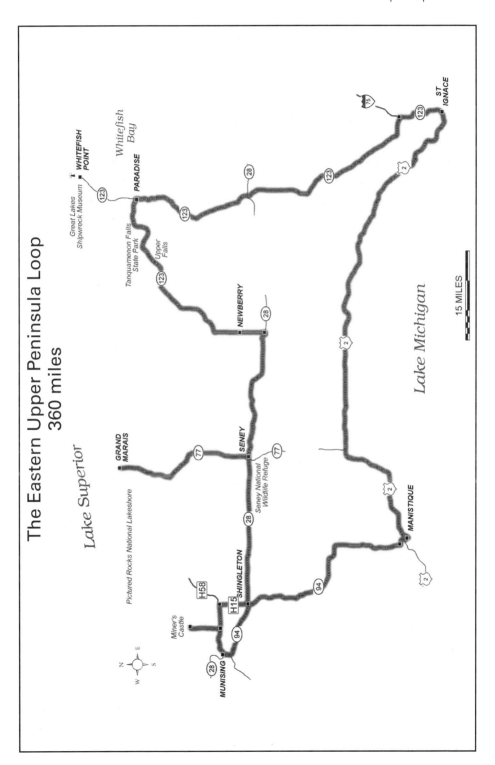

The Eastern Upper Peninsula Loop
360 miles

	THE EASTERN UPPER PENINSULA LOOP 360 MILES	
Miles	**Destination**	**Total**
0	St. Ignace	0
8	M123	8
23	Trout Lake	31
32	Paradise	63
9	Tahquamenon Falls State Park	72
28	Newbery	100
27	Seney M77	127
25	Grand Marais	152
25	M77	177
25	Shingleton	202
10	Munising	212
11	Miner's Castle	223
13	Shingleton/M28/M94	236
36	Manistique/US2	272
88	St. Ignace	360

This tour starts in St. Ignace, following the Mackinac Highway along the coast through town and north about ten miles to M123. This road winds through the coniferous forests of the eastern UP and ultimately along the shore of Whitefish Bay, into the village of Paradise where it swings west. Before following 123 westward, however, I strongly recommend continuing north on the lakeshore road to Whitefish Point. There you can visit the Great Lakes Shipwreck Museum and learn about the maritime history of this region and of the many ships that rest forever on the bottoms of these stormy inland seas. There is also the historic Whitefish Point lighthouse and a bird observatory. Whitefish Point is on a major migratory route for spring and fall migration of many bird species, and is a very popular birding site during those periods.

The stretch of M123 between Paradise and the town of Newberry is great. The road is smooth with many curves and the scenery is grand. You will certainly want to stop at the Tahquamenon Falls State Park to see at least the upper falls.

Tahquamenon Falls in Tahquamenon State Park.

M123 ends at its juncture with M28 south of Newberry. We'll follow M28 west at this point to the town of Seney. Dropping south on M77 a few miles will take you to the headquarters of the Seney National Wildlife Refuge—a 95,500-acre wilderness area located south of M28 and west of M77. Walking tours through part of the refuge are available and there is also a seven-mile self-guided tour for motorized vehicles.

Next you'll want to head north on M77 to the town of Grand Marais on Lake Superior. This town is at the eastern gate of the marvelous Pictured Rocks National Lakeshore. This Lakeshore has it all—majestic coastal cliffs, giant sand dunes, waterfalls, wilderness, and nice hiking trails. The east end has the remarkable Grand Sable sand dunes that are forever moving inland. Beautiful Grand Sable Lake is a great place to canoe or kayak in the company of eagles. There is a visitor center here that has interpretive displays and information about the park. You certainly want to include time in your travel plans for this park. Besides, the trip up and down M77 is worth your time all by itself.

After heading back south to M28 we'll continue west through the famous "Seney Stretch," where you will think you've somehow ended up in the middle of the taiga forests of the sub arctic. This stretch does have a certain tundra-like appearance to it. At the town of Shingleton we go north on county road H-15 to the shoreline and the west end of the National Lakeshore. H-15 takes a four-

Aerial view of Au Sable Point Lighthouse near Grand Marais. (Photo by Raymond J. Malace)

mile westward jog on H-58 en route north. Our stops here include Miner's waterfall along H-15 and the Miner's Castle rock formations at the lakeshore. Miner's Castle was so-named in 1771 by British explorers searching for potential valuable ores in the area. The rock formation sits atop the Northern Michigan Escarpment, which runs about one hundred miles east to west in this part of the state. The Tahquamenon Falls are also on this rock formation. The lakeside cliffs, from which the Pictured Rocks Lakeshore derives its name, are a beautiful palette of colors rising out of the deep and cold steel gray waters of Lake Superior.

Upon leaving the shoreline we retrace out route back south a few miles to H-58 that we take west into the really nice small town of Munising. This town is situated on the water, surrounded by hills and waterfalls. It is a great spot to spend the night or at least to stop for a break. This central coast of Lake Superior is especially treacherous, and Trout Bay and the Munising harbor, protected by Grand Island, provided the only refuge for seafarers for many miles. Native Americans long used the sheltered bay where present day Munising is located. They referred to the spot as *kitchi minissing*—place of the great island. Grand Island, located in the bay just offshore, is indeed a great island. Today it is protected as a National Recreation Area. A day trip to the island to soak in its history and sights is a day very well spent. There are many other interesting things to do out of Munising: Take the Pictured Rocks boat tour; take an airplane ride over the lakeshore for a dramatic view of the sea cliffs and Grand Island (call Skylane at 877-656-4933); or take a glass-bottom boat on the bay to view shipwrecks (call 906-387-4477).

We leave Munising by going south on M94 back to Shingleton and then south to Manistique on the Lake Michigan coast. M94 in this stretch is a really enjoyable riding road with curves and scenery aplenty as it snakes its way through the forest. Once in Manistique head east on US2, enjoying the many blue water vistas all along the shoreline back to St. Ignace. US2 is a wonderful riding road, with mile after mile of good road and great scenery unfolding before you as you reel in the pavement and soak up the unhurried atmosphere of it all. There are many small parks and scenic overlooks along this stretch where you can stop to take in the incredible views of blue water and islands extending beyond the horizon.

The Western Yoop Loop

IF THE EASTERN UP loop is really good, then the western loop is really great. Roads custom made for motorcycling, light traffic, forested hills, and blue water vistas that stretch to the horizon—take your pick, they're all on this tour. Beginning in Gladstone on Little Bay de Noc, we'll head northwest on M35, following it about seventy miles as it twists and turns its way to Negaunee. Once in the Negaunee area there are attractions that one ought to park the bike to enjoy, even though the riding is so great you might feel like just staying aboard and putting on the miles and smiles. In Negaunee there is the Iron Industry Museum with its fascinating displays and stories about Michigan's iron mining industry. The museum is located at 73 Forge Road, phone number 906-475-7857.

Taking US41 west out of Negaunee the next stop is Ishpeming. Like Negaunee this town is in the heart of the UP iron mining district. A new attraction in Ishpeming is the Cliffs Shaft Heritage Park—a site of an old underground mine, complete with towering original mine shafts and equipment. Ishpeming is also home for the National Ski Hall of Fame and Museum, located at 610 Palms Avenue (skihall. com). Da Yoopers Tourist Trap located on US41 just west of town (believe me, you can't miss it!) is a fun stop. After you settle down and stop your giggling following a tour of Da Yoopers Tourist Trap head west on US41 again and follow it west and then north all the way to Copper Harbor and the tip of the Keweenaw Peninsula (meaning "portage" in Native American language). The first leg of this stretch takes us west through the heart of Michigan's moose country, and along the south edge of a large wilderness area that encompasses the Huron Mountains and the McCormick Wilderness tract. US41 then curves northward through the historic village of Alberta (definitely worth a stop), past the Bishop Baraga Shrine near Baraga and then along Keweenaw Bay to the twin cities of Houghton and Hancock. In the Houghton area there are many attractions: Michigan Technological University, the Houghton County Historical Museum, the Quincy Mine Historic Site and tour, and more. Further up the road the City of Calumet is another must-see with its historic district, opera house and The Coppertown Mining Museum.

One of the Michigan roads that always gets mentioned by out-of-state writers is US41 in the Keweenaw. It is definitely worthy of the acclaim, as you shall soon see, as you twist and climb your way to Copper Harbor and the end of the road.

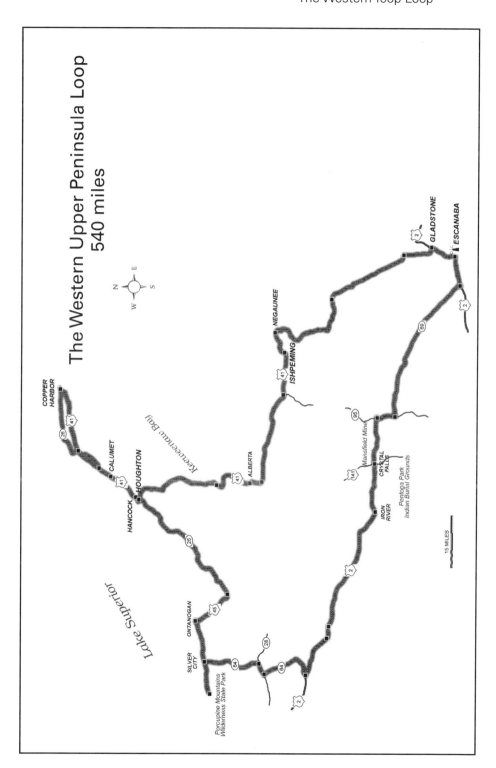

The Western Upper Peninsula Loop
540 miles

N
W E
S

COPPER HARBOR

41

26

CALUMET

41

HOUGHTON

HANCOCK

Keweenaw Bay

26

Lake Superior

45

ONTANOGAN

SILVER CITY

Porcupine Mountains
Wilderness State Park

64

28

64

2

ALBERTA

41

ISHPEMING

41

NEGAUNEE

41

IRON RIVER

95

2

Mansfield Mine

141

CRYSTAL FALLS

Pentoga Park
Indian Burial Grounds

69

GLADSTONE

2

ESCANABA

2

2

15 MILES

THE WESTERN UP LOOP 540 MILES		
Miles	**Destination**	**Total**
0	Gladstone	0
41	Gwinn	41
26	US41/Negaunee	67
59	L'Anse	126
32	Houghton/Canal Bridge	158
52	Copper Harbor	210
55	Hancock	265
57	Ontonagon	322
22	Lake of the Clouds	344
9	Silver City	353
18	Bergland/Lake Gogebic	371
21	US2	392
26	Watersmeet	418
29	Iron River	447
16	Crystal Falls	463
13	Sagola	476
64	Escanaba	540

Twelve miles south of Copper Harbor you'll pass the Delaware Copper Mine which has very interesting tours and displays and just beyond Copper Harbor at the road's end is Fort Wilkins State Park—a fascinating restored fort from Michigan's early history. Copper Harbor is also where you can access the Isle Royale Ferry for a trip across Lake Superior to Isle Royale National Park (leaving your bikes in Copper Harbor; Isle Royale is a hiking and camping wilderness park, not a place where one finds great motorcycling roads).

Don't be in a hurry on the Keweenaw. There is much to explore and see, including ghost towns, old mine sites, waterfalls, lighthouses, lonely shorelines, and much more. For your motorcycling pleasure I recommend at least two loops—one utilizing US41 and the Brockway Mountain Drive, and the second loop utilizing Brockway Mountain Drive and M26 along the coast. If you have time by all means take a third loop—that being along Gay Road on the east coast of the peninsula.

There is so much history on the Keweenaw Peninsula that the Keweenaw National Historic Park was established in 1992. This unique park encompasses communities and attractions in a manner that allows their stories to be told and protected while allowing them to remain in the 'natural' state as functioning entities.

All good things must end and when your time in the Keweenaw is up follow M26 southwest to its juncture with US45, taking 45 back north to the coastal town of Ontonagon. Prior to arriving at Ontonagon you'll pass the Adventure Copper Mine site in Greenland—another very interesting stop. Ontonagon is in the heart of copper mining and forest country. It is a marvelous area with natural wonders aplenty. Take some time to stop at the local history museum and visitors center to get information about the many things to see and do here.

Head west on M64 to Silver City and continue west on M107 as it snakes its way atop a lakeside cliff into the Porcupine Mountains Wilderness State Park, and a fantastic overlook at the end of the road at the Lake of the Clouds. This is incredible motorcycling country. While you're still along the shore of Lake Superior, gather up your nerve and try a dip in the cold water. Even if you just wade up to your knees the shock of the frigid Lake Superior water will give you a renewed respect for those who make their living on the Lake. Besides, it makes for great bragging points after the trip.

Back in Silver City take M64 south all the way to US2, and turn east. The great riding continues unabated on M64 and US2. Along M64 you will follow the west shore of Lake Gogebic—the UP's largest inland lake and a beautiful one at that. The Alligator Eye Scenic Overlook on M64 just north of US2 on Lake Gogebic is a nice rest stop. Following US2 east brings you to even more delights. You'll want to tour the Iron County Museum in Iron River and the Pentoga Park Indian Burial Grounds on the south end of Chicagon Lake just east of Iron River to name just a couple. Further east the Iron County Courthouse in Crystal Falls is a striking building worth a few minute stop to admire its beautiful architecture. Buildings such as this courthouse were built during the peak of the mining and lumbering economies of the Upper Peninsula. Money for public projects was more plentiful during that era, and residents were anxious to demonstrate their public pride through stately and impressive buildings.

In Crystal Falls you will leave US2 and pick up M69 eastbound. M69 is the more lightly traveled and scenic highway back to Escanaba and Gladstone. Though you might not want to ride your bike on the dirt road leading to the site, about six miles east of Crystal Falls, and then about three miles north is the site of the former Mansfield Mine, home to Michigan's worst mining disaster. The mine was

Scenic drive in the Keweenaw Peninsula of Michigan's Upper Peninsula. (Photo by Raymond J. Malace)

dug several layers deep under the Michigamme River and in 1893 the mine caved in under the river, which came roaring into the mine killing twenty-seven miners. Another piece of Michigan history that is nearly forgotten, save for a small marker at the site.

M69 is a very pleasant ride as it angles across Iron, Dickinson, Menominee and Delta Counties to Escanaba. Though this port city is the end of the trip, it doesn't mean an end to things to do. This town has a beautiful waterfront park, there is a museum and archives in town where you can learn about the area's history, and you'll want to see the Sand Point Lighthouse while you're there, and this doesn't even get into the many events such as fairs, parades, car shows and so on.

At 540 miles I recommend making this a three-day trip if possible. You will enjoy every minute and mile of it and you certainly won't be bored.

Great Lakes Circle Tours

B EING SURROUNDED by the Great Lakes provides a special bonus for motorcyclists in this region. Taking trips entirely around the Lakes has long been an objective of many travelers in the Great Lakes basin. Any book about motorcycling in Michigan wouldn't be complete without coverage of these opportunities. Four of the five Lakes—Michigan, Superior, Huron, and Erie—border on Michigan so those are the ones I'll write about.

Because we share three of these Lakes with our neighbor to the north (and to the east, if you live in Michigan), there are certain realities about entering and traveling in a foreign country that need discussion.

For a long time routine trips into Canada and back into the States were a breeze—a friendly border guard asked a few pertinent questions and you were on your way. Unless there was something about what you said or how you answered the questions the whole process seldom took more than a couple minutes. While the border between the U.S. and Canada is still very open and thousands of people routinely cross it each day for business, travel, or recreation, things have noticeably changed since those cowardly and foul acts of 9/11.

Be prepared to answer several questions about your travels and quite likely even have a cursory search made of your belongings—especially when crossing back into the U.S. Years ago I didn't even bother shutting off the engine or taking off my helmet when crossing the border; today I do both as soon as I pull up to the inspection gate. Be prepared to show your driver's license, and when coming back into the States you may well be asked to provide proof of citizenship by presenting your birth certificate, which you should take with you. Whatever you do don't try to be a comedian or wiseass—it won't be appreciated and will definitely complicate your life. And don't try to carry a weapon into Canada. Even if you are fully licensed to carry a handgun in Michigan or another state, it is illegal to take them across the border. If caught with a weapon your trip will definitely take a wrong turn. Border security has become a very important part of our national security so don't view travels across the Canadian border quite the same as we were fortunate enough to have done for generations.

Because I believe that the whole purpose of a Great Lakes circle tour is to see the lakes as much as possible, you will note that some of my routes differ from the standard or official routes, which are based completely on state and provincial or federal highways. After all, shouldn't a rider stay as close to the water as possible and not ride several miles inland just to stay on a major state or federal route? I believe so, and that's why I try to find just those waterside roads rather than simply follow the official routes.

Lake Huron Circle Tour

LAKE HURON IS UNIQUE in that there are actually two routes a rider can take to get around the lake: go all the way around both the main lake and Georgian Bay (which is so large it's sometimes referred to as the sixth Great Lake), or essentially split the lake in two by going up the beautiful Bruce Peninsula and taking a ferry across to Manitoulin Island. Because of my previously stated desires to stay off of main roads as much as possible I prefer the Bruce Peninsula/Manitoulin Island route, so let's talk about that first.

Because a circular tour by definition doesn't have an obvious start and end point, we'll use Port Huron, Michigan as the beginning point. Port Huron is situated at the southern end of Lake Huron, at the beginning of the St. Clair River. A short ride over the Blue Water Bridge puts you in Sarnia, Ontario. Once in Ontario you'll want to stop at the nearby Visitor Centre to exchange some currency and to gather any travel information you might need. I definitely recommend picking up a provincial map and some brochures for the Bruce Peninsula. Ontario is just a marvelous place to visit and roam. There is so much to see and do there that you want to be prepared for various side trips.

The Blue Water Bridge dumps you onto Ontario Route 402—a major expressway that connects Sarnia with all points east. Going east on 402 you can leave the expressway at either exit 15, 25, or 34—it really doesn't matter as they will all get you north to the shoreline road, which is Ontario Route 21. Exit 34 is Route 21 itself. You'll stay on Route 21 all the way to Bruce Peninsula.

Route 21 follows the eastern shore of Lake Huron and is the closest road to the water, but unfortunately it is inland just far enough so that you get only occasional glimpses of the Lake. The various towns that you pass through have parks or roads that will take you to the water's edge, but Route 21 itself doesn't.

This part of Ontario is farm country, and you will pass through miles of green fields, woods, and small towns. Many of the towns have small museums that are interesting to go through, and there are numerous campgrounds and parks if you want to camp.

About one hundred thirty kilometers (keep in mind that measurements in Canada are metric) you will see signs for Point Clark Lighthouse. This lighthouse is a Canadian National Historic Site, and is open to the public for tours and if you feel up to it, a climb to the top. The view is tremendous.

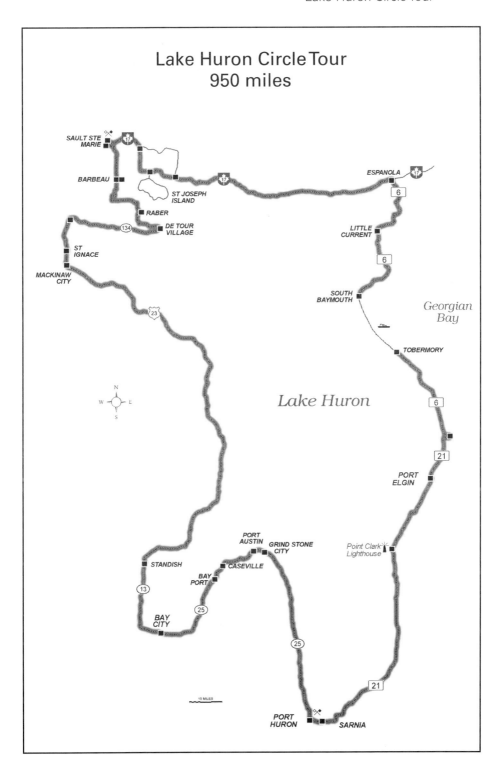

Lake Huron Circle Tour
950 miles

Miles	Destination	Total
	LAKE HURON CIRCLE TOUR **950 MILES**	
0	Port Huron/Blue Water Bridge	0
11	Exit 25/Highway 402	11
67	Goderich	78
26	Point Clark Lighthouse	104
40	Southhampton	144
25	Ontario Route 6	169
48	Tobermory	217
28	South Baymouth (Ferry)	245
42	Little Current/Bridge	287
32	Canada Highway 17	319
59	Blind River	378
34	Ontario Route 129	412
56	International Bridge (Sault Ste. Marie)	468
61	De Tour Village	529
51	Mackinac Bridge	580
57	Rogers City	637
37	Alpena	674
55	Tawas City	729
36	Standish	765
29	Bay City	794
69	Port Austin	863
54	Port Sanilac	917
33	Port Huron	950

About an hour's drive north of the lighthouse is the base of the Bruce Peninsula near Port Elgin. The main road on the peninsula is Route 6, which goes right up the center. I prefer to take Route 13 that you pick up at the very southwest corner of the peninsula just past Southhampton. (Route 13 isn't well marked, but there is an IGA grocery store on the corner. If you miss it don't worry, you can always take Route 6 north through the peninsula.)

Route 13 goes up the west coast of the peninsula for about a quarter of the peninsula's length, and then curves back east to take you to Route 6. Even after Route 13 heads east to Route 6, you can continue going north on a nice paved back road that continues up the west side and finally curves back east and meets Route 6 mid-peninsula at the small town of Ferndale. This road is narrow and curvy and very fun to ride in places and definitely has less traffic than the main road. In the northern half of Bruce Peninsula there are fewer choices, and you'll end up taking Route 6 to the northern tip and the town of Tobermory.

The distance from Port Huron to Tobermory is about 340 kilometers or roughly 225 miles. You'll find that speed limits are generally a little lower in Ontario, so plan accordingly.

Once you're on the peninsula there are many things to see and do. In the Bruce Peninsula National Park, at the northern tip of the peninsula, a hiking trail takes you along the edge of the Niagara Escarpment—the same limestone cliff that creates Niagara Falls. From the escarpment you can look out over Georgian Bay to the east of the peninsula. The cliffs at the water's edge are spectacular. Fathom Five National Marine Park off the northern tip of the peninsula is famous for its scuba diving opportunities, and glass-bottom boat tours, lighthouse tours, dinner cruises and more are available for those who want to spend some time on Bruce.

A memorable part of this tour will be the ferry boat trip across the channel from Tobermory at the tip of Bruce Peninsula to South Baymouth on the southern coast of Manitoulin Island. While the Bruce Peninsula separates the main portion of Lake Huron on the west from Georgian Bay on the east, Manitoulin Island (and other nearby islands) form what is called the North Channel—that part of Lake Huron that lies between the islands and the Canadian mainland to the north. This is a remarkably beautiful area with islands and blue water as far as the eye can see.

A ferry called ChiCheemaun (meaning The Big Canoe in Ojibwa) makes regular passages across the open water to and from Tobermory and South Baymouth. The ferry is operated by Ontario Ferries, and information can be obtained from ontarioferries.com or by calling 800-265-3163. Reservations are highly recommended. Motorcyclists have the privilege of being the first vehicles loaded on the ferry, and the first vehicles unloaded. There is a special motorcycle parking area on the lower level of the ferry, with tie-down brackets in the floor and ropes provided to secure the bikes. You want to be sure to secure your bike, as the water can get quite choppy and rough even in a moderate wind.

This is a popular route for motorcyclists, and you meet an interesting group of fellow bikers from all around the U.S. and Canada. I even encountered a couple from England making a two-year trip around the world on their Yamaha Secas. The ferry trip takes about two hours.

Manitoulin Island—the largest freshwater island in the world—is so large that it has a mainland feel to it. There are things to do on the island, but making the roughly forty-mile trip across it on Route 6 is great fun by itself. The road is enjoyable, with curves and hills enough to keep it interesting while passing through a landscape of stone and forests, with the occasional hard rock farm trying to make a go of it. As is the case on all good riding roads you have to choose whether to ride fast to enjoy the curves, or ride more slowly and enjoy the scenery.

You leave the island at the north end from a small town called Little Current. There is an interesting one-lane swing bridge here that connects Manitoulin to the next island. The bridge swings open to allow boat traffic through. It is quite rough so you want to have both hands on the bars. Route 6 makes it way north to the mainland, eventually terminating at the town of Espanola and the Trans-Canada Highway (Canadian Route 17). Route 17 follows the northern shore of Lake Huron westward from this point all the way to Sault Ste. Marie (The Soo) Ontario. From Espanola to the Soo is approximately 245 km / 160 miles.

While not a wilderness area, this stretch of area is only lightly developed. Because it is a main trans-continental highway, there is a fair amount of traffic on the road, including large trucks. Route 17 does have a good number of passing lanes constructed at strategic points to allow faster traffic to get by slow vehicles.

Due to the bilingual nature of Canada, you'll have a chance to brush up on your high school or college French courses. All road signs are in both French and English, as are many brochures and other printed materials.

About one hundred fifty-five miles west of Espanola you will see Ontario Route 129 going north from Route 17 to Chapleau, ON. If you feel adventuresome, and you have a full tank of gas and a trouble-free bike, this is a beautiful stretch of road across two hundred twelve kilometers of near wilderness. Not a place you want to break down, however, and don't count on using your cell phone.

An interesting side trip, and one which continues the island hopping theme, is to follow the Canada National Park signs about sixty miles east of Sault Ste. Marie and take Road 548 onto St. Joseph Island. The road makes a scenic circular tour of the island, and takes you to Fort St. Joseph Historic Park. This fort was the most westerly of the various British frontier posts during the War of 1812.

The twin cities of Sault Ste. Marie anchor the International Bridge connecting Michigan and Ontario. The St. Mary River connecting Lake Superior and Lake Huron was named by French explorers in 1641. Because there is a fall of eighteen

Blue Water Bridge linking Port Huron to Sarnia, Ontario, Canada. (Photo by Rich Kelly)

feet in this short stretch of river, tremendous rapids were found by early explorers. Two Jesuit priests in 1641 gave the river the name of St. Mary in honor of an Indian mission by that name that they operated east of Georgian Bay. The Jesuits gave the name of Le Sault de Sainte Marie to this location meaning the falls (or rapids) of the St. Mary.

In the Canadian Soo an interesting stop is at the Canadian Bush Plane Heritage Center, located at 50 Pim Street downtown on the river not far from the Bridge. Go to bushplane.com/ or call (877) 287-4752 for more information.

Sault Ste. Marie Michigan was first established in 1668 when Father Marquette and others founded a mission there. French trappers, explorers, and missionaries had traveled through the area prior to this, but warring bands of Iroquois Indians from the east made any kind of settlement impossible. Even indigenous native tribes were forced out of what is now Michigan due to the Iroquois. In 1653 a series of major battles between Iroquois war parties and tribes from what is now Michigan and Wisconsin occurred. One of these battles is still remembered by the place name of Point Iroquois west of Sault Ste. Marie, Michigan. There is a lighthouse and an Indian mission cemetery at the spot today.[1] By 1668 peace with the Iroquois was achieved and exploration of the Great Lakes region by French explorers began in earnest. Sault Ste Marie is either the second or third oldest city in the nation, depending on which reference resources are cited.

Sault Ste. Marie has many interesting things to see and do. It is worth a few hours of your time to explore this unique city. Certainly watching the freighters going through the locks is a must for anyone visiting the Soo. Seeing these huge freighters just a few yards away is an amazing sight. The ultimate experience is to take a tour boat through the locks system. You can't get any closer to the workings of the locks than this. The Tower of History is another attraction worth your time. At 210 feet high it provides a great panorama of the entire area, as well as a museum of Native American and missionary artifacts. Taking a tour of the museum ship Valley Camp provides a unique opportunity to see the inner workings of an actual Great Lakes freighter.

One of my most enduring and evocative memories of Upper Peninsula vacations both as a child and adult is the haunting sound of ship whistles and fog horns in the night while sleeping in a local motel or campground.

Upon leaving the Soo to continue on the circle tour the "official" route will have you take M-129 south from Sault Ste. Marie. The problem is this road is straight, inland, not especially attractive and not very fun. Interesting sites along the eastern portion of the St. Mary River are missed by taking M-129. A better route is to take Portage Street—the main east / west street in Sault Ste. Marie—all the way east until you see signs for the Sugar Island Ferry, with Sugar Island just offshore. The road then turns south, becoming Riverview Road. It follows the shoreline for several miles, allowing great views of the river, islands, and freighter traffic. Unfortunately, even this road runs inland for a bit, but it is much more enjoyable and scenic than the state highway.

Stay on Riverside Dr. for about thirteen miles to the four-corner town of Barbeau, which brings you to 15 Mile Road. If you wish at this intersection you can go east for three miles to the Village of Neebish, and then south along the shoreline to the Village of Munuscong on what appropriately enough is called Scenic Drive. Neebish Island is just across the channel. There is no outlet so you'll have to retrace your steps back to Barbeau but this scenic detour is well worth it.

Back in Barbeau continue south on Riverside Drive. After a couple of easy to follow jogs it finally ends at 22 Mile Road. At this point go west one mile, and then continue south again on Pennington Road for two miles where you will hit Gogomain Road. Take Gogomain Road east about eleven miles and you'll once again

---

[1]*Michigan, A History of the Wolverine State.* Willis F. Dunbar © 1970. Wm. B. Eerdmans Publishing Co.

A freighter making its way through the Soo Locks.

be on the shores of the St. Mary River. The pavement curves south and becomes Raber Road. Gogomain / Raber is a great road to ride. There is very little traffic and good scenery. Raber Road will take you through the small village of Raber on the water, and then finally south to state highway M-48. Be careful in Raber as there is a deceptively tight curve coming out of town on which you can easily end up on the wrong side of the double yellow line.

We have no option but to take M-48 south for four miles to North Caribou Road. Turn east on North Caribou Rd and take it to the road's end in DeTour Village. Spending some time in DeTour is a good idea. It's a working waterfront town with a ferry to Drummond Island. While Drummond Island has lots to see, some of the good sights really aren't accessible by touring or sport bikes. (You adventure bikers will have a ball, however) Taking the ferry over is a fun experience just the same, and there are many miles of motorcycle-friendly roads on the island.

Following the waterfront in DeTour will bring you to State Route 134. While I try to stay off main roads M-134 is fine because it's a great riding road in its own right, and besides, there's no alternative. M-134 hugs the northern Lake Huron shore with islands and blue water, dotted with white sail boats on the left and cedar forests on the right, from DeTour Village west to the Mackinac Trail, which will take you south along the shoreline and through St. Ignace to the Mackinac Bridge. There really isn't much to see if you take the I75 expressway from M-134 south to St. Ignace.

Crossing the five-mile wide Straits of Mackinac on the Mackinac Bridge is a thrill in itself. Suspended high above the water with Lake Michigan on your right and Lake Huron to the east, the view is a montage of islands, lighthouses, working tugs, sailboats, Mackinac Island ferries with their proud rooster tail plumes of water, and freighters loaded with goods and raw materials coming and going on this water highway. Take your time and enjoy the few minutes that you have to take pleasure in this unique ride and splendid scene.

Throughout the Lower Peninsula of Michigan it is very easy to hug the shoreline of Lake Huron—simply follow U.S.-23 from Mackinaw City all the way south to Standish. This will put you as close to the water as you can be without getting wet, and is a very nice scenic ride. In the town of Standish you will want to get on M-13 and take this south along Saginaw Bay to the small town of Kawkawlin. Just south of Kawkawlin you have a choice: either take Connecter 13 south and get on I75 for a few miles until you hit M-25 eastbound, or take Huron Road where it splits off Connector 13 just south of Kawkawlin and take it the four miles into downtown Bay City where you'll intersect with M-25. Huron Road turns into Euclid Avenue in Bay City.

In Bay City you have the opportunity to take a three-hour sailing trip on the Bay on one of two large schooners operated by BaySail, 901 Water Street, located near Wenonah Park. Call 888.229.8696 or go to baysailbaycity.org for more information. Reservations are strongly recommended.

Picking up M-25 in Bay City and heading east will take you back up and around the Thumb on the east side of Saginaw Bay and finally south again along the Lake Huron shore back to our starting point of Port Huron. Remain on M-25 the entire way past Bay City except for any side trips you may wish to make following signs to lighthouses, parks, and other attractions.

There are innumerable things to see and do along the entire stretch of shoreline road in Lower Michigan. You will pass museums, lighthouses, monuments, huge limestone quarries, wildlife refuges, parks and many other points of interest. There is also no shortage of restaurants, campgrounds, motels, and other facilities. Fortunately US23 hasn't been replaced by an expressway and you can leisurely travel for an entire day and almost never be out of sight of the lake. The east coast of Michigan is referred to as the sunrise coast, and in general is less developed and less hectic than the west side of the state.

On the Thumb portion of the route you will have the opportunity to have a real fish sandwich at Bay Port, lie on the beach at Caseville, or Port Austin, see the old grindstones at Grindstone City, view lighthouses, take a charter boat fishing for Great Lakes salmon or Lake Trout, or just ride along and enjoy the scenery all the way south back to Port Huron. If you really want to treat yourself or your riding partner, start or end the trip with an overnight stay and meal at the Edison Inn in Port Huron, which is situated just off the river very close to the Blue Water Bridge. Luxurious accommodations and great food start at $89.00 per night.

If you choose to go all the way around Lake Huron and Georgian Bay, simply stay on Ontario Route 21 as it turns eastward and don't take the turn onto Bruce Peninsula. O21 will turn into Ontario Route 26 at Owen Sound, and continue east to Barrie. Ontario Route 400 is an expressway that takes you north from Barrie to Parry Sound, where the expressway ends and you continue north on Ontario Route 69 to Sudbury.

Sudbury is a mid-sized industrial and mining town and while there you'll want to explore the local nickel mining industry and visit the large Science North Museum. Going west out of Sudbury on Trans-Canada Highway 17 will take you back to Sault Ste. Marie.

Unfortunately the route east of Georgian Bay is for the most part inland far enough so that side trips are necessary to see the lake.

So there you have it—a tremendous trip of about 955 miles (add about 150 miles if you go all the way around Georgian Bay) through a variety of countryside ranging from forested and wild to resort areas, small urban locations, and prime agricultural land. And the whole time you're never more than a few miles at most from the shore.

Lake Superior Circle Tour

ALL OF THE GREAT LAKES circle tours are unique and great trips in their own right, but I've always thought that the trip around Lake Superior was the crown jewel. It's probably because I'd rather be in the middle of Lake Superior Provincial Park in Ontario surrounded by cliffs and forests than in any large city in the world that prejudices my thinking. The Lake Superior trip is just stupendous. No matter where you are on the trip—Michigan, Minnesota, Wisconsin or Ontario—you're never far from magnificent vistas, waterfalls, historic lighthouses, islands, small towns with great stories to tell and lots of history, majestic overlooks, and always that view of the lake itself with its watery horizon stretching seemingly forever into the distance. Adjectives fall short when it comes to describing this area. Superlatives like tremendous and spectacular are overused today and thus watered down. The Lake Superior region is one place where they really are applicable.

Knowing that you're riding through a land that is populated with wolves, moose, bears and woodland caribou adds to the flavor of the trip. This is still mostly wild lands not conquered by man's hand. The roads are wonderful, with hills and curves aplenty. They run the gamut from waterside pavement to magnificent roads that snake through valleys and over hills with cliffs on each side and blue sky above. Sounds like a dream-come-true trip for any motorcyclist!

For those unfamiliar with the Lake Superior region I do want to warn you of some realities. First, the weather in that area can change rapidly, and even in the summer the temperature frequently drops into the forties. Cold roadside fog can develop, and the nights can get very cool. This isn't meant to discourage anyone, but be prepared with cold and wet weather clothing in case it's needed. Chances are it won't be, but I've been caught in some sudden cold spells where it went from eighty degrees to fifty in short notice along the lake and a good wind suit was mandatory for comfort and safety. Be prepared for pleasantly cool nights if you camp.

Secondly, make sure your machine is in good working order and that you keep the gas tank topped off. While we're not talking about the roadless artic here, it is still someplace where you don't want to run out of gas or have a mechanical problem due to lack of maintenance. Motorcycle dealers and repair shops are few and far between.

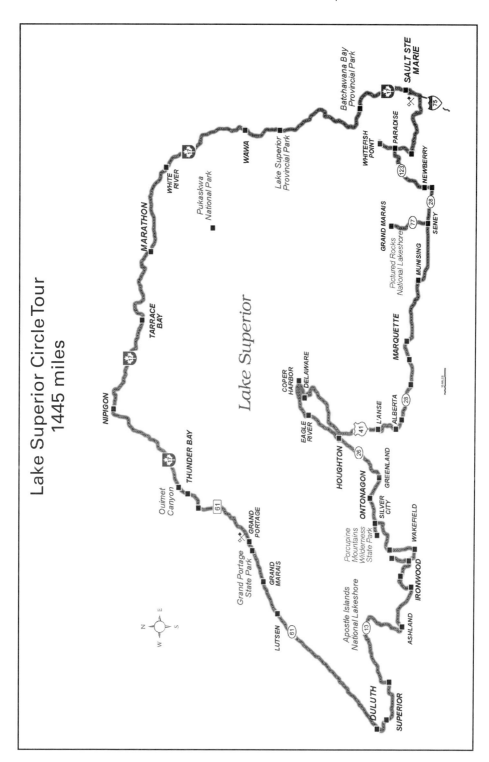

Lake Superior Circle Tour
1445 miles

Lake Superior

SAULT STE MARIE

Batchawana Bay Provincial Park

PARADISE

WHITEFISH POINT

NEWBERRY

123

28

SENEY

77

GRAND MARAIS

Pictured Rocks National Lakeshore

MUNSING

MARQUETTE

28

ALBERTA

L'ANSE

41

COPER HARBOR

DELAWARE

EAGLE RIVER

26

HOUGHTON

ONTONAGON

GREENLAND

SILVER CITY

WAKEFIELD

Porcupine Mountains Wilderness State Park

IRONWOOD

ASHLAND

13

Apostle Islands National Lakeshore

Lake Superior Provincial Park

WAWA

WHITE RIVER

17

Pukaskwa National Park

MARATHON

TARRACE BAY

17

NIPIGON

THUNDER BAY

17

Ouimet Canyon

61

GRAND PORTAGE

Grand Portage State Park

GRAND MARAIS

LUTSEN

61

DULUTH

SUPERIOR

75

17

N
W E
S

LAKE SUPERIOR CIRCLE TOUR 1445 MILES		
Miles	**Destination**	**Total**
0	Sault Ste. Marie	0
85	Lake Superior Provincial Park	85
60	Wawa/Ontario Route 101	145
56	White River	201
55	Marathon	256
60	Schreiber	316
59	Nipigon	375
25	Dorion	400
45	Thunder Bay	445
42	Grand Portage, MN	487
43	Grand Marais	530
66	Split Rock Lighthouse State Park	596
43	Duluth	639
11	Superior, WI	650
80	Bayfield	730
22	US2/Ashland	752
55	Black River Scenic Drive, MI	807
13	Lake Superior	820
15	Bessemer	835
22	Porcupine Mountains Park South Boundary Road	857
31	Lake of the Clouds	888
23	Ontonagon	911
13	Greenland	924
38	Hancock	962
45	Lac Le Belle	1007
6	Delaware Mine	1013
12	Fort Wilkins State Park	1025

LAKE SUPERIOR CIRCLE TOUR 1445 MILES		
Miles	**Destination**	**Total**
10	Eagle Harbor	1035
9	Copper Harbor	1044
22	Eagle River	1066
15	Calumet	1081
14	Houghton	1095
42	Alberta	1137
22	Michigamme	1159
36	Marquette	1195
41	Munising	1236
36	Seney	1272
25	Pictured Rocks Lakeshore/Grand Marais	1297
25	Seney	1322
26	Newberry	1348
37	Paradise	1385
25	Point Iroquois	1410
35	Sault St. Marie	1445

Finally, watch out for wildlife. It's a thrill to see them in the woods or swamps near the road, but you certainly wouldn't want to hit a thousand pound moose that chose that moment to cross the road in search of greener pastures.

As with any circular trip there is no one start and end point—just what happens to be most convenient. For me, that was always the Soo, so we'll arbitrarily begin at Sault Ste. Marie, Michigan and head north by crossing the International Bridge into Sault Ste. Marie, Ontario. Because you will be in Canada for about 350 miles a stop at the Visitor Centre just beyond the bridge to pick up some brochures and maps and exchange some currency is highly recommended. Though most things cost more in Canada the exchange rate for the U.S. dollar has been running anywhere from 20–30 percent more than the Canadian dollar so it pretty much evens out in the end. Besides, given the wonderful trip ahead of you and the friendly Canadians you're about to meet, it isn't unreasonable to pay a little for the experience. Save your receipts because upon leaving the country you can get a refund of Goods and Services Taxes that you pay on all goods and services, as the name implies.

It is extremely easy making the Ontario portion of the loop—just get on and stay on the Trans-Canada Highway / Route 17, from the Canadian Soo all the way to Thunder Bay. In Sault Ste. Marie, Ontario you will be on 17B when you get off the bridge. This road changes names as it goes through town, but it's always 17B. (Bay Street, Queen Street, Church Street, Pim Street, and finally, Great Northern Highway) Once you reach the northern city limits and Route 17/ Great Northern Highway, you don't have to think about directions for the next three hundred miles.

As you head north along the east shore of the lake the surroundings and the road gradually improve for the better. After about a half-hour you'll start enjoying what the trip is all about—great scenery and great riding. Between the Soo and the town of Wawa there are so many things to see that one just has to be willing to stop occasionally and smell the flowers—or watch the moose. You'll see signs for attractions such as waterfalls, scenic overlooks, lighthouses, historical markers and so on. To really savor the flavor of this area take the time to make side trips to the many things to see along the way. The stretch from Batchawana Bay Provincial Park north to the town of Wawa is just one scenic delight after another. In fact, this is true for the entire trip! Lake Superior can be said to be lacking in only two things—warm water and sandy beaches.

South of Wawa in Lake Superior Provincial Park an enjoyable trip through the park should include walking to the Agawa Rock Indian Pictographs. These ancient drawings on the shore of the lake are reached by a trail that is fascinating in its own right. You walk in a deep cleft between two rock walls, which are actually massive boulders and uplifted rock that has split forming a narrow 'tunnel' to walk through. The Magpie Falls are also a short but very nice side trip.

Wawa (Ojibwa for Land of the Wild Goose) is a good place to stop and refuel both yourself and your bike. You will know you're there when you see the famous Wawa Goose. If you haven't seen it yet, you will know it when you do.

Route 17 curves inland for a stretch north of Wawa around Pukaskwa National Park, a huge wilderness park on the lake. The next town you'll come to is White River. If you're into canoeing, fishing, wilderness hiking or hunting then this is your place. It is far from Lake Superior, but surrounded by hundreds of lakes and streams, and miles of forest. White River has gained some fame in a most unusual manner. In 1914 a veterinarian in the Canadian Army on his way to Europe and World War I bought a bear cub he named Winnie at White River as a mascot for his unit. The bear was left in the care of the London Zoo in England where a certain A.A. Milne and his son Christopher Robin noticed it and fell in love with it because of its playful ways and personality. That bear of course became the basis for the famous lovable bear known by children everywhere as Winnie-The-Pooh.

Upon leaving White River Route 17 begins its westward march. Lake Superior curves north to meet the road near the village of Marathon. Shortly west of there is Terrace Bay and just west of Terrace Bay is Aquasabon Falls and Gorge. They're just off the highway and are a must see. Not far west of Terrace Bay and the falls is the town of Schreiber located on the Lake. Schreiber hosts a Ride for Sight motorcycle fund raising event in late June. These have turned into major events in Canada and are very popular. Check out rideforsight.org for more information and dates the rides are to be held in various Canadian communities.

The town of Nipigon is nestled at the northwest corner of Lake Superior, just before the shoreline starts angling southwest. Of interest to bikers is a new motorcycle rally started by American visitors that were so impressed with the Nipigon area that they organized an annual event based there called the Say Eh! Rally. The event was to take place annually on Labor Day weekend—time will tell if it becomes a northern version of Sturgis.

Southwest of Nipigon the next must see stop is Ouimet Canyon. This marvel of nature was formed by rock faulting and is a spectacular sight. It is accessed just off Highway 17 near the town of Dorion.

Continue following Route 17 to the City of Thunder Bay (previously Port Arthur and Fort William prior to their 1970 amalgamation). There is very much to do in and near this town. Make time for a visit to historic Old Fort William—billed as the world's largest recreated fur trading post—for a look at late 18th and early 19th century Upper Canada.

Route 17 joins Canada Route 11 near Thunder Bay and these two roads are combined through the city. In the southwest portion of Thunder Bay Routes 17 & 11 intersect with Route 61, and Routes 17 & 11. Continue straight west through western Ontario and all points west. From Thunder Bay southwest along the coastline you'll ride Route 61 for the remainder of the Ontario portion. Thunder Bay has many attractions and great natural beauty. It is surrounded by high hills on one side and the Lake on the other. Definitely plan to spend time exploring this appealing city.

By good planning or just serendipity the road remains numbered as Route 61 after you enter Minnesota so you'll stay on Route 61 from Thunder Bay to Duluth. The "arrowhead" country of Minnesota is as spectacular as the Ontario portion of the trip. Lake side cliffs, waterfalls, forests, hills, light traffic and a wonderful riding road make this a stretch you'll want to come back to time and again.

Shortly after entering Minnesota you'll find yourself in Grand Portage State Park with its High Falls—the state's highest waterfalls. Not far down the road in Magney State Park are the Devil's Kettle Waterfalls on the Brule River. Next comes

The Quincy Mine Shaft, located in Hancock, in the Upper Peninsula. (Photo courtesy of Travel Michigan)

the city of Grand Marais and a bit further the small town of Lutsen, located in the Sawtooth Mountains (okay, we're talking about Midwestern mountains here, not the Rockies). Lutsen Mountain Ski Area offers the longest and tallest ski runs in the Midwest and the gondola on Moose Mountain or the chairlift on nearby Eagle Mountain offer rides to the top in the summer for spectacular views of the surrounding area.

As I noted earlier, the attractions on this route are just too numerous to write about them all. Just be willing to take the time to explore sites as you pass them on the road, and I guarantee you won't be disappointed. The only way you'll be disappointed is if you just keep riding (which is tempting because the riding is so great!) and don't stop to enjoy the natural beauty and sights.

Duluth, MN is the next large town on the tour. This port city, located in the heart of the continent, looks like it was custom made to fit in this part of the country. There is nothing pretentious or phony in the town or the people. One of the quickest ways to learn about this area and its history and culture is a stop at The Depot. Technically it's the St. Louis County Heritage and Arts Center Historic Union Depot. You can understand why it's known locally simply as The Depot. The Depot houses everything from old railroad cars and locomotives to historical and cultural artifacts and displays that span two centuries. The Depot once served seven different rail lines and 5,000 people per day walked through its doors. It has been beautifully restored and is a highly recommended stop on your journey through the Superior region.

Finally, before leaving Duluth take a trip down Skyline Parkway, which forms a 38-mile long semicircle around Duluth on the high lands on the edge of town. You'll drive on a cliff hundreds of feet above the city and the lake, with stupendous views being your reward.

In the city of Duluth Route 61 will merge into I35 for a short distance until its juncture with US2 where the tour turns east toward Superior, Wisconsin. On your way to Superior you will be on US2/I53 for much of the way. In order for you to stay near the lakeshore and take a much more scenic route, at the southeast portion of Superior you want to head east on Wisconsin Route 13. Route 13 takes you out to the tip of the Bayfield Peninsula and to the Apostle Islands National Lakeshore, a beautiful archipelago of twenty-two islands, rock formations and a great collection of historic lighthouses. Boat tours through the islands are very popular, as are hiking trails on the islands themselves.

After leaving the Apostle Islands area Route 13 curves back south and rejoins US2 just west of Ashland, WI. Get back on US2 and take it through Ashland. Almost exactly twenty-five miles east of Ashland turn left onto Wisconsin Route 122. This great stretch of road goes north to the lake then east along the lake several miles, turning into CR505 when you enter Michigan. Continue taking CR505 as the pavement meanders east and southerly. CR505 ultimately heads straight south towards the town of Ironwood, MI. Just north of town it intersects with CR204, an east and west road. 204 runs past the Gogebic County airport and 2.8 miles later it ends at Black River Drive/CR513, a National Scenic Byway.

Turn left and take this road up to the Black River Harbor on Lake Superior, even though it requires that you double back on the same road to get back on US2 (believe me, you won't mind having to ride this road twice!). The Black River

Drive is a beautiful fifteen-mile stretch of winding road along the Black River, replete with waterfalls, hills, curves, forests and wildlife. Eagle sightings are common in this area and five waterfalls are easily accessible from the road. You will also pass the Copper Peak Ski Flying Hill—the world's tallest ski jump. The view from atop the 18-story observation deck is unlike any other in the Midwest. Even when just viewed from a distance this structure will give you a whole new perspective on ski jumping, and respect for the men and women who fly off the lift with nothing but a lot of cold air beneath them!

After completing the Black River Drive diversion take it south to US2 and head east again a few miles to Wakefield where US2 intersects with M28. Turn north on M28 for about a mile and you'll intersect with CR519—the road you want. Take 519 north to the South Boundary Road of the Porcupine Mountains Wilderness State Park. Follow this great stretch of road as it meanders through the south portion of this large wilderness park, ultimately turning north and ending at M107. Turn west on M107 and climb it to the overlook at the Lake of the Clouds—a must-see on this trip. There are many hiking trails in the park—some short and some long wilderness trails. Bears are very common in this area so if you camp or hike follow the advice of the park rangers and take appropriate precautions regarding food storage.

Once finished in the park head east on M107 to Silver City where the road joins M64, which will take you to the town of Ontonagon. (In Ontonagon you will see the northern terminus of US45. President Lincoln commissioned this road, called the Military Road, during the Civil War in order to ensure a safe supply of copper ore for the Union.) Take M38 (The Ontonagon-Greenland Road) out of Ontonagon all the way past the small town of Greenland, where you will turn east onto M26 which you will take up to the Keweenaw Peninsula.

In Greenland, on M38 you'll see the Adventure Mine—an early copper mine that operated from 1850–1920. Daily-guided tours into the mine are offered. It's a very informative and interesting diversion.

Continue on M26 all the way to Houghton, cross the Portage Canal Bridge, and turn right again on M26 in the town of Hancock. The Keweenaw Peninsula is a place that deserves a day or two all to itself. There are several great routes on the peninsula so don't be in a hurry. This tour describes the various circle tours that the Keweenaw offers. You can either just take US41 up to Copper Harbor and head back south—missing much of what the Keweenaw has to offer—or you can take the several small tours that I spell out here in order to see the peninsula the way it should be seen and experienced.

If you're in a hurry and must do the peninsula in one round trip then take US41 to the end at Copper Harbor and head south on Brockway Mountain Drive out of town. Brockway Mountain Drive is a must-do. The Drive ends at M26 at its south end and 26 then joins U.S.-41 making the loop very easy to do.

However, I highly recommend that you don't just do the US41 / Brockway Mt. Drive loop. You'll miss out on so much!

Instead, when you enter the peninsula at Hancock, follow M26 as it goes easterly, then north, to the town of Lake Linden. In the small town of Lake Linden you will see Bootjack Road going east off M26. Take this road a short distance and you will see Traprock Valley Road going to the north. (The very names of these roads evoke adventure!) Take Traprock Valley Road a little less than two miles to Gay Road where you will turn right and follow it all the way to the water where it will swing to the north and hug the coast of Keweenaw Bay.

Follow this scenic road along the water's edge almost twenty miles to the small crossroads town of Lac La Belle. Turning left on Lac La Belle Road will take you to U.S.-41 near the town of Delaware, and the Delaware Copper mine site. This underground mine was in operation from 1847–1887 and guided or self-guided tours of the mine are available. The mine is a very interesting place to visit. In addition to the well lit mine tunnels they also have a display of antique machinery and engines. The mine is located on US41 and is open 7 days per week from June–October.

When you're done touring the mine, head north on 41 to Copper Harbor. Whether you're on a Gold Wing, Harley or GSX you will find yourself leaning forward and playing road racer on this renowned motorcycling road.

Copper Harbor is Michigan's northernmost city and is literally at the end of the road, but there are two loops you really need to take out of town—requiring doubling back—but what a reward there will be for this effort.

Head out of town on south M26 (though you will actually be heading west, not south) for about eight miles to the junction with Brockway Mountain Drive. Head back to Copper Harbor on BMD. You won't find a better road for many miles around. Once back in Copper Harbor I recommend a stop at the Harbor Haus restaurant for a great lunch with an outstanding view. As the sign atop the restaurant asserts you really will be breathing some of the purest air on earth. A boat tour of the islands in the bay and to the Copper Harbor lighthouse is a great way to really appreciate this unique area and see the 1800s lighthouse up close.

Fort Wilkins State Park is literally at the end of the road just outside of Copper Harbor and is a very interesting stop. The fort was built in 1844 and manned by army troops to keep the peace between settlers and Indians. You can imagine that the soldiers stationed there must have felt that they were truly at the end of the world, especially in the long cold winters. The need for the fort quickly faded and it was abandoned in 1870. As a state park the fort has been reconstructed and has very interesting displays of military and frontier life during the 1800s in the Lake Superior wilderness. As I've noted in other sections, depression-era programs to get people working (WPA, in particular) were largely responsible for the restoration of this fort. The park is a wonderful place to camp if the day is near its end.

When you're done enjoying all that the Copper Harbor area has to offer turn around and head right back on Brockway Mountain Drive, as it's a delightfully new and different perspective from the opposite direction. If camping isn't your thing a night spent at the Keweenaw Mountain Lodge (906-289-4403) on US41 will be an experience you'll never forget. The Lodge is a fascinating building, built during the worst of the Depression when the local mines had shut down and unemployment in the region was severe. The building of the Lodge was actually a federal WPA project, not a private enterprise. Today in addition to the Lodge there is a beautiful golf course for those skilled enough to play on the rough and hilly terrain.

Once back to M26 you can then follow 26 along the Lake Superior coast through the wonderful towns of Eagle Harbor and Eagle River, before finally rejoining US41 and reluctantly heading south out of the Keweenaw. There are many wonderful things to see in Copper Harbor, Eagle River and Eagle Harbor so don't be in too much of a hurry. The lighthouse and associated museums in Eagle Harbor is an especially good stop.

Sooner or later you will have to leave the Keweenaw, and when you must take US41 south through the villages of Baraga and L'Anse. About 3.3 miles southeast of L'Anse on US41 Old 41 veers off. Old 41 is a much more interesting and enjoyable riding road, so I recommend taking the Old 41 loop. It rejoins the new highway just north of the town of Alberta, and then Old 41 veers off again a mile later just south of town, this time for quite a bit longer stretch.

It is no accident that Old 41 goes through the Village of Alberta. This village has a very interesting history. It was a company town built out of the wilderness by Henry Ford and Ford Motor Company in 1935. Ford at one time had huge holdings in the UP—in the range of 500,000 acres. Ford wanted a dependable supply of the right kind of timber guaranteed for his automobiles, which in the 1920s and 1930s had a great amount of wood in them. Ford built several large sawmills in the UP, and in fact in the town of Kingsford at one time 8,000 people worked in his various plants and mills.

Ford wanted his workers to live near the land and to work on the land. As a former farm boy Henry Ford never lost his love of the land and his belief that working the land was one of man's highest callings. Alberta was built out of the forests with comfortable homes for the workers and a state-of-the-art sawmill.

In the 1950s when wood was no longer utilized in cars or trucks, Ford Motor Company donated the town and 2,000 acres of surrounding land to Michigan

Technological University for use as a forestry research and education center. There is a museum in Alberta that has great displays and tells the story of Alberta and Henry Ford.

After splitting off of the new highway just south of Alberta, Old 41 eventually rejoins the new highway in the burg of Tioga. This is moose country so if you're alert you may see one of these large animals in a nearby swamp with its head submerged eating aquatic vegetation.

Head east on US41 all the way through and just past Marquette. In Marquette you can tour the beautiful and historic county courthouse, made famous in the movie and book *Anatomy of a Murder*. The Marquette Maritime Museum is another stop you should make while in this enjoyable city. (300 Lakeshore Blvd. (906) 226-2006). But for the lack of tides and saltwater Marquette could easily be mistaken for a coastal town on Maine's rocky coast.

Where M28 and US 41 split east of Marquette you want to stay on M28 as it hugs the shoreline east all the way to Munising. There are so many things to see and do in this area it's difficult to list them all. Watch the road signs for waterfalls, scenic overlooks, lighthouses, and other attractions. In Munising, boat trips to the Pictured Rocks formations on Lake Superior make a very enjoyable diversion.

M28 east of Munising cuts inland as there are no paved roads in the vicinity of the lakeshore for much of this area. Just outside Munising you will see signs for H13 / Miner Road and the Miner's Castle rock formations on Lake Superior. This is all part of the Pictured Rocks National Lakeshore and is definitely worth a side trip to see.

Past the small town of Shingleton you enter the famous "Seney Stretch"—a stretch of M28 that is perfectly straight and flat for twenty-five miles. It isn't as boring as one might think, however, as the road goes through a wild area of forests, lakes and streams, including a long stretch along the large Seney Wildlife Refuge. In the town of Seney M77 will take you north again to the town of Grand Marais and Lake Superior. This is another worthwhile side trip. M77 takes you to the east end of the Pictured Rocks National Lakeshore, where a surprise in the form of huge sand dunes awaits you just west of Grand Marais. There is a short paved road going from the town of Grand Marais west to the dunes and the park's visitor's center.

Unless you want to ride on gravel and sand you will have to take M77 back to Seney and M28 where we once again head east to the junction of M123 where we head north into Newberry (designated by the state legislature as the Moose Capital of Michigan) and beyond. M123 is a delightful road to ride. The main attraction between Newberry and Paradise are the Tahquamenon Falls. The Tahquamenon River gained its name from Native Americans. It means 'dark waters', a name derived from the river's dark copper-colored waters, which is caused by high levels of tannic acid as a result of flowing through the coniferous forests of the area.

The Upper Falls of the Tahquamenon is an impressive sight that you don't want to miss as the 200-foot wide river plunges fifty feet over a cliff. The well-marked entrance to the state park where the falls are located is on M123. This is also Ernest Hemmingway country. The setting for Hemmingway's 'The Nick Adams Stories' is the country north of Newberry and Seney, where the Big Two-Hearted and Fox rivers flow today much as they did nearly one-hundred years ago when Hemingway's character Nick Adams camped along them and fished for trout.

When someone tells you that you can go to both Hell and Paradise in Michigan they're not pulling your leg. Hell is in southeast Michigan and Paradise is on the Superior coast near Whitefish Point where M123 hits Whitefish Bay. From Paradise we ultimately need to follow M123 south, but first another side trip, this time to north to Whitefish Point, is in order. Going north out of Paradise on Whitefish Point Road will take you to the Point, with its shipwreck museum (including the two-hundred pound brass bell from the *Edmund Fitzgerald*), the Audubon Bird Observatory, and lighthouse. It is well worth making the approximately twenty miles round trip to the Point and back. In the spring and fall this is a favorite spot for birders as the Point is a funnel for a wide variety of birds migrating across Lake Superior.

Leaving Paradise on M123 will take you south along the shore of Whitefish Bay. Almost ten miles south of Paradise you'll see a paved road going east—take it. This is a shoreline road that hugs the coastline, rather than going inland as the designated Circle Tour route recommends. This road, the Curley Lewis Highway which later becomes Lakeshore Road, (also designated as the Whitefish Bay Scenic Byway) takes you past Iroquois Point lighthouse, an old Indian Mission, and the Bay Mills Indian Reservation with its very large gambling casino. Iroquois Point was the site of a major battle between Native American tribes in 1662. The invading Iroquois were defeated in a surprise attack by outnumbered local Chippewa Indians. The two surviving Iroquois warriors were sent back east to warn other Iroquois bands to stay out of the upper lakes area. This battle was instrumental in opening up the upper Great Lakes region for further exploration by eliminating the Iroquois threat which up to that time had significantly hindered movement by Europeans and Natives alike.

Lakeshore Drive will ultimately turn into 6 Mile Road just southwest of the Soo, and the last few uneventful miles will take you to Old Mackinaw Trail where a left turn takes you back into Sault Ste. Marie, Michigan, marking the end of an incredible trip around a truly superior lake. Depending on how many of the side trips one takes, the total tour will be in the range of 1,500 miles in length. Scheduling a five or six-day trip around Lake Superior makes for a very enjoyable tour with time to do some additional things such as boat rides, waterfall excursions, exploring historic lighthouses and museums, short hikes, and much more.

This is definitely a trip you'll be telling your friends and family about for many years.

Lake Erie Circle Tour

THIS BOOK IS PRIMARILY about motorcycling opportunities in Michigan, so even though the majority of the Lake Erie tour is in other states and Ontario we'll start at Michigan's main Lake Erie port city of Monroe. The City of Monroe has a long history—having its start in 1780. It also has a strong French flavor and until 1817 was called Frenchtown. It may be most famous for being the boyhood home of George Custer, renowned General of the Civil War and of course remembered mostly for the demise of him and his Seventh Cavalry by the Sioux at the battle of the Little Bighorn. There is a General Custer exhibit in the Monroe County Historical Museum which follows the famous General's life from birth in Ohio through his shortened military career. The museum is easily accessible on Dixie Highway / Monroe Street just south of the river.

Monroe's long and interesting history is due to its location on the water highway used by the very earliest explorers. For a hundred years, there were skirmishes involving the French, British, and native tribes before the original Frenchtown was established at this site. Frenchtown was the site of one of the largest battles in the War of 1812. In what was called the River Raisin Battle only thirty-three out of nine hundred thirty four soldiers escaped death or capture in January 1813. This is the largest battle ever fought on Michigan soil. The day after the battle a massacre of wounded and captured soldiers took place which enraged the Americans and energized them to fight all the harder. "Remember The River Raisin" became a rallying cry for American soldiers during the remainder of the War.

Visit the River Raisin Battlefield museum at 1403 Elm Street in Monroe.

If you were looking for someplace that really appreciates a good plateful of cooked Muskrat (more elegantly known as marsh beef), but didn't want to drive all the way to Louisiana, you've found the place. Eating Muskrat has been a tradition for over two hundred years in Monroe. Muskrat as cuisine got its start during the War of 1812 when Frenchtown inhabitants were starving. Had it not been for the ubiquitous Muskrat providing a source of food, many people would have died of starvation. While it's become difficult to find it in restaurants because of state health regulations, it is still a staple of local barbecues, feasts, and civic celebrations.

Saying *au revoir* to Frenchtown we'll head north on the historic Dixie Highway and start our tour. Dixie Highway was the earliest road designed to connect

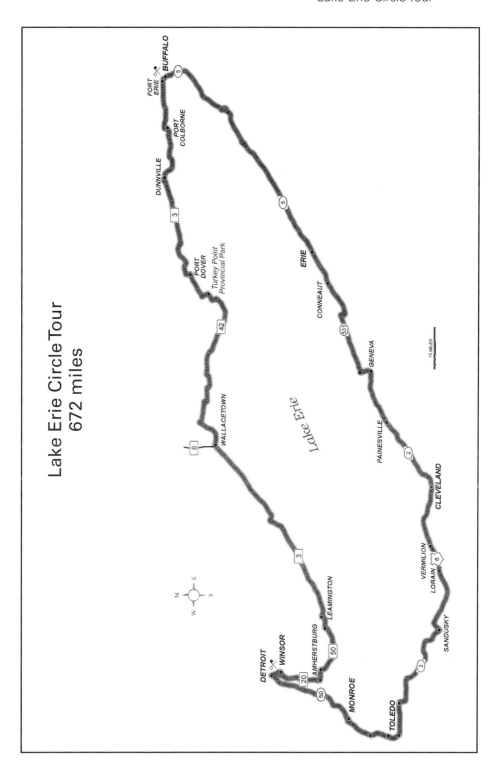

Lake Erie Circle Tour
672 miles

LAKE ERIE CIRCLE TOUR 672 MILES		
Miles	**Destination**	**Total**
0	Monroe	0
35	Ambassador Bridge	35
18	Amherstburg	53
35	Leamington	88
5	Point Pelee Provincial Park	93
38	Blenheim	131
36	Wallacetown	167
42	Port Burwell	209
21	Port Rowan	230
23	Port Dover	253
33	Dunnville	286
23	Port Colborne	319
15	Fort Erie	334
4	Peace Bridge / Buffalo	338
14	Old Lakeshore Road	352
60	Pennsylvania	412
19	Erie. PA	431
44	Ashtabula, OH	475
10	Geneva State Park	485
48	Cleveland	533
41	Vermillion	574
21	Sandusky	595
35	Ottawa National Wildlife Refuge	630
18	I280/Toledo	648
24	Monroe	672

Michigan and Florida, and various points in between. There were actually several variations of the Dixie Highway, even here in Michigan, but they were all part of the original network of main north-south roads that were the first to connect the eastern portion of the country in this manner. Within the City of Monroe Dixie Highway is called Monroe Street. It shares the roadway with M50 for a short distance going north out of town where it crosses I75 and it soon splits off M50 and heads northeast near the shoreline. Because Dixie Highway is now replaced by I75 it carries less traffic than it did in the past. Crossing over the Huron River and into Wayne County, Dixie Highway becomes River Road, and then Jefferson Avenue. It follows very closely to the Detroit River shoreline all the way to the Ambassador Bridge where we will cross into Canada.

There are a number of small parks along the entire stretch that allow access to the river itself, with its impressive vistas of strong currents, islands, and ocean-going ships heading up and down the waterway. This river now also supports a world-class Walleye fishery thanks to efforts of many in both the public and private sectors that cleaned up the river from its industrial sewer status of fifty years ago to the vibrant and attractive waterway it is today. Only thirty-five years ago Lake Erie was declared dead. It was little more than a huge cesspool largely unfit for swimming or recreational use. Thanks to a great deal of work, implementation and enforcement of environmental protection laws, and a major financial investment by all involved the lake itself is greatly improved. The economic boost that a healthy Detroit River and Lake Erie has brought to this area can't be measured.

The last few miles of the ride up Jefferson Avenue are an eye-opener. This stretch of road is definitely not the usual byway sought out by motorcyclists, but it isn't very long and it's worth seeing. You'll pass by huge industrial complexes in places like Ecorse, River Rouge and Zug Island that served as the manufacturing backbone of our economy for many decades. Huge factories and steel mills—both active and abandoned—line the road and waterway in this stretch. It's the kind of place not a lot of people see, but is critical to our economic well-being. The hard part is ensuring that we have the industrial infrastructure necessary for our modern economy while at the same time making sure that our quality of life and environment isn't harmed. It's a delicate and expensive balancing act to be sure. There are few places where the economic and environmental tug of war has taken place to the degree it has on the lower Detroit River.

Just up the road from Ecorse and River Rouge you'll see the massive Fort Wayne complex on the east side of the street. Fort Wayne has unfortunately fallen into disrepair, but it has a long and interesting history. The fort was built in 1854 on what is the narrowest stretch of river in that area because of serious border tensions with British Canada. Fort Wayne was to have the latest in artillery to defend shipping lanes and be capable of reaching the opposite shore. The fort was named after General 'Mad Anthony' Wayne, who defeated a coalition of Indians (Shawnee, Miami, Delaware, Ottawa, and Ojibwa) in the 1796 battle at Fallen Timbers on the Maumee River in northern Ohio. The Indians regrouped at Fort Miami but the British commander there refused to provide any further military assistance. That decision effectively secured U.S. occupation of the Northwest Territory.

The fort was fortunately never used in combat but it did serve as an induction center for every war from the Civil War to Viet Nam. Untold thousands of men, myself among them, have vivid memories of the long lines and bad attitudes of the E-4 paperwork processors who considered themselves to be just one step below Commanding General. Several original buildings at the fort still survive.

At this point just follow the signs to the Ambassador Bridge and head south to Windsor, Ontario. Yes, that's right, south. Detroit is the only border crossing point in the nation where you travel south to get to Canada. The Detroit River turns in an east / west direction at this point, with Windsor situated on the south shore. The Ambassador Bridge is unique in several ways. First, it is the busiest international crossing point in North America, and second, it is privately owned. One might assume that an international bridge would be a government-owned piece of infrastructure, but that's not the case. The Bridge was built with private funds in 1929, and is jointly operated by The Detroit International Bridge Company and The Canadian Transit Company. Over one-quarter of all Canadian / U. S. trade occurs over the Ambassador Bridge.

Detroit and Windsor share a very close relationship. They are sister cities in many ways with common links involving families, economics, sports, and recreation activities.

The Windsor area like Detroit is also steeped in history. As one might expect it has a more-decidedly British flavor, and is graced with beautiful gardens and parks along the riverfront. It has also become famous for its casinos—an activity that Detroit also has begun to gamble on as a means to economic prosperity.

Crossing the Bridge will put you on Ontario Route 3, so just stay on 3 until its junction with Ontario Route 20, on which you'll start south along the east coast of the Detroit River. Route 20 will initially be Ojibway Parkway, and later turn into Front Street for much of its length south to Amherstburg. Going south along the east shore is a bit like downriver Detroit—it's where a good deal of Ontario's chemical industry is located thanks to the same underground salt deposits that spawned the chemical industry on the Michigan side.

Fort Malden National Historic Site in Amherstburg is a reconstructed fort built by the British shortly after the War of 1812. A restored 1819 brick barracks, earthworks from the 1840s, and various other buildings are preserved at the site.

As with other Canadian forts it tells the other side of the story. This fort, which was built twenty years after the original Fort Amherstburg just south of here at the mouth of the Detroit River, was built for the purpose of defending British North America from what they perceived as American ambitions on the land east of the river. The original Fort Amherstburg was a major British base during the War of 1812. It's fascinating to take oneself back two hundred years when the open and welcoming border between our two nations that we all so take for granted wasn't the case.

Shortly after passing through Amherstburg O20 swings eastward, and shortly after that you'll encounter CR50, which heads south to the lake. Take CR50 and follow it along the shoreline all the way to the town of Kingsville, where O20 rejoins it. Continue east until you reach Leamington, where O20 ends and you pick up Ontario Route 3, which will be your host for about eighty miles to the small town of Wallacetown.

Pillar commemorating the Monroe Massacre.

In Wallacetown you will turn south on county road 8 to route 16, which will take you to route 20, and finally 24. The route numbers change quite frequently, but if you just stay on the road that follows the coastline the most closely, you'll be all right. Route 24 will take you along the coast to Route 42. This stretch of road from Wallacetown east to Port Rowan takes you past four Ontario Provincial Parks that are located on the lakeshore. Head east on Front Street from Port Rowan, and follow this road along the shoreline for several miles as it takes you through Turkey Point Provincial Park and finally back to Route 24 then Route 6 to Port Dover.

Follow Route 6 east out of Port Dover to RR-3 (Dover-Dunville Road) and follow this road all the way through the town of Dunville. RR-3 will continue along the shoreline (known as Lakeshore Road in that stretch) and finally take you back to Ontario Route 3 near Port Colborne. Follow Ontario 3 to Fort Erie where you will cross the Niagara River to Buffalo, NY.

Fort Erie, Ontario is a nice place to take a break and discover a little about Ontario history and learning more about our own history at the same time. The Old Fort Erie—another major War of 1812 site—is an interesting place to visit, especially for Americans. It provides a glimpse into the Canadian and British side of the story of that war. Two American warships were captured at Fort Erie (The Ohio and Somers). Lake Erie of course played a very significant part in that war with Commander Oliver Perry engaging the British in fierce naval battles on the lake in an attempt to free Detroit and Lake Erie from British control.

The nearby Ridgeway Battlefield Museum also describes a fascinating period of history from the Canadian perspective that most Americans aren't aware of. In 1866 a group of Irish-American Civil War veterans (The Fenian Brotherhood) invaded British North America (now Canada) in an attempt to obtain freedom for Ireland. Obviously it was a doomed attempt, but it is an example of the continuing animosity between the British and Americans during that time period, and of course it shows that the British / Irish issue has been stewing for a very long time. There were several other excursions into what was to become Canada during that period, all of which had the effect of speeding up the process of confederation of Canada as a nation to preserve its territorial integrity. The USS Michigan even played a role in the ill-fated Fenian Brotherhood excursion by forming a blockade at Buffalo preventing reinforcements from reaching the invaders.

After crossing over the Peace Bridge into Buffalo, follow I190 / Route 5 south out of town. When the expressway ends, Route 5 continues along the shoreline all the way to Ohio. In several stretches along the New York shore of Lake Erie you'll see Old Lakeshore Road veer off from Route 5 and more closely follow the shore. Taking Old Lakeshore Road will put you nearer the shoreline in these areas, although Route 5 is usually also very close to the water.

Route 5 is easy to follow through Erie, Pennsylvania—a city you will want to go through in order to visit some very interesting historic sites along the shoreline. There are a number of museums, lighthouses, parks, and monuments—including the Commodore Perry monument of interest.

Continue west on Route 5 until just before the Ohio border where Route 5 joins US20. Stay on 20 for just a few miles until Conneaut, Ohio where you'll get on Route 7, which goes north to Ohio Route 531. O531 in turn will take you along the coast until Geneva State Park where it meets Ohio Route 534 and swings back south to US20. Go west on US20 to Painesville then north on Ohio Route 44 a short distance to Ohio Route 283 (Lake Shore Blvd.). Take 283 west to where it joins I-90 / Ohio Route 2 in Cleveland at exit number 177.

Stay on I-90 / O2 a short distance and when I-90 veers south stay on O2 to Lakewood where it too turns south near the Rocky River Bridge. When O2 heads south you'll continue straight ahead on US-6 (West Lake Road) hugging the shoreline. These shoreline roads in the greater Cleveland area have less traffic than you might imagine, and are enjoyable to ride. (This route is also a National Scenic Byway) This shoreline route also takes you near many attractions on the Lake and in Cleveland, such as the 1819 Dunham Tavern, the USS Cod Submarine, the Rock and Roll Museum, Jacob's Field, and much more. A day trip south to the Cuyahoga Valley National Park makes for a very nice diversion. West of Cleveland Route 6 hugs the shoreline all the way to Sandusky, home of world famous Cedar Point Amusement Park. Past Sandusky you will pick up Ohio Route 2 again. In this vicinity there are many side trips available to various attractions (lighthouses, monuments, parks, beaches and much more). Ferries to the several islands in Put-In-Bay deliver explorers to a variety of one-of-a-kind attractions ranging from fascinating glacial grooves on Kelley's Island to the Perry Victory and International Peace Memorial on South Bass Island.

Ohio 2 west of Sandusky is a scenic coastal road that will take you all the way to Toledo and then onto I280 for a short distance, then to I75 which will deliver you back to Monroe. There isn't a good coastal road along the water from Toledo to Monroe. Ironically the closest lakeshore road that goes all the way through this stretch is I75. The Dixie Highway (Michigan Route 125) parallels I75 about two miles inland. It can be reached by exiting the expressway at exit 5 or 6, and going west two miles to the Dixie, taking it north into Monroe. Thus completes this very interesting, and yes, even scenic, tour around a great lake.

Lake Michigan Circle Tour

OF ALL THE GREAT LAKES, Lake Michigan is unique because it is the only one situated completely within the U.S. It is, of course, the largest lake in the country and home to over 11 million people. It's also unique due to the vast difference between the sparsely populated northern lake and the heavily industrialized and populated southern portion. The greater Chicago urban area makes a trip around Lake Michigan a difficult proposition. One must either skirt around Chicago and never see the lake or go through many miles of heavy urban congestion in order to stay near the water.

But there is another option—take a ferry across the lower lake. This option adds a special flavor to the trip, as well as allowing one to avoid that portion of the lake from Milwaukee, Wisconsin south through Chicago, and Gary and Michigan City, Indiana. There are now two ferry options. The first, and oldest, is to take the *SS Badger* from Ludington, MI, to Manitowoc, WI. This ferry is larger and a bit slower than the newer option, which is a smaller twin-hulled vessel that crosses the lake further to the south, and it has more of a cruise ship feel. Call 888.337.7948 or surf over to ssbadger.com for schedules and reservations. The second ferry is the *Lake Express,* which sails between Muskegon and Milwaukee. This service started operations in 2004 and takes a different approach to crossing the lake. It is a high speed but smaller vessel, just under two hundred feet in length. Call 866-914-1010 or go to lake-express.com for reservations or sailing times. Port information for the two ferries is as follows:

SS Badger

Ludington   Take US10 west to downtown Ludington, on east side of downtown James Street will take you south to the port.

Manitowoc   Take W42 south to 10nd Street, a one-way street going south. Follow 10th Street south to Madison Street, then east a short distance to the docks.

Lake Express:

Muskegon   Located on the south shore of Muskegon Lake, at 1920 Lakeshore Drive, at the Great Lakes Marina.

Milwaukee   Located at the Port of Milwaukee, on Lincoln Memorial Drive. Get off at exit 3 of the I794 expressway, or follow Lincoln Memorial Drive south along the shoreline.

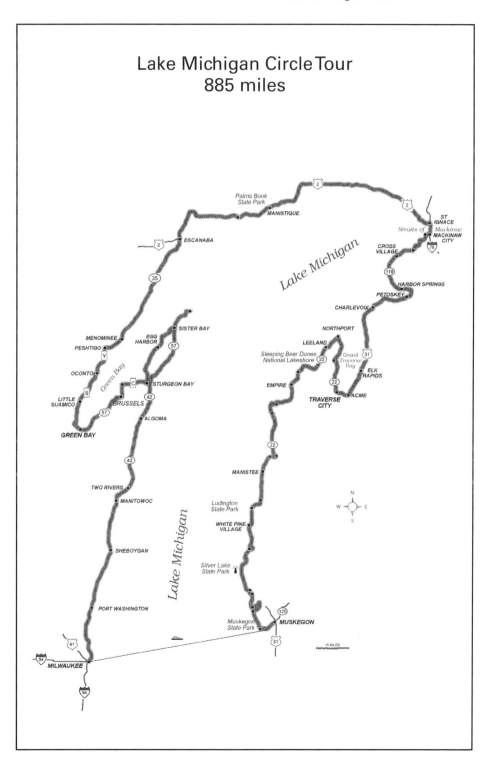

Lake Michigan Circle Tour
885 miles

LAKE MICHIGAN CIRCLE TOUR 885 MILES		
Miles	**Destination**	**Total**
0	Muskegon	0
24	Montague/White Lake	24
28	Silver Lake/Silver Lake State Park	52
26	Ludington/White Pine Village	78
30	Orchard Beach State Park	108
32	Frankfort	140
24	Empire/Sleeping Bear Dunes Lakeshore	164
27	Leland	191
24	Suttons Bay	215
34	Elk Rapids	249
34	Charlevoix	283
16	Petoskey	299
33	Cross Village	332
22	Mackinac Bridge	354
88	Manistique	442
54	Escanaba	496
55	Menominee	551
8	Pestigo, WI	559
48	Green Bay	607
47	Sturgeon Bay	654
45	Northport/Peninsula Point	699
61	Algoma	760
36	Two Rivers	796
7	Manitowoc/Port	803
82	Milwaukee/Port	885

This tour and the accompanying map data will assume a Muskegon-Milwaukee crossing—not because of any recommendation of one ferry over the other, but simply because this will provide the greatest amount of road information. If one takes the Ludington ferry then that road data south of Ludington and south of Manitowoc is irrelevant.

As with the other Great Lakes circle tours, I also avoid the official route as much as possible to get off major highways and expressways, and onto lakeshore roads.

The city of Muskegon is a fairly large old industrial town which in recent years has taken great pains to change its image as old chemical and manufacturing plants have closed, or been replaced with new and cleaner and more attractive operations. If you have interest in World War II fighting ships then a stop at the Great Lakes Naval Memorial & Museum is a must. It is the home to *USS Silversides*, a WWII Pacific Theater submarine. A tour onboard the submarine is a fascinating and humbling experience. The museum also is home to the *USCGC McClane*, a Coast Guard cutter built in 1927. There is a large selection of various naval paraphernalia as well. The museum is located at the west end of Muskegon Lake at the channel. The museum is accessible from the south shore of the lake only. Take Sherman Road to Lakeshore Road to get there.

To avoid riding through heavy traffic in Muskegon itself the best place to start this motorcycle trip is on the north side of Muskegon Lake. From the U.S.-31 expressway take state highway M120 west. The state highway quickly turns south, but you want to continue following the pavement straight ahead as it becomes Memorial Drive along the north shore of Muskegon Lake. Memorial Drive terminates within the boundaries of Muskegon State Park and at this point you turn north on Scenic Drive, which runs along the Lake Michigan coast for roughly the next eight miles. This is a very nice stretch of road.

The Lake Michigan coast is lined with what are technically called drowned river mouths. These are lakes that formed when a river has been 'impounded' by the sand dunes at the shoreline, creating a lake with a narrow opening or channel at the point it empties into Lake Michigan. Many of these drowned river mouth lakes don't have bridges across them at their channels resulting in the need to skirt around them by going inland. This was not only the case with Muskegon Lake, but with White Lake, located eight miles north, and several others up the line.

Scenic Drive becomes Shore Drive as it skirts White Lake on the south shore. Cross the White River on BR-31 then make a west turn again right after the bridge on Old Channel Trail which follows the north shore of White Lake and will deliver you back to the Lake Michigan shore. The shoreline road makes an east, and then a west, jog as it continues north into Oceana County, becoming 48nd Avenue. At this point you're about a mile inland, but one-and-a-half miles into Oceana

County a left turn puts you back on Scenic Drive and more coastline travel. No turns are involved, but Scenic Drive becomes 16th Avenue on its way north. At Buchanan Road our road takes a half-mile jog east then continues north until it Ts at Silver Lake Road—also called Lighthouse Road heading west to the Lake Michigan shore. I recommend taking this short ride out to Lake Michigan to see Little Sable Point Lighthouse. This light reaches over one-hundred feet high and makes a very pretty picture as it stands alone surrounded by sand dunes on one side and the blue water of Lake Michigan on the other.

Heading east on Silver Lake Road will take you to Silver Lake State Park and the famous Silver Lake sand dunes. This park has a wonderful beach of unlimited sand, and several dune buggy concessionaires will take you for very enjoyable rides on the dunes in their specially modified buggies. The Silver Lake area is a very popular summer vacation destination. You'll either love it or want to leave it as quickly as possible. It is a beehive of activity.

We have to skirt around Silver Lake to its east shore, then head north again, first on Shore Drive for a short distance then onto Ridge Road. Ridge Road closely follows the Lake Michigan shore heading north. The circumnavigation process has to be repeated again several miles up the road to get around Pentwater Lake. This time BR-31 will be the road we take back west once beyond Pentwater Lake. As BR-31 makes its way back east toward the expressway you'll see Lakeshore Road heading north on a narrow strip of land squeezed between Bass Lake on the east and Lake Michigan on the west. Take Lakeshore Road north about eight miles to Iris Road which we must take east to get around Pere Marquette Lake—yet one more drowned river mouth—this time for the Pere Marquette River.

Before turning east on Iris Road, I recommend you head north a short distance to White Pine Village—a reconstructed community of over twenty-five old buildings that recreate Ludington's past. It's a 'living' interpretive village museum that has thousands of fascinating displays and artifacts.

About halfway between Bass Lake and Pere Marquette Lake you'll pass the giant Consumers Energy Company pumped storage facility perched on the hillside to the east. This is an electrical power generating plant where water from Lake Michigan is pumped uphill to the lake-sized pond during low energy demand periods, and then released through tubes that feed waterpower to generators to create energy during high-energy demand periods.

Upon reaching Old US31 take it north two miles to the intersection with US10. I recommend taking US10 west at this point to Lake Michigan, and then turning north on M116. M116 is a dead end road that takes you out to Ludington State Park. The Park itself isn't the destination here as much as the ride out there along the lakeshore. It's a great place to stop and enjoy the shoreline and scenery.

(On the way out to the shore you'll pass by Piney Ridge Road—a two-mile long dead end road going north off of M116. It's a very fun four mile round trip on this curvy road.)

If you just want to continue north and don't want to take the M116 side trip, then just forget most of the previous paragraph. You do want to take US10 west, but only for less than a half mile to Jebavy Drive, where you resume northward. Four and a half miles north on Jebavy will take you Angling Road which veers off at a 45 degree angle before finally straightening out and heading straight east to Stiles Road, and a resumption of northward riding. After one small easterly jog at Townline Road Stiles Road turns into Maple Road in Manistee County and it will take you north all the way to the city of Manistee.

Take US31 across the river in Manistee and about one mile north of town you will see M110 going straight north along the shoreline. Follow 110 along this very pretty stretch and it will eventually swing easterly to get around Portage Lake. In so doing it will connect with M22, a wonderfully scenic road that will be our riding companion for many miles, taking us to the tip of the Leelanau Peninsula and to Traverse City where we finally leave it behind.

M22 between Portage Lake and Traverse City is a wonderful mix of hills, curves, farms and forests, and perhaps most of all, great scenery. There are many things to stop and see along the way. In Empire, for instance, you should definitely take the short ride to the Empire Bluffs—high dunes that overlook Lake Michigan and offer a stunning vista of forested hills and endless deep blue water.

Stop at the Sleeping Bear Dunes National Lakeshore headquarters at the intersection of M22 and M72 to learn more about this marvelous geologic wonder. While at the M22/M72 intersection, also head west on what will be Front Street for three blocks, then north a couple of blocks to the parking lot on Empire Beach. At the north end of this park you'll find the beautiful Manning Memorial Light. This is Michigan's newest lighthouse, built in 1991 in honor of a local citizen.

As you follow M22 north into the Leelanau Peninsula you'll pass through wonderful small towns like Leland and Northport where you should park your bike and explore the towns on foot. You'll pass lighthouses and wineries, grand overlooks and historic sites, and all the time riding with an appreciative smile and uttering the occasional WOW! to yourself or your partner. After Northport M22 takes you south along the east side of the Leelanau Peninsula, and along the west coast of Grand Traverse Bay.

A half-mile north of M72, just prior to entering Traverse City, you'll see a business called Traverse Tall Ship Company on the water's edge. They have a large sailing vessel, the tall ship *Manitou,* on which one can sail Grand Traverse Bay. According to their literature *Manitou* is one of the largest sailing vessels on the

Great Lakes. Sailing on this ship is a blast. You sit back and watch the crew work the sails and enjoy the scenery and the sound the wind. Call (231) 941-2000 for more information.

All good things must end, including M22. When it does you're left eastbound on M72 for a short distance and then US31, which runs east and west through Traverse City along the south shore of Grand Traverse Bay. Follow US31 through town and take it up the east side of Grand Traverse Bay. Just northeast of Traverse City near the town of Acme you will see the Music House. If you're into music, especially automated musical instruments, be sure to stop here. Plan on over an hour for the guided tour and demonstrations. The museum has one of the world's largest collections of rare and historical automated instruments.

Like M22, US31 will transport us through great countryside and lakeshore for many miles. The upcoming area—Elk Rapids, Charlevoix, Petoskey, and Harbor Springs—is a fairly upscale area, with old resorts and resort towns that have served many generations of families. It's a land of well-kept houses, flower-lined streets, and lots of history. You might call it Michigan's Gold Coast. It is also Ernest Hemmingway's youthful stomping grounds, vacationing with his family on Walloon Lake near Petoskey. There's a small Hemmingway museum display at the Little Traverse History Museum Center—located in an old railroad depot in Petoskey on the waterfront.

We'll stay on US31 all the way to the east side of Petoskey where a north / left turn onto M119 takes us to the next very nice part of this journey.

M119 isn't a great motorcycle road for the first few miles. First you have to get through the upscale town of Harbor Springs—another town where you may want to park and walk around. Once beyond Harbor Springs M119 gets progressively better, until it turns into the "Tunnel of Trees", as it is called. M119 is the only state highway where special rules apply. There is no shoulder and the trees are literally right on the edge of the pavement. There is also a severe shortage of any straight sections. Many of the curves are tight, so even though it is very tempting to go fast, try to show some semblance of restraint and keep your speeds reasonable for the road you're on. M119 runs along the crest of a high bluff overlooking Lake Michigan. Unfortunately the land all along it is private, with many drives heading down the bluff to palatial second homes. M119 is a blast to ride, to put it succinctly.

The state highway ends in the village of Cross Village, but the lakeshore route continues north several more miles. Continue following Lakeview Drive north along the coast until it finally gives up and curves inland heading east. Follow the easterly pavement and it becomes County Road 81 that after going east for several miles turns and goes straight north to the shoreline and Wilderness Park Drive.

A 100-year-old fishing village in the town of Leland. (Photo by Rick Lahmann)

Turn right on Wilderness Park Drive and follow it into Mackinaw City and the Mackinac Bridge.

Common questions are: Why is the word mackinac spelled two ways? What or who the heck is a mackinac anyway?

Well as is common in Michigan the word has its origins in Native American language. Mackinac is a French derivation of michilimackinac which itself is a shortened version of the Ojibwa word "missilimaahkinaank" which means "at the territory of the mishinimaki," which was an Indian tribe that lived in the straits area long ago. The correct spelling is Mackinac, but the British anglicized it to Mackinaw when they conquered the area.

Mackinaw City is a great place to park yet again and walk. You won't be the only biker there. It's a favorite gathering place for motorcyclists, and you'll see quite a selection of machines parked in the lot that runs the length of downtown. Relax, eat some fudge, and watch the other people who are watching you, with everyone trying to figure out which T-shirt or tourist knick-knacks to waste their money on. Fort Michilimackinac and the old Mackinac Point Light are favorite sites to explore. Old Mackinac Point Light in particular is a great spot to sit in the shade near this marvelous old structure and watch the activity on the Straits and be amazed at the size and beauty of the Bridge.

After downing your last bite of fudge it's time to head across the Mackinac Bridge. If you've never been across it before you're in for a real treat. I've ridden across it dozens of times and it is still a thrill each time. The view from the top of this five-mile long suspension bridge is just incredible. Water horizons stretch forever to the east and west, freighters are making their way through the center channel of the straits, and smaller boats leave their white wakes in the dark blue water nearly two hundred feet below you. Riding on the inside lane of the suspension portion of the bridge, where an iron grid rather than concrete forms the roadway, is an extra source of excitement as you can look down through the grid while riding across and see the water below you. If this isn't your idea of fun, the outside lanes in each direction are paved and very solid.

Once in St. Ignace head west on US2 and relax. This wonderful lakeshore route will carry us for almost one hundred fifty miles to the town of Escanaba. Along US2 you will find many opportunities to pull over to enjoy the lake views and take a walk. Signs for various attractions are all along the route so you can pick and choose just how much you want to do. Just west of Manistique you will find M149 and signs pointing north for a short detour to the Palms Book State Park and Michigan's largest spring, called Kitch-itIkipi (the big spring). The spring is 200 feet across and forty feet deep. Ten thousand gallons a minute pour from underground fissures. The water is sparkling clear and a glass-bottom boat allows a unique perspective on this natural wonder.

The town of Escanaba is located on the west shore of Little Bay De Noc (as opposed to Big Bay De Noc which is east of the Stonington Peninsula). Escanaba is a good-sized city with lots of services, including motorcycle repair shops and dealers. Escanaba hosts a large antique car show called Krusin' Klassics the first weekend of June each year. This large event includes cruises, car shows, tractor pulls, food, dancing, and in general a good time for young and old.

The origin of the name Bay De Noc is another of those questions that frequently arises. Well, again, you can thank the Indians and the French. The Nokay (spelled Noquet in French) were a small Algonquin tribe that lived in the area of Green Bay north to the vicinity of what is now Escanaba. The French called these bays the bays of the Noquet, or Bay De Noc for short.

With that piece of arcane knowledge under your belt, our journey now turns southward along the west shore of Lake Michigan—specifically Green Bay which extends from near Escanaba south to the city of Green Bay, Wisconsin.

We leave US2 in Escanaba as it continues its westward journey to the State of Washington, and we head south on M35 to Menominee. M35 is about as close to the water's edge all the way between Escanaba and Menominee as you can get without getting wet.

I know you're thinking about how a city gets the name Menonimee, so I'm going to tell you. You guessed it—Native American language. There is a tribe, still

Raft carrying individuals across Kitch-iti-kipi Spring. (Photo by Jerry Bielicki)

very active and healthy, in the Green Bay area called the Menominee. According to research, the Menominee called themselves Mamacoqtaw, meaning The People. Other tribes referred to them as Menomini—a derivation of the Algonquin word for wild rice—that was a staple of the diet for Indians in that region.[2] Prior to settlement, the mouth of the Menominee River was a large marsh where wild rice was abundant.

Lakeside travel gets a little dicier in Wisconsin because there isn't one road such as US2 or M35 that provides a water side route. A person either takes one of the major roads and stays away from the water, or whenever possible take the many county roads that do provide a pleasurable ride near the water, away from the crowds and major highways.

US41 joins M35 just north of Menominee and you cross the Menominee River on US41 into Marinette, Wisconsin. In Marinette stay on US41 as it heads out of town taking you to the town of Peshtigo.

While almost everyone has heard of the famous Chicago fire of October 8, 1871 few people have heard of the much more disastrous fires that struck Wisconsin and Michigan on the same day. Peshtigo was caught in the middle of the worst recorded forest fire in North American history. The fire burned a huge tract of Wisconsin and the Upper Peninsula of Michigan, killing between 1,200 and 2,400 people in its path. Due to the near wilderness nature of the area at that time, and the lack of communication systems and roads, the true number of victims was never determined, but entire communities were wiped out. While the Chicago fire became part of our country's history and lore, this much worse fire has largely faded from our collective memory.

The Peshtigo fire museum located at 400 Oconto Avenue, Peshtigo [(715) 582-3244] is a very interesting stop.

On the west side of Peshtigo County Road Y heads south from US41. Follow 'Y' as it heads south, then southwesterly along the lakeshore. Just prior to the Oconto River it curves inland a bit and in the village of Onconto the lakeshore road swings south again as County Road S. CRS continues south for a number of miles and at the village of Little Suamico the pavement's name changes to CR-J. Further south still, on the outskirts of the city of Green Bay CR-J becomes Lakeview Drive, which you stay on and after it crosses US141 you get on the I43 expressway to get across town and over the Fox River. Shortly after crossing the river we'll start our northward journey up the Door Peninsula by exiting I43 on Shore Road. As the name suggests Shore Road takes you along the shore of Green Bay, and ends at Nicolet Road, where a left turn will continue your northward trip. Along the way north Nicolet Road becomes CR-A, but the pavement alignment is unchanged. As I've said before, just follow the pavement.

CR-A will eventually end at Wisconsin Route 57. We'll follow 57 for many miles as it winds its way up the peninsula. At the small village of Brussels turn left onto County Road C and follow it straight north for a number of miles and then east as it goes across the peninsula to the town of Sturgeon Bay.

Take the Madison Street Bridge across the Sturgeon Bay Shipping Canal, and just beyond the bridge turn left onto CR-B. After many coastal miles CR-B becomes CR-G, and later still it becomes Horseshoe Bay Road in the vicinity of Egg Harbor. Just north of the village of Egg Harbor CR-B merges onto Wisconsin Route 42 which we will follow all the way to the very tip of the peninsula, and the end of the road, at Northport.

Leaving Northport we have to backtrack on 42 for a bit, to the town of Sister Bay and the junction with W57 on which we turn south. We'll stay southbound on W57 for many miles, all the way to just north of Sturgeon Bay, where it rejoins W42 for the trip through town.

Southbound we'll take the W42 bridge across the ship canal, and just on the south side of the canal we'll turn south onto CR-U and follow it south along the coast for several miles. Just north of the town of Algoma CR-U becomes CR-S that we take into town. In Algoma CR-S joins Wisconsin 42 for a few miles as the coastal road but just south of town 42 swings inland and we turn south on Lakeshore Road and take Lakeshore all the way south to the town of Kewaunee where W29 takes us over to W42 once again south through town. Just south of Kewaunee Lakeshore Road again splits off W42 and heads along the coast. Lakeshore and W42 join together once again further south but 42 again swings west and Lakeshore continues straight south on the coast.

Just north of the town of Two Rivers Lakeshore Road becomes Sandy Bay and then CR-O, continuing south on the shoreline. In the town of Two Rivers our coastal road will once again rejoin W42, which we'll stay on all the way into Manitowoc. In downtown Manitowoc we turn south from W42 onto 10nd Street, and follow it south for a number of miles as it becomes CR-Ls. (If you're taking the *SS Badger* back across the lake the port is on 10nd Street south of Wisconsin 42)

As you travel further southward the CR-Ls pavement becomes Lakeshore Road, and then 15th Street in the city of Sheboygan, and joins W28 also. Taking Wisconsin 28 southward out of Sheboygan you'll come to a point where it veers straight west and CR-OK keeps going south ahead of you—take this county road. CR-OK will eventually become the Sauk Trail, which we'll continue to follow south—this time on the inland side and parallel to the I43 expressway. Eventually Sauk Trail becomes CR-LI and goes south many miles to Port Washington, where it joins Wisconsin Route 32 for a short distance. Heading south out of Port Washington turn south on Wisconsin Street and follow it south as it turns into County Road C and then Lakeshore Road and once again it is called CR-C (just follow the pavement). County Road C does eventually turn westward and just after crossing over I43 you want to leave it behind once and for all by turning south on Port Washington Road, which runs parallel to the expressway on the west side. Take Port Washington Road south to where it joins W32, then taking Wisconsin Route 32 south along the shoreline. You'll finally see Lincoln Memorial Drive veer off of W32 and follow the lakeshore. Take LMD south as it winds through several large lakeshore parks, finally ending in Milwaukee at the I94 expressway.

I have this trip ending there because if you want to take the ferry back across Lake Michigan to Muskegon the Port of Milwaukee is located at the south end of Lincoln Memorial Drive just off of the expressway.

By the way, if you're not like me and don't mind expressways, you can pick up the I43 Xway just west of Manitowoc and take it south to Milwaukee for the last leg of this trip, rather than the shoreline routes described above.

This trip is approximately 885 miles in length. If a ferry ride across Lake Michigan is included in the trip this will take anywhere from at least three to five hours when loading and offloading are considered as well as actual time underway. I recommend at least three days for this trip. As usual, there is just too much to see and do along the way to hurry it.

If you can arrange the trip so as to be in Wisconsin the first week of June you can also plan to attend the American Motorcyclist Association-sponsored Superbike motorcycle races at Road America, located about an hour northwest of Milwaukee at Elkhart Lake, WI. A fabulous time is guaranteed, and there is great riding to be enjoyed in the Kettle Moraine area near Elkhart Lake. Advance tickets and additional information are available at roadamerica.com or by calling 800-365-RACE.

Some Good Local Rides

1. **Stevensville, Baroda, Hills, Snow, Tabor Mountain Roads and Red Bud Trail**. (Stevensville to Buchanan, Berrien County). This trip starts in Stevensville, about six miles south of St. Joseph, and meanders southeast through vineyard, hill, and orchard country. The last five miles follow the twists and turns of the St. Joseph River into the town Buchanan. The pavement changes name several times as it heads southeast. Other than a mile stretch near the quite unattractive village of Baroda, where some folks apparently feel that converting orchards and vineyards to subdivisions is progress, the trip has plenty of hills, curves, and great scenery. Start on Stevensville Road, which turns into Baroda, which in turn becomes Hills Road, turning left onto Snow Road. When Snow Road turns east, just keep going straight on Mt. Tabor Road which curves around and rejoins Snow Road. When you get to the stop sign at Red Bud Trail turn right and follow the hilly curves along the river into Buchanan. The well-known Red Bud Motorcycle Track-N-Trail Motocross track is located on this stretch of Red Bud Trail (269-695-6405 will get you the track office).

2. **Huron River Drive / Savage Road / Willow Road.** This stretch of road follows the Huron River from Ypsilanti to the river mouth at Lake Erie south of Gibraltar. There are essentially parallel roads winding along both sides of the river, so a round trip can be had by switching sides of the Huron River.

3. **Huron River Drive II.** From the north side of Ann Arbor, where M14/BL23 cross the Huron River, (on the west side of the river) take Huron River Drive northwest along the Huron River. The road crosses over to the east side of the river about three miles north of town and then goes through Dexter and the Hudson Mills Park. There are several more really good riding roads in northern Washtenaw and southern Livingston County once you reach the vicinity of the county line. Return to A^2 on the west side of the river on Dexter-Pinckney and Dexter-Ann Arbor Roads.

4. **Edward N. Hines Drive.** Follow the drive from the southeast corner of Northville, south and then easterly along the Middle Branch of the Rouge River.

Hines Drive begins at Seven Mile Road across from the Northville Downs race track. The road is as nice a twisty and winding road as can be found in southeast Michigan, and for the most part is within various public parks that line the river. In Dearborn Heights, about 1.5 miles east of Telegraph Road, turn left onto West Outer Drive, following it north through more parkland along the main branch of the Rouge River. When you hit the I-96 expressway, turn around and retrace your route back to Northville. It's a very enjoyable approximately 40-mile round trip with very few straight stretches and plenty of curves. The wooded parks and the river will make it seem that you're far from the urban congestion of Wayne County.

5. **North Territorial Road.** Pick it up Plymouth in northwest Wayne County, ride all the way across Washtenaw County, ending at Berryville in northwestern Jackson County. This is a very pleasant ride across its entire length, and a historical road to boot.

6. **Seymour Road/Waterloo-Munith Road/Coon Hill Road/Wooster Road.** Jackson County, Waterloo Recreation Area. Pick up Seymour Road just east of the State Prison at Jackson, off Parnall and O'Leary Roads. Follow Seymour as it winds northeast all the way to Waterloo-Munith Road, where you turn north/left. Follow W-M as it heads northwest then straight west to Randolph Road, then south to Coon Hill Road Take Coon Hill to Wooster, then back south to re-join Seymour. A fun loop for an hour's diversion in the Jackson area.

7. **Lansing to Saugatuck.** Many people from Lansing head west to the Lake Michigan coast for day trips or weekend stays. Most take a roundabout way via expressways but there is a much nicer and more direct route that motorcyclists especially would enjoy.

    Head west on Vermontville Highway—accessible by taking M99 three miles south of Lansing and turning west onto Vermontville Highway - all the way through the town of Vermontville and west into Barry County where the road changes to State Road. Continue west on State Road as it jogs one mile north and ultimately takes you to M43 and then south into the town of Hastings. Follow M43 as it jogs south into town and then swings west again. Three miles after turning west M43 turns to the south and Gun Lake Road/M179, the road you want, keeps going straight west. Stay on M179, a designated scenic highway, all the way to just over the US131 expressway overpass. During this stretch you will pass through the Barry State Game Area and the Yankee Springs State Recreation Area, with very nice scenery and hilly roads.

Immediately after you go over US 131 you will see a road heading south along the freeway. In fact, the entrance onto the expressway is off of this adjacent road. Take it south for a mile then turn west on the first road you encounter, which will be 128th Avenue. You will stay on this road for about fifteen miles, all the way to M40. It's a very nice ride, first taking you through farmland then the Allegan Game Area, a large heavily wooded stretch.

Turn south on M40 and take it about three miles to M89 and then head west. M89 will continue through the Allegan State Game Area to the town of Fennville. A nearly forgotten piece of Michigan and US history lies two miles south of M89 just west of M40. On the west shore of Lake Allegan, in what is now the Allegan Game Area, is an old Civilian Conservation Corps camp that was used to house German prisoners of war during WWII. The more trustworthy prisoners worked at local orchards, fruit farms and other businesses in the southwest part of the state that were desperate for manpower. A number of them stayed on after the war.

On the west side of Fennville 58th Street goes north. Take this for four miles, turning west on 132nd Avenue and follow it as it meanders west into Saugatuck. This trip from Lansing to Saugatuck, basically as the crow flies, is a very enjoyable 95-mile ride.

8. **Goodrich to Memphis.** Genesee, Lapeer, St. Clair, Macomb and Oakland Counties. This is a very pleasant two-hour ride that takes you through enjoyable rolling lake country of southern Lapeer and northern Oakland Counties. Starting in Goodrich, head east on Hegal Road, taking it five miles to Hadley Road. Jog south a half-mile and continue east on Brocker Road to M24. Follow M24 north two miles and turn east on Dryden Road. Follow Dryden Road over hills and through nice farm country eighteen miles until it intersects with Capac Road. Make a slight jog north on Capac Road and continue east on Belle River Road as it meanders southeast about ten miles to Memphis. You can either retrace your route back, or drop south on M19 to the small town Richmond and take Armada Center Road on its indirect path to 32 Mile Road just east of Romeo. Head west on 32 Mile (which becomes Romeo Road in Oakland County) about ten miles to Rochester Road. Rochester Road from this point north back to Dryden Road is a fun riding road with plenty of curves to keep it interesting.

9. **Barry County** has some of the best riding roads in southern Michigan. Its hills, lakes and forests are a recipe for winding roads and nice scenery. A very enjoyable local ride for folks in the Grand Rapids to Kalamazoo area begins

in Middleville in northwest Barry County. From Middleville go south on M37 for about three miles. When M37 turns to head east continue south on Yankee Springs Road / CR 611. Follow CR611 about fifteen miles south through the Barry State Game Area to where it finally swings east becoming Milo Road, and intersecting with M43. Jog south one mile on M43 to Hickory Road and take it east, through Hickory Corners. Go north out of Hickory Corners on CR 601 and follow it as it winds its way almost twenty miles northeast to the town of Hastings. North of Hickory Corners 601 is called Gilkey Lake Road. After a jog at Pifer Road 601 is called Cedar Creek Road. It's called CR 601 through the entire stretch, however, and it will ultimately take you to downtown Hastings and M43. Go north on M43 one mile in Hastings and you'll see State Road / CR 438 going west. Follow 438 northwest back to Middleville.

10. **Old M20** from Big Rapids to White Cloud, then south on M37 to the city of Newaygo and Croton Road—east on Croton Road past Croton Dam, then north on Croton Road to Hardy Dam, and then east to Old US131 and back north to Big Rapids. Curves aplenty, two large earthen dams and impoundments, and nice scenery. Mecosta and Newaygo Counties.

11. **Blanchard Road and County Road 548** from Shepherd to Stanwood. Isabella and Mecosta Counties. Pleasant farmland and a few hills and curves. A nice laid-back ride.

12. **County Road B15 from Montague to Pentwater.** Muskegon and Oceana Counties. Nice Lake Michigan shoreline route. Busy on summer weekends.

13. **Caberfae and Harrietta Loop.** From the intersection of M55 and M115 near Cadillac, go west on M55 about nine miles to No. 21 Road, taking this south for a mile, then west and southwest, following the pavement. Continue west on No. 48 Road until the pavement turns north again, following it north and northwest until it hits M55. Go east on M55 three miles, turning north on the pavement on No. 13 Road, past the Caberfae Ski Area and a series of great hills and curves, plus a scenic overlook, as you make your way north to Harrietta. As you enter town a paved road next to the railroad tracks heads east. Take this for almost five miles to No. 21 ½ Road where a north turn takes you to M115. Turn right on 115 and follow it back into Cadillac. This stretch of M115 is very scenic and has a lot of character. This roughly fifty-mile loop has it all.

14. **M55/M37/M115 Loop.** This loop to the west of Cadillac is on three state highways, but is a nice one. These three roads are all very good motorcycling roads in their own right as they curve through forests and over hills. It is about fifty miles in length and makes for a very fun short ride.

15. **The Mission Peninsula**, using Bluff Road on the east coast, M37 up the spine of the peninsula, and Peninsula Drive on the west coast. A prettier drive is hard to find. While you're there donate a couple of bucks to the Grand Traverse Regional Land Conservancy to help them protect this and other irreplaceable jewels of land. (231.929.7911)

16. **County Road 58** from Petoskey to Wolverine. Curves and hills, forests and fields.

17. **Emmett County C81** from Harbor Springs to Mackinaw City. Ditto.

18. **The Au Sable River Road and M65** from Oscoda to Curran. A designated scenic highway along the famous Au Sable River in northeast Michigan. Then onto M65 as it curves through the Au Sable River Valley. Great riding roads with scenery in spades.

19. **County Road H-40/Old US2 and Old M48** from Rudyard to Engadine in Chippewa and Mackinac Counties. Now a quiet blacktop running through eastern UP farm and forest lands.

20. **Forest Highway H13** from Nahma Junction to Munising. A very pretty road through the forest with light traffic and loads of scenery. Home to deer, bears, moose and wolves.

21. **County Road 426/G67/581** from Gladstone to Felch. Delta, Marquette and Dickinson Counties. It may sound like I'm repeating myself, but if you like curves, hills, scenery, solitude, and in general a great ride, give this stretch of pavement a try.

22. **Big Bay Road** (Marquette to Big Bay). Loads of scenery, tons of history, a great old lighthouse, and good food at an old inn. Who could ask for more?

23. **County Road H16** from US2 to M38. Iron, Houghton and Ontonagon Counties. Let's see; all this road has is great curves, hills, scenery that won't quit,

very light traffic, forests, wildlife, pure air, and blue skies. So it's not perfect, give it a try anyway. You'll be very glad you did.

24. **Black River Drive** (Bessemer to Lake Superior). Gogebic County. A designated scenic highway. Don't miss this one, even if you have to ride hundreds of miles to get there.

25. **Gogebic County Road 519** / Porcupine Mountains South Boundary Road. Gogebic and Ontonagon Counties. Ditto.

Frankenmuth's covered Bridge. (Photo courtesy of Travel Michigan)

Desirable Destinations and Events

THE FOLLOWING DESTINATIONS are towns, attractions, or places that are worth your time to go see, and may not be on any of the above tours. Some don't fall on good touring roads or in scenic areas, or they occur in differing places and dates, and therefore you're not likely to see them unless you make a special effort. Some of these sites or events are common knowledge if you've lived in the state for any length of time, but assuming that not everyone who reads this book is intimately familiar with the state, hopefully this list will provide insight into some fun and very interesting things to see or do here. They aren't listed in any particular order.

Henry Ford Museum & Ford Rouge Plant Tour

If you have a passion for cars and the automobile industry in general the Henry Ford Museum and Rouge Plant tour will be of great interest. Located in Dearborn the museum is open every day except Thanksgiving and Christmas. The museum has a fascinating display of cars, equipment, antiques, and articles of Americana that go far beyond automobiles. You may have visited Greenfield Village and the Henry Ford Museum as a schoolchild, but going as an adult is so much more enjoyable because you can talk, you don't have to stand in straight lines and you can go where you want, not where the teacher tells you to go.

The factory tour where F-150s are made is part of the overall package and Ford provides the transportation. There's a special effects theater, antique cars, a plant walk-through to see trucks being made, and much more. There are lots of displays that take you through over one hundred years of automotive history and development. It's a very interesting way to spend a day!

The tour starts at The Henry Ford, 20900 Oakwood Blvd., Dearborn. For more information, call 313-982-6001 or 800-835-5374; go to the website: thehenryford.org; or email: info@thehenryford.org.

The City of Frankenmuth

Willkommen to Michigan's Little Bavaria. Frankenmuth doesn't just have a tourist attraction—it *is* a tourist attraction. For years the city was Michigan's number one tourist attraction with three million visitors annually. (In recent years they may have been upstaged by the Cabela's Store near Monroe, however).

View of the waterfall at River Place specialty stores in Frankenmuth. (Photo courtesy of Frankenmuth Conventionand Visitors Bureau)

The town was formed in 1845 by Lutheran missionaries from the Bavarian province of Franconia. Everything about the town has a German flavor. It is probably most famous for Zhender's and The Bavarian Inn - two huge restaurants that serve family style dinners on a mass-production scale. They've been local institutions since 1856 and 1888. The Frankenmuth Brewery, a local institution for almost 150 years, closed after being damaged in a storm in 1996 is reopened with locally brewed beers and ales, and out-of-the-ordinary menu fare. There is much more to do here than just eat and imbibe, however. Frankenmuth is a very walkable town, with many small gift shops, art galleries and unique specialty stores selling cheeses, leather goods, woolen clothing, handmade fudge and candy, and much more. Bronner's Christmas Wonderland, with a building the size of five-and-a-half football fields is open year around, and bills itself as the world's largest Christmas display store. Take a cruise on a paddle wheel boat down the Cass River, sample wine at local wineries, or relax in its riverside parks. The biggest event of the year in Frankenmuth is the Bavarian Festival, held in early June each year. Call 989-652-8155 for festival information. It's definitely worth a ride to Frankenmuth to see what it's all about, even though it is located in an area that is somewhat short of great scenery and riding roads.

The Steam Railroading Institute (Owosso, MI)

Anyone who loves railroading, especially steam locomotives, owes it to themselves to make the trip to Owosso to the Steam Railroading Institute. They are located at 405 South Washington Street in Owosso, at the Tuscola & Saginaw Bay RR crossing. Phone (989) 725-9464 (mstrp.com). The Institute has two working steam locomotives and a number of old rolling stock on display. They also have a museum with many railroading and telegraph artifacts. This large facility is very active and growing fast with many new displays in the works. The Institute has excursions from May through December.

Folks who lived in East Lansing or attended Michigan State University prior to 1981 may recall seeing Pere Marquette steam locomotive 1225. For years it was parked next to the old campus boiler building with the MSC smokestack. In 1983, after being given to the Institute by MSU the locomotive was moved to a facility in Owosso. It has been fully restored and is used for a variety of short excursions and for educational purposes. It's an amazing sight to see up close even when not running. When it's operating its size and power are beyond description. Engine 1225 was the model for the locomotive used in the 2004 movie *The Polar Express* and made several trips for the movie's premier showing. Flagg Coal Company Steam Engine 75 is also on display and is utilized on excursions.

If you want to see even more railroading paraphernalia drive the short distance from Owosso to Durand while you're at it to see the Durand Union Station and Railroad Museum, located at 200 Railroad Street, Durand, MI (989) 288-3561. The museum is located at the Durand Union Station, which is claimed to be one of the most photographed depots in the nation due to its unique architecture. Durand was built up around railroads in the late 1800's. Few Michigan communities have a deeper railroading heritage than Durand. Union Station was originally built in 1903 and after it was almost completely destroyed by fire it was rebuilt in 1905. The depot reflects the golden age of railroading in this country that sadly has faded away.

According to information distributed by the museum, during the early 1900's when the railroad industry was at its peak, 42 passenger trains, 22 mail trains, and 78 freight trains passed through Durand every day! Durand Union Station handled about 3000 passengers per day. Grand Trunk Railway abandoned the depot in 1974 and its destruction appeared imminent but local citizens rallied to save it and in 1979 the City of Durand purchased it for $1.00. Local citizens have restored it and it has become the State Railroad History Museum.

Lobby of Kalamazoo Air Zoo. (Photo courtesy of Kalamazoo County Convention and Visitors Bureau)

While in the Owosso area, you might wish to ride a couple of miles east of town on M21 to view the sight of Michigan's first coal mine. A historical marker marks the spot. Michigan's coal mining past isn't well known, but from roughly 1850 to 1950 there were many coal mines in a region stretching from Bay City to Jackson. A fairly low-quality coal was mined, and it was always a battle making the small mines profitable.

About twelve miles west of Owosso on M21, at the southeast corner of M21 and Shepherdsville Road, is a sign marking the site of the first professional football game played in Michigan, and likely in the U.S. A picture of this sign will be necessary if you ever want to impress your buddies with this arcane piece of trivia. Otherwise nobody will believe you.

Kalamazoo Air Zoo

The Air Zoo was recently expanded and renovated and is again open to the public. It has a very impressive collection of more than eighty vintage and more modern aircraft, including the only existing SR-71B Blackbird spy plane. The 119,000 square foot Air Zoo has many rare military planes as well as hands-on exhibits, flight simulators, an indoor balloon ride, and two new 4-D theaters showing movies depicting military planes in action, among other features. As an added bonus, the price of admission also gets you into the Kalamazoo Aviation History Museum and Guadalcanal Memorial Museum adjacent to the Air Zoo.

These facilities are both great places for anyone who enjoys aviation-related displays, aircraft, military history, and related artifacts. Call (269) 382-6555 or go to airzoo.org for additional information.

Michigan Historical Museum

The state's historical museum in downtown Lansing is the kind of place that draws you back for repeated visits. If you have preconceived ideas that this is just another stuffy and uninteresting museum, well, all I can say is you're wrong. The state really did it right with this facility—called the Michigan Library and Historical Museum—built in 1989. The state library is an impressive facility in its own right and is located in the west half of this unique building, with the museum in the eastern portion. A large living White Pine tree grows in the courtyard separating the two facilities. The museum is a very high-quality public museum maintained with tax revenues, and there is no admission charge.

Military Monuments in Lansing

Dedicated to the innumerable thousands of young men and women who didn't get the chance to pursue their dreams.

When visiting the Michigan Historical Museum in Lansing, take time to walk the grounds of the nearby state capitol building to view the various military monuments honoring veterans who fought in all of America's wars over the last one hundred fifty years.

Especially sobering is the Viet Nam Veteran's Memorial located two blocks west of the Capitol, directly north of the Historical Museum / State Library Complex. Like the Wall in Washington, D.C., seeing the names of all 2,654 veterans from Michigan that died in that war inscribed in granite is a powerful statement.

Motorsports Hall of Fame

The Motorsports Museum & Hall of Fame is operated by the Motorsports Museum and Hall of Fame of America Foundation. The museum houses over 40 racing and high performance vehicles. The collection features racers from the world of Indy cars, stock cars, Can Am, TransAm, sprint cars, powerboats, truck racing, drag racing, motorcycles, air racing, and even snowmobiles.

The Museum showcases exhibits and photographs of the personalities, manufacturers and machines of all kind of racing. Other features include racing videos, driving simulation, games, driver uniforms, memorabilia displays and a gift shop.

The Museum is located at the southwest corner of I-96 and Novi Road, exit 162 in Novi. They have well over 100 items on exhibit, most of them rare racing vehicles, including land and water speed record holders, both antique and current. The Hall of Fame enshrines "Heroes of Horsepower" covering nine motorsports categories. Inductions are held each June. (This facility will likely move in 2006. Call them at 800-250-7223 for more information.)

Motown Historical Museum

Anyone who came to age after the late 1950s owes a debt of gratitude to Detroit musicians who set a standard for a new form of popular music. These performers, writers, musicians, and producers created something new and exciting within the music industry, something that came to be called the Motown sound, and Detroit came to be known around the world as Motown. The influence of these Detroit artists is still felt today. All of our lives were touched by the music of The Temptations, The Four Tops, The Supremes, Smokey Robinson, and many, many more. How many of our memories directly relate to a song or a dance that came out of Motown?

The Motown Historical Museum tells the story of Motown music and its impact on society. Starting with a small house that Barry Gordy christened Hitsville USA (now home to the museum) Detroit music started a phenomenon.

Whether you get there by bike or car, this museum and the story it tells is part of us. Going there is more like a pilgrimage, a trip back to our youth, rather than simply a visit to a museum. You too can stand in Studio A, where Motown's hit songs were recorded.

The museum is located at 2648 W. Grand Blvd., near the Lodge Freeway. Open Tuesday–Saturday. Phone 313-875-2264.

Selfridge Military Air Museum and Air Park

Aircraft, especially military aircraft and historical artifacts, hold a special place in the heart of many motorcyclists, lots of whom are veterans themselves. At the Selfridge museum and air park a wide variety of aircraft, dating from throughout the twentieth century, are on display. An interesting collection of additional military paraphernalia is also on display. The museum and air park are located at Selfridge Air National Guard base near Mt. Clemens, and is operated by the Michigan Air Guard Historical Association. Open weekend afternoons. Call 586-307-6768 for more information.

A fun alternative to get to Selfridge is by train. Operated by the Michigan Transit Museum near Mt. Clemens, a train leaves the museums station in Joy Park each Sunday, and on both weekend days in October. Go to mtmrail.com or call 586.463.1863 for information. The museum is located on Cass Street just west of Groesbeck Highway.

Mackinac Island

Because no motor vehicles are allowed on this island in the Straits of Mackinac, I'm obviously not recommending it for its great riding roads. (Although the perimeter road would be an absolute blast on a motorcycle! This road, designated as M185, is the only state highway in Michigan on which motor vehicles are not allowed.) Mackinac Island is unique in the country. You explore the island on foot, by bicycle or horse and buggy. The only way to get to it is by way of one of the ferries that serve the island. Besides tourist and fudge shops there are many worthy things to see and do on the island.

Much of Mackinac Island is a state park. It had formerly been a national park—the nation's second national park following the establishment of Yellowstone National Park. After the federal government transferred the land to the state, it became Michigan's first state park in 1895.

Mackinac Island State Park consists of 1,800 acres of land and many buildings. The most important of the buildings is Fort Mackinac. The French first built the fort at what is now Mackinaw City in 1715. In 1780 during the American Revolutionary War the British took over the fort, dismantled it, moved it to the island and then rebuilt it. Fort Mackinac has been painstakingly restored.

The British occupied the Island during the War of 1812, and the British Landing site on the west shore is marked with a historic monument.

The second main building on the island—and perhaps its most famous—is the Grand Hotel, the world's largest. Unlike no other hotel in the world, this is first class lodging in the extreme. It was built in 1886 by a consortium of railroad and steamship lines, hoping to cash in on the growing luxury tourist business. They succeeded fabulously.

Gilmore Car Museum

This museum isn't as well known as it should be. It's a fascinating place where eight historic barns hold nearly two hundred classic vehicles covering 100 years of automotive history. You can see everything from an 1899 Locomobile, to 1960s muscle cars.

It all started in 1963 when Donald Gilmore's wife bought him a 1920 Pierce-Arrow for restoration. The Gilmores never looked back. In addition to cars, there are wonderful displays of various automotive artifacts and rare parts.

To make it even better, the museum hosts a vintage motorcycle show each June. Anyone interested in showing a pre-1985 motorcycle can send an email to info@gilmorecarmuseum.org and put "cycle flyer" in the subject line.

The Kalamazoo Valley Antique Tractor, Engine and Machinery club also sponsors a three-day show at the museum in June.

The Gilmore Car Museum is located at 6865 Hickory Road, Hickory Corner, MI, near Kalamazoo. Their phone number is (269) 671-5089, and their web site is gilmorecarmuseum.org.

This museum should be high on your list of places to see!

The National Cherry Festival in Traverse City

Held every July since 1926 this huge event is a must for anyone who loves crowds of people, music, a large variety of events, parades, crowds of people, games, more parades, blue water, air shows, crowds of people, cherry pies, cherry ice cream, cherry sundaes, cherry tarts, cherry burgers, cherry wine, cherry... well you get the point. Cherries are big business in Michigan, especially in the northwestern Lower Peninsula. According to the National Agricultural Statistics Service, Michigan ranks first in the nation in the production of tart cherries.

The National Cherry Festival has come a long way from its original purpose of promoting the local cherry growing and processing industry. While that is still the pit of the festival's purpose, it has grown into a huge week-long party with so many events, bands, games, contests, people, music, food, celebrities, and so on that it boggles the mind. It's the place to see large crowds of people, including a lot of bikers that show up each year to see and be seen, eat a lot of food, and just have a lot of fun.

If you plan to go make room or campsite reservations well in advance—like six months. Go to cherryfestival.org for many more details and dates.

Michigan Motorcycling Resources

In the past writers of travel guides went to great lengths to list every applicable organization, facility, phone numbers, names, and so on. The problem of course was that this information was no sooner in print than it started to become obsolete. Companies go out of business or move, event dates change or are cancelled, stores close, and the like.

In the current electronic age it is much easier to locate up-to-date information and one doesn't have to thumb through a book to find things. Below I've listed a number of web sites that should be of interest to motorcyclists in general. Keeping in mind that readers new to Michigan and motorcycling will view this list, it contains sites that are fairly basic to veteran riders or long-time Michigan residents, but could be helpful to new residents or riders. Phone numbers for chain motels are also included, as well as a listing of Michigan motorcycle dealerships, and phone numbers for County Sheriff Departments and State Police posts across the state.

Handy Web Sites

ASSOCIATIONS AND CLUBS

11th Cavalry Motorcycle Club of America: 11thcavalrymc.com/
ABATE of Michigan: abateofmichigan.org/
Airheads Beemer Club: airheads.org/
All American Indian Motorcycle Club: ourworld.cs.com/dayoh6/
American Biker Association: americanbikerassociation.com/
American Firefighters Motorcycle Association: .aff-mc.com/
American Gold Wing Association: agwa.com/
American Historic Racing Motorcycle Association: ahrma.org/
American Motorcycle Network: .americanmotor.com/
American Steel Motorcycle Club: americansteelmc.com/
American Veterans MC: aaa-ammo.com/avmc-1.htm
Antique Motorcycle Club of America: antiquemotorcycle.org/TheClub/theclub.
    html
Aprilia USA Owner's Club: aprilia-usa.com/
Bald Guys Motorcycle Club: baldguysmc.com/
Bent Wheels Competition Club: bentwheels.com/1/bw/index.asp
Bikers Against Child Abuse: bacausa.com/
Bikers For Kids: bikers4kids.org/
Blood Brothers MC: bloodbrothersmc.org/

Blue Knights International: blueknights.org/
Blue Knights of Michigan MC 1: bkmichiganone.com/
Blue Knights of Michigan MC 2: an2wan.tripod.com/
BMW Motorcycle Owners of America: BMWMOA.org
BMW Oilheads Club: oilheadsclub.org/
BMW Riders Association: bmwra.org/
BMW Touring Club of Detroit: bmwtcd.org/
Bonneville Owners Club: autos.groups.yahoo.com/group/
    bonnevilleownersclub/
Brothers of the Third Wheel: btw-trikers.org/uploads/home.php
BSA Owners' Club: bsaoc.demon.co.uk/
Buell Riding Club (BRAG): buell.com/en_us/brag/bragmain.asp
Buffalo Soldiers MC of Michigan: buffalosoldiersnational.com/mi.htm
CB 750 Preservation Society: cb750.org/
Christian Motorcyclists Association: cmausa.org/
Christian Riders Ministry: christianriders.org/
Christian Sportbike Association: christiansportbike.com/
Combat Veterans Motorcycle Association: combatvet.org/
Concours Owners Group: concours.org/
Corrections Officers MC: Grey Dragons 810-796-9069 (pathfy4545@aol.com)
Detroit Hot Girlz MC: detroithotgirlz.com/
Ducati Women: ducatiwomen.com/home.html
Ducatis Unlimited Connection: duc.org/
Excelsior – Henderson Riders Club: ehridersclub.com/
Fellowship Riders: fellowshipriders.org/
FJR Owners Club: fjrowners.ws/fjro4/usa.html
Flint Motorcycle Club: flintmotorcycleclub.com/index1.html
Gold Wing Road Riders Association / Michigan District: gwrra-mi.org/
Gold Wing Road Riders Association: gwrra.org/
Gold Wing Touring Association – Michigan Chapter:
    gwta-of-michigan.tripod.com/
Grand Rapids Harley Owners Group: grhog.com/
Harley Owners Group – Muskegon: angelfire.com/mi/muskegon/index.html
Harley Owners Group – Great Lakes Southeast Michigan: glsem-hog.com/
Northern Chapter – Harley Owners Group: northernchapter.com/
Harley Owners Group – Port Huron: phhog.com/
Superior Chapter – Harley Owners Group: superiorchapterhog.com/
Harley Owners Group: harley-davidson.com/ex/hog/template.
    asp?fnc=hog&bmLocale=en_US

Herd of Turtles Motorcycle Club: pjgillam.tripod.com/herd_of_turtles.htm

Hogs In Ministry: h-i-m.org

Honda CB1100R Owners Group: eskimo.com/~carcosa/1100R.html

Honda Sport Touring Association: ridehsta.com/

Honda VTX Owners Association: .vtxoa.com/

Huron Valley Night Hawks MC: bikergazette.com/members/ShaggyHVNH.
    html

Husqvarna Motorcycle Club: huskyclub.com/

In Country Vets Motorcycle Club: icvmc.com/

Indian Motorcycle Club of America: indian-motorcycles.com/

International Brotherhood of Motorcycle Campers: ibmc.org/

International CBX Owners Association: cbxclub.com/

International Norton Owners Association: inoanorton.com/welcome.htm

International Order of Old Bastards MC: home.inreach.com/ioob/index.htm

Internet BMW Riders: ibmwr.org/

Iron Butt Association: ironbutt.com/about/default.cfm

Iron Butt Goldwingers Association: .ironbuttgoldwingers.com/

Iron Indian Riders: .ironindian.com/

Jus Brothers Motorcycle Club: jusbrothersmc.com/

Kawasaki Good Times Owners Club: kawasaki.com/gtoc/main.html

Latin American Motorcycle Association / Women's Section: latinbikers.com/
    Damas/Damas.htm

Latin American Motorcycle Association: latinbikers.com/

Leathernecks Motorcycle Club: leathernecksmc.org/

Long Riders Association: longridersmc.org/

Long Riders MC Magazine: longridersmagazine.com/index_lr_online.htm

Magna Riders Association: magnariders.com/

Marines Motorcycle Club: marinesmc.com/

Metro (Detroit) Triumph Riders: metrotriumphriders.com/

Michigan Classic Muscle Bikes Association: geocities.com/MotorCity/
    Downs/2263/main.html

Michigan Independent Riders Group: angelfire.com/mi/MIRG/

Michigan Norton Owners: (419) 882-2943

Mid-Michigan BMW Touring Club: angelfire.com/mi4/bmwtc/

Mid-Michigan Riders MC: angelfire.com/ri/cycleclub/

Military Veterans Motorcycle Club: militaryveteransmc.com/

Moto Guzzi National Owners Club: mgnoc.com/

Motor Maids, Inc.: motormaids.org/

Motorcycle Beginners: motorcyclebeginners.com/

Motorcycle Touring Association: mtariders.com/

Muskegon Motorcycle Club: (231) 798-1552

Norton Owners Club: nortonownersclub.org/

Para-Dice Motorcycle Club: para-dicemc.org/para-dice_025.htm

Pioneers Motorcycle Club: members.cox.net/pioneers/Preamble.htm

Port Huron Motorcycle Club: (810) 982-4894

POW_MIA Riders MC: powmiariders.com/

Proud Veterans Motorcycle Club: kevinandteri.com:8080/pvmc/html/

Red Knights Motorcycle Club: redknightsmc.org/

Ride Motorcycle Club: ridemotorcycle.com/

Ride To Work Association: ridetowork.org/home.php

Saginaw Valley BMW Riders MC: dnesbitt.com/svbmwriders/

Shadow Club USA: shadowclubusa.com/

Sister Cycle: sistercycle.com/

Southern Cruisers Riding Club: southerncruiser.net/chapters1.htm#Michigan

Sportsbike Web Site: sportbikes.ws/index.php

Star Touring & Riding Association: startouring.org/

Suzuki Owners Club: soc-usa.org/

Trike Riders International: trikes.org

Triumph International Owners Club: members.aol.com/JohnTIOC/tioc.htm

Triumph Online Motorcycle Club: autos.groups.yahoo.com/group/triumphmotorcycleclub2/

Triumph Owners Motorcycle Club: tomcc.org/index.html

United Sidecar Association: sidecar.com/

United States Patriots M/C: uspatriotsmc.com/

USA Eagle Riders / Deaf Bikers of Michigan: usaeagleridersdeafbikersofmichigan.com/

USA Highway Riders M/C: usahighwayriders.com/

Valkyrie Owners Association International: valkyrie-owners.com/

Valkyrie Riders Cruiser Club: valkyrieriders.com/

Ventures (Yamaha) Motorcycle Club: venturers.org/

Victory Motorcycle Club: thevmc.com/start.html

Vincents Owners Club: voc.uk.com/sections/index.html

Vintage BMW Motorcycle Owners Club: vintagebmw.org/current/

Vintage Japanese Motorcycle Club: vjmc.org/

Virago Owners Club: viragoownersclub.org/

V-Max Owners Association: v-max.com/

V-Twin Sports Riders: geocities.com/flootiebuell/

Warrior Brotherhood Veterans MC: warriorbrotherhood.com/

Wide Open Sport Bikes.Com: wideopensportbikes.com/WOShomepage.htm
Wolverines Motorcycle Club: wolverinesmc.com/
Women In The Wind, Inc.: womeninthewind.org/
Women on Wheels: womenonwheels.org/
Women's International Motorcycle Association: wimausa.org/
Yamaha Owners Club: autos.groups.yahoo.com/group/yamahaownersclub/
Zen Riders: zenriders.com/main.htm

MAGAZINES AND JOURNALS
American Iron Magazine: americanironmagazine.com/
American Motorcycle Network: americanmotor.com
Beginner Bikers Magazine: beginnerbikes.com/
Bike Week Report: bikeweekreport.com/
Biker Threads Magazine: .bikerthreadsmagazine.com/
Cycle News Magazine: cyclenews.com/
Cycle World Magazine: cycleworld.com/
Easy Riders Magazine: easyriders.com/
Hot Bike Harley-Davidson Magazine: hotbikeweb.com/
Metric Bikes Magazine: metricbikes.com/index.htm
Midwest Motorcyclist: midwestmotorcyclist.com/
Motorcycle Consumer News: mcnews.com/mcn/
Motorcycle Cruiser Magazine: motorcyclecruiser.com/
Motorcycle Daily Magazine: motorcycledaily.com/
Motorcycle Explorer Internet Magazine: motorcycleexplorer.com/
Motorcycle USA: motorcycle-usa.com
Motorcyclist Magazine: motorcyclistonline.com/
Rider Magazine: riderreport.com
Road Racing World Magazine: venus.13x.com/roadracingworld/
RoadRUNNER Cruising & Touring Magazine: rrmotorcycling.com/
Superbike Magazine: superbike.co.uk/
Twistgrip Magazine: twistgrip.com/new%20twistgrip.html

MANUFACTURERS
Aprilia Motorcycle Company: aprilia.com/portale/eng/company02.phtml
BMW Motorcycle Company: bmwmotorcycles.com/home
Britten Motorcycle Company: britten.co.nz/
Buell Motorcycle Company: buell.com/selector.asp
Cagiva MotorcycleCompany: cagivausa.com/
Ducati Motorcycle Company: ducati.com/

Harley-Davidson Motorcycle Company / US: harley-davidson.com/en/homef.
   asp?bmLocale=en_US
Honda Motorcycle Company: powersports.honda.com/motorcycles/
Husqvarna Motorcycle Company: husqvarnausa.com/
Kawasaki Motorcycle Company: kawasaki.com/
KTM Motorcycle Company: ktmusa.com/frameset.asp
MV Agusta USA: mvagustausa.com/web-mvagusta/news_columbus04.html
Norton Motorcycle Company: nortonmotorcycles.com/
Royal Enfield Motorcycle Company: enfieldmotorcycles.com/
Suzuki Motorcycle Company: suzukicycles.com/Products/Motorcycles/Default.
   aspx
Triumph Motorcycle Company: triumph.co.uk/
Ural Motorcycles: ural.com/
Victory Motorcycle Company: victorymotorcycles.com/victory/default.aspx
Yamaha Motorcycle Company: yamaha-motor.com/products/categories/2/mcy/
   yamaha_motorcycles.aspx

MISCELLANEOUS

Bed & Breakfast Inns: bedandbreakfast.com/michigan.html
Enforcers Motorcycle Links: enforcersmc.com/links.htm
Fasttrack Riders: fastrackriders.com/
FIM (English Version): fim.ch/en/default.asp?
GingerMan Raceway: gingermanraceway.com/home.html
Grattan Raceway: grattanraceway.com/
International GPS Waypoint Registry: .waypoint.org/default.html
Michigan Biker Events Web Site: michiganbikerevents.com
Michigan Lighthouse Conservancy: michiganlights.com/
Motorcycle Events: gmasw.com/bikelist.htm
Motorcycle Resources and Reviews: powersportsnetwork.com/
   ?d=d&menucat=Enthusiasts
Motorcycle Hall of Fame Museum: amadirectlink.com/museum/index.asp
National Motorcycle Museum: nationalmcmuseum.org/default.asp
Ride To Work: ridetowork.org/home.php
State of Michigan Motorcycle Endorsement Information: michigan.gov/
   sos/0,1607,7-127-1627_8666_9062---,00.html
State of Michigan, Dept. of Natural Resources / Parks: michigan.gov/dnr
Michigan Road Construction / Repairs / Conditions: michigan.gov/
   mdot/0,1607,7-151-9615---,00.html

Michigan Motorcycle Operators Manual: motorcycletraining.accn.org/mi%20m
   otorcycle%20operater%20manual.pdf
State of Michigan Travel Site: travel.michigan.org/
Sturgis Motorcycle Museum & Hall of Fame: sturgismotorcyclemuseum.org/
Upper Peninsula Travel Planner: uptravel.com/
WERA Racing: wera.com/
Woman Biker.Com: womanbiker.com/home.php3

MOTORCYCLE INSURANCE
Auto-Owners: auto-owners.com/our_prods/car_products/rv.htm
Foremost: foremost.com
Geico: geico.com
GMAC: gmacinsurance.com
Markel / BikeLine: protectmybike.com/
Progressive: motorcycle.progressive.com/motorcycle_homePolicyAccess.asp
Sentry: sentry.com/consumer_auto_specialty_insurance.htm
Motorcycle Racing Insurance – Armor: amadirectlink.com/ATVA/ARMOR.htm

MOTORCYCLE RENTAL
Cruise America: cruiseamerica.com/motorcycle_rentals/default.asp
Eagle Rider: eaglerider.com/

MOTORCYCLE SHIPPING
1AA Motorcycle Transport: 1aamotorcycles.com/
American Auto Transporters: shipcar.com/motorcycle-shipping.html
Auto Car Transport: auto-car-transport.com/
Dependable Auto Shippers: dasautoshippers.com/dasnew/web_order/lp/move-
   cars.asp
Discount / American Baggage: discount-shipping.net/vehicles/motorcycles.cfm
Federal: funtransport.com
Moving.com: moving.com/guide/moving/motorcycle.asp
The Auto Mover: theautomover.com/motorcycle.htm

ORGANIZATIONS
American Motorcyclist Association: ama-cycle.org/
Canadian Motorcycle Association: canmocycle.ca/
Michigan Bikers Association: michiganbiker.com/home.shtml
Michigan Confederation of Clubs: /mcoc.us/

Motorcycle Riders Foundation: mrf.org/
Motorcycle Safety Foundation: msf-usa.org/
National Coalition of Motorcyclists: aimncom.com/

TRAINING AND SCHOOLS

Alpha Training Center, Lansing: alphatrainingcenter.com
CLASS Motorcycle Schools: classrides.com/
Ferris State University – Motorcycle Rider Course: ferris.edu/cpd/motorcy-
    clerider/
Keith Code Motorcycle School: superbikeschool.com/
Michigan Rider and Safety Education Program: michigan.gov/sos/0,1607,7-127-
    1627-87875--,00.html
Michigan State University Motorcycle Training Program: msu-htsp.org/cycle.
    htm
Motorcycle Racing School – Ed Bargy: edbargyracingschool.com/
Motorcycle Racing School – Kevin Schwantz: schwantzschool.com/
Motorcycle Racing School – Penguin Roadracing School: penguinracing.com/
Motorcycle Rides in America Track Days & Schools: motorcycleridesinamerica.
    com/schedules.htm
Northeast Sportbike Association: nesba.com/
Schoolcraft Community College Motorcycle Safety Classes:
    motorcycle@schoolcraft.edu
Stayin' Safe Motorcycle Training – stayinsafe.com/

Emergency Phone Numbers

Over the years I've found that in rural areas and on county roads you're more likely to have success getting a Sheriff Deputy to the scene if help is needed than you are a Michigan State Police Trooper. On a State or Federal highway the MSP will likely be the closest and your best bet for assistance, but on the back roads I'd bank on the county Sheriff Department. In addition, most Sheriff Deputies are locals. They were probably born and raised in that county, whereas a Trooper was most likely born in another part of the state and transferred to the local Post. Deputies know the back roads of their county well and can also advise as to things such as the best wrecker service for your particular predicament, local repair facilities, or straighten you out should you be temporarily directionally disoriented.

Michigan State Police phone numbers for all Posts are printed on the Michigan state map, but I've included them here for your convenience. Phone numbers for Sheriff Departments are harder to come by, so they're also printed below for your convenience and safety.

County Sheriff Departments

Alcona	989-724-6271	Crawford	989-348-4616
Alger	906-387-4444	Delta	906-786-3633
Allegan	269-673-0500	Dickinson	906-774-6262
Alpena	989-356-4128	Eaton	517-543-3512
Antrim	231-533-6335	Emmett	231-347-2036
Antrim	231-533-8627	Genesee	810-257-3407
Arenac	989-846-4561	Gladwin	800-553-0911
Baraga	906-524-6177	Gogebic	906-667-0203
Barry	269-948-4805	Grand Traverse	231-995-5000
Bay	989-895-4050	Gratiot	989-875-5214
Benzie	231-882-4484	Hillsdale	517-437-7317
Berrien	269-983-7141	Houghton	906-482-0055
Branch	517-278-2325	Huron	989-269-9910
Calhoun	269-969-6450	Ingham	517-676-2431
Cass	269-445-8644	Ionia	616-527-5737
Charlevoix	231-547-4461	Iosco	989-362-6164
Cheboygan	231-627-3155	Iron	906-875-6669
Chippewa	906-635-6355	Isabella	989-772-5911
Clare	989-539-7166	Jackson	517-768-7922
Clinton	989-224-5200	Kalamazoo	269-385-6173

Kalkaska............	231-258-8686	Oakland.............	248-858-5001
Kent...............	616-632-6357	Oceana..............	231-873-2121
Keweenaw..........	906-337-0528	Ogemaw.............	989-345-3786
Lake...............	231-745-2712	Ontonagon..........	906-884-4901
Lapeer.............	810-667-0443	Osceola.............	231-832-2288
Lenawee............	517-263-0524	Oscoda..............	989-826-3214
Livingston..........	517-546-2440	Otsego..............	989-732-3555
Luce...............	906-293-8431	Ottawa.............	616-738-4000
Mackinac...........	800-643-1911	Presque Isle.........	989-734-2156
Macomb............	810-469-5151	Roscommon.........	989-275-5101
Manistee...........	231-723-3585	Saginaw.............	989-790-5456
Marquette..........	906-225-8435	Sanilac.............	810-648-8351
Mason.............	231-843-3475	Schoolcraft.........	906-341-2122
Mecosta............	231-592-0150	Shiawassee..........	989-743-3411
Menominee..........	906-863-4441	St. Clair.............	810-985-8115
Midland............	989-839-4627	St- Joseph...........	269-467-9045
Missaukee..........	231-839-4338	Tuscola.............	989-673-8161
Monroe............	734-240-7401	Van Buren..........	269-657-2006
Montcalm..........	989-831-7590	Washtenaw..........	734-971-8400
Montmorency.......	989-785-4238	Wayne.............	313-224-2222
Muskegon..........	231-724-6236	Wexford............	231-779-9211
Newaygo...........	231-689-6623		

Michigan State Police Posts

Detroit Area

Detroit Metro

    Emergency........800-495-4677

Brighton.............810-227-1051

Ypsilanti.............734-482-1213

Eastern Michigan

Bad Axe.............989-269-6442

Bay City.............989-684-2235

Bridgeport...........989-777-3700

Caro................989-673-2157

Corunna.............989-723-6761

East Tawas...........989-362-3435

Flint................810-732-1111

Gladwin.............989-426-3068

Lapeer..............810-664-2906

Sandusky............810-648-2234

West Branch.........989-345-0956

Southern Michigan

Adrian..............517-263-0033

Battle Creek..........269-968-6115

Coldwater...........517-278-2373

Jackson.............517-780-4580

Hillsdale.............517-849-9922

Lansing.............517-322-1907

Monroe.............734-242-3500

Niles................269-683-4411

Paw Paw............269-657-5551

White Pigeon.........269-483-7612

West Michigan

Bridgman	269-465-6525
Grand Haven	616-842-2101
Hart	231-873-2171
Hastings	269-948-8283
Ionia	616-527-3600
Lakeview	989-352-8445
Newaygo	231-652-1662
Rockford	616-866-4411
South Haven	269-637-2126
Wayland	269-792-2213

Northern Lower Peninsula

Alpena	989-354-4101
Cadillac	231-779-6040
Cheboygan	231-627-9974
Gaylord	989-732-5141
Houghton Lake	989-422-5103
Ithaca	989-875-4112
Kalkaska	231-258-4112

Manistee	231-723-3536
Mt- Pleasant	989-773-5952
Petoskey	231-347-8102
Reed City	231-832-2221
Traverse City	231-946-4647

Upper Peninsula

Calumet	906-337-2211
Gladstone	906-428-4412
Iron Mountain	906-774-2122
Iron River	906-265-9916
L'Anse	906-524-6162
Manistique	906-341-2102
Munising	906-387-4551
Negaunee	906-475-9922
Newberry	906-293-5152
St- Ignace	906-643-7582
Sault Ste- Marie	906-632-2217
Stephenson	906-753-2276
Wakefield	906-224-9691

Major Hotel and Motel 800 Numbers

Adam's Mark Hotels	800-444-ADAM
Americinn	800-634-3444
AmeriHost Inn	800-434-5800
Baymont Inn	800-301-0200
Best Inns and Suites	800-BESTINN
Best Western	800-528-1234
Clarion Hotels	800-CLARION
Comfort Inns	877-4CHOICE
Courtyard by Marriott	800-321-2211
Days Inn	800-325-2525
Doubletree Hotels	800-222TREE
EconoLodge	877-4CHOICE
Embassy Suites	800-EMBASSY
Fairfield Inn	800-228-2800
Four Seasons Hotels	800-332-3442
Hampton Inns	800-HAMPTON

Hawthorn Suites	800-527-1133
Hilton Hotels	800-HILTONS
Holiday Inns	800-HOLIDAY
Howard Johnson	800-446-4656
Hyatt Hotels	800-233-1234
Knights Inn	800-843-5644
La Quinta Inns	800-531-5900
Marriott	800-228-9290
Microtel Inns	(888) 771-7171
Motel 6	800-4MOTEL6
Omni Hotels	800-THEOMNI
Quality Inns	877-4CHOICE
Radisson Hotels	800-333-3333
Ramada Inn	800-228-2828
Red Roof Inns	800-THE ROOF
Regent International	800-545-4000

Renaissance Hotels 800-228-9898

Residence Inn 800-331-3131

Rodeway Inns 800-228-2000

Sheraton Hotels
and Inns 800-325-3535

Shoney's Inn 800-222-2222

Signature Inn 800-822-5252

Stouffer Hotels
and Resorts 800-468-3571

Super 8 Motels, Inc. 800-800-8000

Suisse Chalet 800-5CHALET

Travelodge and
Viscount Hotels 800-578-7878

Westin Hotels
and Resorts 800-228-3000

Wyndham Hotels
and Resorts 800-822-4200

Lost or Stolen Credit Card Phone Numbers

American Express: 1-800-668-2639
Diner's Club: - 1-800-2Diners
Discover: 1-800-DISCOVER
Mastercard: 1-800-MASTERCARD
VISA: 1-800-847-2911

Michigan Motorcycling Regulations

Motorcycle—A two or three-wheeled motor vehicle which has a gasoline engine with more than 50 cc piston displacement and two brake horsepower, and can achieve a top speed of 30 mph on level surfaces.

Helmets—Required for all riders. Must be DOT approved.

Helmet Speakers—No Restrictions

Eye Protection—Shatterproof glasses, helmet face shield, or windshield required at speeds over 35 mph.

Headlight—Required. Modulating headlight allowed.

Riding Style / Lane Use—No more than two abreast allowed. Lane splitting not allowed.

Mirrors—Required.

Horn—Required

Passenger Age Restrictions—None

Passenger Footrests—Required if carrying a passenger.

Passenger Seat—Required if carrying a passenger.

Training—Required under age 18.

Handlebars—A maximum of 15 inches allowed between highest point of handlebar hand grips and lowest point of an unoccupied seat.

License—Must have motorcycle endorsement on driver's license.

Speed Limits—Locally-maintained roads and state highways—55 mph unless otherwise posted. Expressways—70 mph unless otherwise posted. Motorcycle must be at least 125 cc for use on expressway or other limited access highway.

Signaling Turns—Use of electric or arm signals required for lane changes and turns.

Insurance—Must be insured with at least a 20/40 thousand dollar public liability policy and ten thousand dollar property damage coverage.

Radar Detectors—No Restriction

Maximum Sound Level—86dBA at speed over 35mph measured from 50 feet. 82dBA at speed less than 35mph measured from 50 feet. 95dBA in stationary run-up test at 75 inches.

Adjacent States and Provinces

Indiana, Minnesota, Ohio & Wisconsin—Helmet use required until age 18.

Illinois—No helmet required.

Ontario—Helmet required (throughout Canada)

Motorcycle Dealers & Repair Facilities

APRILIA

Detroit Eurocycles LLC
18301 Nine Mile Road
Eastepointe, MI
586-778-8900

Full Throttle Motor Sports
9555 Woodlane Drive
Lansing, MI 48821
517-646-9850

K&W Cycle
4090 Auburn Road
Utica, MI
586-731-5959

TNT Motorsports & Equipment
5812 South Division Street
Kentwood, MI
616-534-8928

BENELLI

North Side Recreational Vehicles
10586 South Williams Road
DeWitt, MI 48820
517-668-8056

Geiger Farms
6947 Sand Beach Road
Harbor Beach, MI 48441
989-479-0918

BMW

BMW Motorcycles of Detroit
34080 Van Dyke Avenue
Sterling Heights, MI 48312
586-274-4000

Southeast Michigan BMW
39933 Ford Road
Canton, MI 48187
734-981-1479

BMW Motorcycles of Grand Rapids
5995 South Division Street
Grand Rapids, MI 49548
616-530-6900

DUCATI

Classic Cycle, Inc.
30478 Groesbeck Hwy
Roseville, MI 48066
586-447-1340

Gar's Sports Center, Inc.
2531 South Division Street
Grand Rapids, MI 49507
616-452-6951

Great Lake Powersports
4211 Fenton Road
Burton, MI 48529
810-233-7800

Mid Michigan Honda Triumph
4108 Page Avenue
Michigan Center, MI
517-764-0900

Rosenau Powersport
24732 Ford Road
Dearborn Heights. MI 48127
313-278-5000

Section 8 Superbike
2287 East West Maple Road
Commerce Township, MI 48382
248-669-6633

HARLEY-DAVIDSON

Detroit Harley-Davidson / Buell
25152 Van Dyke
Center Line, MI 48015
586-756-1284

Biker Bob's Harley-Davidson / Buell
14100 Telegraph Road
Taylor, MI 48180
734-947-4647

Jim Bailey's Harley Davidson
6315 Illinois Street
Fort Wayne, IN 46804
260-489-2464

Motor City Harley-Davidson / Buell
34900 Grand River
Farmington Hills, MI 48335
248-473-7433

Wolverine Harley-Davidson / Buell
44660 North Gratiot Avenue
Clinton Township, MI 48036
586-463-7700

A.B.C. Harley-Davidson / Buell
4405 Highland Road / M59
Waterford, MI 48328
248-674-3175

Brighton Harley-Davidson / Buell
5942 Whitmore Lake Road
Brighton, MI 48116
810-225-2915

American Harley-Davidson and Buell
5436 Jackson Road
Ann Arbor, MI 48103
734-747-8008
800-234-7285

Tecumseh Harley-Davidson / Buell
8080 Matthews Highway
Tecumseh, MI 49286
517-423-3333

Gilbert's Harley-Davidson
3350 Lapeer Road
Port Huron, MI 48060
810-982-4351

Harley-Davidson of Port Huron
3450 24th Avenue
Fort Gratiot, MI
810-385-3763

Ray C's Harley-Davidson / Buell
1422 Imlay City Road
Lapeer, MI 48446
810-664-4505

Cummings Harley-Davidson / Buell
5350 Davison Road
Burton, MI 48509
810-234-6646

Toledo Harley-Davidson / Buell
7960 West Central Avenue
Sylvania, OH 43617
419-843-7892

Town & Country Sports Center
US12 & US127
Cement City, MI 49233
517-547-3333

Shiawassee Harley-Davidson / Buell
11901 North Beyer Road
Birch Run, MI 48415
989-624-4400

Capitol Harley-Davidson
9550 Woodland Drive
Dimondale, MI 48821
517-646-2345

Mahrle's Harley-Davidson / Buell
5738 Beckley Road
Battle Creek, MI 49015
269-979-2233

Wild Boar Harley-Davidson / Buell
624 28th Street
Grand Rapids, MI 49548
616-243-1111

Perry's Harley-Davidson / Buell
5331 Sprinkle Road
Kalamazoo, MI 49002
269-329-3450

Wild Boar Harley-Davidson / Buell
2977 Corporate Grove Drive
Hudsonville, MI 49426
616-896-0111

C & S Harley-Davidson
4741 Pickard Road
Mt. Pleasant, MI 48858
989-772-5513

Snell Harley-Davidson / Buell
590 Ottawa Street
Muskegon, MI 49442
231-722-3653

Sandy's Harley-Davidson
11940 North Maple Island Road
Fremont, MI 49412
231-924-3020

Saginaw Valley Harley-Davidson / Buell
3850 South Huron Road
Bay City, MI 48706
989-686-0400

Gildner's Cycle Shop
2723 South M76
West Branch, MI 48661
989-345-1330

Northwoods Harley-Davidson / Buell
980 South Wisconsin Avenue
Gaylord, MI 49735
989-732-8000

Classic Harley-Davidson / Buell
3939 South Blue Star Drive
Traverse City, MI 49683
231-943-9344

Northwoods Harley-Davidson / Buell
276 South Huron Avenue
Mackinaw City, MI 49701
231-436-5331

Harley-Davidson of Green Bay
2728 Manitowoc Road
Green Bay, WI 54311
920-406-3900

Bald Eagle Harley-Davidson
2080 US41
Marquette, MI 49855
906-228-5330

HONDA

Dynamic Powersports
17416 East 9 Mile Road
Eastpointe, MI 48021
586-445-8100

Rosenau Powersports
24732 Ford Road
Dearborn Heights, MI 48127
313-278-5000

Honda of Warren
30788 Ryan Road
Warren, MI 48092
586-751-1200

Metro Powersports
44600 Michigan Avenue
Canton, MI 48188
734-397-5880

Macomb Powersports
46860 Gratiot Avenue
Chesterfield, MI 48051
586-949-4000

Anderson Sales & Service
1645 South Telegraph Road
Bloomfield Hills, MI 48302-0049
248-858-2300

Ray's Honda
959 South Telegraph Road
Monroe. MI 48161
734-241-8444

Al Gaskills Honda City
65700 Gratiot Avenue
Lenox, MI 48050
586-727-2777

Nicholson Honda
4405 Jackson Road
Ann Arbor, MI 48103
734-769-9815

C & C Sports. Inc.
8090 Grand River Road
Brighton, MI 48114
810-227-7068

College Bike Shop
340 North Larch Street
Lansing, MI 48912
517-484-6413

Groves Motorsports
525 North Cedar
Mason, MI 48854
517-676-5667

Albins Honda
325 Vermontville Hwy
Potterville, MI 48876
517-645-7611

US27 Motorsports
5301 North US27
St. Johns, MI 48879
989-224-8874

Route 66 Powersports
3613 South State Road
Ionia, MI 48846
616-527-0130

Holiday Power Sports
4501 Page Avenue
Michigan Center, MI 49254
517-764-3600

C & C Sports. Inc.
8090 Grand River Road
Brighton, MI 48114
810-227-7068

Great Lakes Powersports
G4211 Fenton Road
Burton, MI 48529
810-233-7800

Town & Country Sports Center
US12 &US127
Cement City, MI 49233
517-547-3333

M & M Cycle
3825 Lake Street
Kalamazoo, MI 49048
269-381-5800

Paw Paw Cycle
134 Ampey Road
Paw Paw, MI 49079
269-657-2574

Mid Michigan Honda Triumph
4108 Page Avenue
Michigan Center, MI
517- 764-0900

Team D & D Cycle
695 East Chicago Road
Coldwater, MI 49036
517-278-5532

North End Cycle Shop
2426 Cassopolis Street
Elkhart, IN 46514
574-264-0618

Gars Honda
2531 South Division Avenue
Grand Rapids, MI 49507
616-452-6951

Harbor Sports & Cycle
2188 State Route 139
Benton Harbor, MI 49022
269-927-6186

Shawmut Hills Sales
2807 Lake Michigan Drive NW
Grand Rapids. MI 49504
616-453-5467

Michiana Cycle, Inc.
50715 State Road 933
South Bend, IN 46637
574-272-4484

Village Motorsports
3661 Plainfield Avenue NE
Grand Rapids, MI 49525
616-364-8481

Birch Run Motorsports
8230 Main Street - Pob 678
Birch Run, MI 48415
989-624-2160

Bay Cycle Sales
3800 South Huron Road M13
Bay City, MI 48706
989-684-0754

Stevens' Sport Center
1911 East Airport Road
Midland, MI 48642
989-631-6450

Linwood Cycle Sales Co.
1517 North Huron Road
Pinconning. MI 48650
989-697-4425

Lapeer Honda
757 South Main Street
Lapeer, MI 48446
810-245-0400

Central Motor Sports
905 Corporate Drive
Mount Pleasant, MI 48858
989-773-6025

Honda Sales
3045 Pigeon Road
Elkton, MI 4873 I
989-375-2391

Great Escapes Motor Sports
I36 North US Highway 31 South
Traverse City, MI 49684
231-943-9800

Galmores Inc.
105 2nd Street
East Jordan, MI 49727
231-536-7582

Terry's Sports Center
8307 West M72 Hwy
Grayling, MI 49738
989-348-7513

Extreme Power Sports
2572 South Otsego Avenue
Gaylord, MI 49735
989-732-4331

Hacker's Honda
3901 West Houghton Lake Drive
Houghton Lake, MI 48629
989-366-7015

Peacock Ltd. of Baldwin
276 South M37
Baldwin, MI 49304
231-745-4606

Whites Sales & Service
9611 North Straits Hwy
Cheboygan, MI 4972!
231-627-9919

Scooter's Motorsports
4250 US Highway 41 West
Marquette, MI 49855
906-228-4040

Cycle City, Inc.
1415 Lincoln Drive
Escanaba, MI 49829
906-786-5834

Spread Eagle Marine
HC 2 Box 251 Pob 49
Florence, WI 54121
715-696-3292

North Honda Motorsports
3700 10th Street
Menominee, MI 49858
906-863-5592

Ayes Motor Center
Highway 51 North
Hurley, WI 54534
715-561-2720

Leitz Sports Center. Inc.
2512 I75 Business Spur
Sault Sainte Marie, MI 49783
906-632-8291

Galmores Inc.
105 2nd Street
East Jordan, MI 49727
231-536-7582

HUSQVARNA
Claerhaut's Husqvarna
Unionville, MI
9890883-9887

Classic Cycle
Roseville, MI
586-447-1340

Reimbold's Sales & Service
Reese, MI
989-755-0612

SNS Cycle
880 Chicago Drive
Jenison, MI
616-457-7433

BOSS HOSS
Detroit Boss Hoss
20315 East 9 Mile
St. Clair Shores, MI 48080
586-777-0578

KAWASAKI
Romeo Motorsports Kawasaki
410 East Saint Clair Street
Romeo, MI 48065
586-752-696!

Bright Power Sports Kawasaki
4181 Dix Highway
Lincoln Park, MI 48146
313-382-1220

Michigan Powersports Kawasaki
1196 Ecorse Road
Ypsilanti, MI 48198
734-482-4386

Anderson Sales & Service
1645 South Telegraph Road
Bloomfield Hills, MI 48302
248-858-2300

Ray's Powersports Kawasaki
959 South Telegraph Road
Monroe. MI 48161
734-241-8444

Michigan Powersports Kawasaki
1196 Ecorse Road
Ypsilanti, MI 48198
734-482-4386

J & J Kawasaki Sales & Service
475 SE Catawba Road
Port Clinton, OH 43452
419-734-2754

Honda East Kawasaki
1230 Conant Street
Maumee, OH 43537
419-891-1230

Power Sports Kawasaki
4340 West Maumee Street
Adrian, MI 49221
517-265-3727

Macomb Powersports Kawasaki
46860 Gratiot Avenue
Chesterfield, MI 48051
586-949-4000

Pilgrim Kawasaki
260 Ann Arbor Road West
Plymouth, MI 48170
734-451-7200

Al Gaskill Kawasaki
17416 East 9 Mile Road
Eastpointe, MI 48021
586-445-8100

K & W Cycle Kawasaki
4090 Auburn Road
Shelby Township, MI 48317
586-731-5959

Nicholson Enterprises
4405 Jackson Road
Ann Arbor, MI 48103
734-769-9815

Olson Power Sports
24841 Grand River Avenue
Detroit, MI 48219
313-541-7200

Holiday Kawasaki
450! Page Avenue
Michigan Center, MI 49254
517-764-3600

Holiday Kawasaki
4501 Page Avenue
Michigan Center, MI 49254
517-764-3600

Town & Country Sports Center
US12 & US127
Cement City, MI 49233
517-547-3333

Nevins Motorsports Kawasaki
116 West Chicago Street
Jonesville, MI 49250
517-849-5399

Power Sports Kawasaki
4340 West Maumee Street
Adrian, MI 49221
517-265-3727

M/C Supply Ltd
2310 South M37 Hwy
Hastings. MI 49058
269-945-2783

M & M Cycle
3825 Lake Street
Kalamazoo, MI 49048
269-381-5800

Sister Lakes Kawasaki
67990 M152
Benton Harbor, MI 49022
269-944-5577

Vanderzee Shelton Kawasaki
02951 73rd Street
South Haven, MI 49090
269-637-8788

John Hoeksema
11483 East Lakewood Boulevard
Holland, MI 49424-9663
616-396-8132

Paw Paw Kawasaki
134 Ampey Road
Paw Paw, MI 49079
269-657-2574

Wise Motors
106 West Main Street
Mendon, MI 49072
269-496-3414

Great Lakes Kawasaki
G4211 Fenton Road
Burton, MI 48529
810-233-7800

Nord-Ride Kawasaki
7415 Enterprise Parkway
Mount Morris, MI 48458
810-564-1929

Howell Cycle
2445 West Grand River Avenue
Howell, MI 48843
517-546-3310

Reinbold's Sales & Service
110 North Gera at M46 & M83
Reese, MI 48757
989-755-0612

JD Motorsports Kawasaki
245 Columbia Street
Caro, MI 48723
989-673-8400

Cycle Land
3482 Lapeer Road
Port Huron, MI 48060
810-987-3963

Off Road Outlet Kawasaki
955 South Van Dyke Road
Bad Axe, MI 48413
989-269-7979

Steven's Kawasaki
3640 South Huron Road
Bay City, MI 48706
989-667-0880

Ray C's
1381 Imlay Road
Lapeer, MI 48446
810-664-9800

Grove's Motorsports
525 North Cedar Street
Mason. MI 48854
517-676-5667

College Bike Shop
340 North Larch Street
Lansing, MI 48912
517-484-6398

Joe Brooks Kawasaki
2593 North State Road
Ionia, MI 48846
616-527-0985

Treads & Sleds Kawasaki
2715 29th Street SE
Grand Rapids, MI 49512
616-575-0130

Team Alpine Kawasaki
4790 Alpine Avenue NW
Comstock Park, MI 49321
616-784-1221

Country Turf & Kawasaki
8325 Broadmoor Avenue SE
Caladonia, MI 493 I 6
616-891-7200

John Hoeksema
11483 East Lakewood Boulevard
Holland, MI 49424
616-396-8132

Babbitt's Sport Center
3712 Airline Road
Muskegon, MI 49444
23!-737-924!

Finish Line Kawasaki
2284 West US10
Ludington, MI 49431
231-757-8946

Peacock Ltd of Baldwin
276 South M37
Baldwin, MI 49304
231-745-4606

Powers Motor Sports Kawasaki
11995 North Maple Island Road
Fremont, MI 49412
231-924-1924

Recker Motor Sports Kawasaki
1604 West High Street
Mount Pleasant, MI 48858
989-772-9197

Classic Motor Sports Kawasaki
3939 South Blue Star Drive
Traverse City, MI 49684
231-943-9344

Gaylord Kawasaki
928 South Otsego Avenue
Gaylord, MI 49735
989-732-6737

White Sales & Service
9611 North Straits Hwy
Cheboygan, MI 49721
231-627-9919

Au Sable Valley Kawasaki
5660 F41
Oscoda, MI 48750-8610
989-739-7774

Zambon's North Country Sales
2020 Ludington Street
Escanaba, MI 49829
906-789-0360

Zambon's North Country Sales
2223 US Hwy 41 West
Marquette, MI 49855
906-228-7010

Evert's Hancock Kawasaki
315 Dakota Street
Hancock, MI 49930
906-482-2811

KTM
Detroit Eurocycles
18301 Nine Mile Road
Eastpointe, MI
586-778-8900

Lansing Cycle
6081 South Martin Luther King
Lansing, MI 48911
517-393-6477

Life Cycle
3103 Lake Street
Kalamazoo, MI
269-388-5590

MOTO-GUZZI
Detroit Eurocycles
18301 Nine Mile Road
Eastpointe, MI
586-778-8900

GT Motors
816 East Howe Avenue
Lansing, MI 48906
517-485-6815

MV AGUSTA
Classic Cycle
30478 Groesbeck Hwy
Roseville, MI 48066
586-447-1340

MZ MOTORCYCLES
Indian & MZ Motorcycles of Leslie
101 North Main Street
Leslie, MI
517-589-9933

SUZUKI
Bright Powersports
4181 Dix Highway
Lincoln Park, MI
313-382-1220

Suzuki of Warren
30822 Ryan Road
Warren, MI 48092
586-751-1200

Pilgrim Motorsports Suzuki
260 West Ann Arbor Road
Plymouth, MI 48170
734-451-7200

Macomb Powersports
46860 Gratiot Avenue
Chesterfield, MI 48051
586-949-4000

Ray's Powersports
959 South Telegraph Road
Monroe, MI 48161
734-241-8444

Ray C's Extreme Store
422 Imlay City Road
Lapeer, MI 48446
810-664-4505

Rosenau Powersports
24732 Ford Road
Dearborn Heights, MI
313-278-5000

Anderson Sales & Service
1645 South Telegraph Road
Bloomfield Hills, MI 48302
248-858-2300

Champion Powersports
9700 Belleville Road
Belleville, MI 48111
866-GOCHAMP

Wheels USA 1
1559 North Lapeer Road.
Oxford, MI 48371
248-628-5000

Kensington Motorsports
56605 Pontiac Trail
New Hudson, MI 48165
248-446-0000

C & C Sports
8090 West Grand River Avenue
Brighton, MI 48114
810-227-7068

Nicholson Enterprises
4405 Jackson Road
Ann Arbor, MI 48103
734-769-9815

Full Throttle Motorsports
9555 Woodlane Drive
Lansing, MI 48821
517-646-9850

Holiday Power Sports
4501 Page Avenue
Michigan Center, MI 49254
517-764-3600

Joe's Motorcycle Tires & Accessories
2593 North State Road
Ionia, MI 48846
616-527-0985

M & M Motorsports
3825 Lake Street
Kalamazoo, MI 49001
269-381-5800

MC Supply Ltd.
2310 South M37
Hastings, MI 49058
269-945-2782

US27 Motorsports
5301 N. US27
St. Johns, MI 48879
989-224-8874

Shawmut Hills Sales
2807 Lake Michigan Drive NW
Grand Rapids, MI 49504
616-453-5467

Paw Paw Lake Sports & Marine
5270 Paw Paw Lake Road
Coloma, MI 49038
269-468-8600

Brickyard Road Motor Car Ltd.
682 East Chicago Road
Coldwater, MI 49036
517-279-2886

Grace Performance
2203 Wadhams Road
Kimball, MI 48074
810-989-9050

Great Lakes Powersports
4211 Fenton Road
Burton, MI 48529
810-233-7800

Grove's Motorsports
525 North Cedar Street
Mason, MI 48854
517-676-5667

Town & Country Sports Center
US12 & US127
Cement City, MI 49233
517-547-3333

Snyder Suzuki
5684 East Broadway Street
Mt. Pleasant, MI 48858
989-773-5024

Harvey Motors
42800 Red Arrow Highway
Paw Paw, MI 49079
269-657-2913

Treads & Sleds
2715 29th Street SE
Grand Rapids, MI 49512
616-575-0130

J. T. Cycle
825 Golden Avenue
Battle Creek, MI 49015
269-965-0571

Village Motor Sports
3861 Plainfield Avenue NE
Grand Rapids, MI 49525
616-364-8481

Michiana Cycle
50715 North US31
South Bend, IN 46637
574-272-4484

Babbitt's Sports Center
3712 Airline Road
Muskegon, MI 49444
231-737-9241

Suzuki Sales
3045 Pigeon Road
Elkton. MI 48731
989-375-1391

Laethem Equipment Company
245 Columbia Street
Caro, MI 48723
989-673-3939

Stevens Sport Center
1911 East Airport Road
Midland, MI 48642
989-631-6450

Great Escapes Motorsports
136 North US31 South
Traverse City, MI 49684
231-943-9800

Extreme Power Sports
2752 South Otsego Avenue
Gaylord, MI 49735
989-732-4331

Brandt's Sports Center
6398 State Route 33
Cheboygan, MI 49721
231-625-2567

Zambon's North County Sales #2
2020 Ludington Street
Escanaba, MI 49829
906-789-0360

Falls Action Sports
5050 Highway 141
Oconto, WI 54153
920-834-2600

Stevens Cycle Sales
3636 South Huron Road
Bay City, MI 48706
800-292-5017

Dave's Suzuki
1655 Plett Road
Cadillac, MI 49601
231-775-3796

Lakeshore Motor Sports
4690 East Ludington US10
Ludington, MI 49431
231-843-4770

Big Jim's Sports Unlimited
3137 US23 South
Alpena, MI 49707
989-356-4141

Scooter's Motor Sports
4250 US41 West
Marquette, MI 49855
906-228-4040

U.P. Cycle & Sport
W7730 US2
Iron Mountain, MI 49801
906-779-2983

Ayes Motor Center
701 Highway 5l North
Hurley, WI 54534
715-561-2720

TRIKES

Trikes of Oxford
248-770-3423
trikesofoxford.com

American Harley-Davidson
5436 Jackson Road
Ann Arbor, MI 48103
734-747-6143

Signature Bikes & Trikes
1918 Georgetown Center Drive
Jenison, MI 49428
616-457-4488

3-Wheel Enterprises
594 Kenowa Avenue SW
Walker, MI 49544
616-453-0588

Voyager Trikes
131 28th Street SW
Wyoming, MI 49548
616-340-0786

TRIUMPH

Triumph Detroit
30478 Groesbeck Hwy
Roseville, MI 48066
586-447-1340

Classic Motor Sports
480 US 31 South
Traverse City, MI
231-943-9344

Mid-Michigan Honda Triumph
4108 Page Avenue
Michigan Center, MI 49254
517-764-0900

Life Cycle
3103 Lake Street
Kalamazoo, MI 49001
269-388-5590

North Coast Motorcycle
Toledo, OH
1-877-northcoast

URAL

Crawford Sales Company
10138 Colonial Street
South Lyon, MI 48178
248-437-3950

Reinbold's Sales and Service
110 North Gera Street
Reese, MI 48757
989-755-0612

VICTORY

Champion Powersports
9700 Belleville Road
Belleville, MI 48111
800-GOCHAMP

Michigan Powersports
1196 Ecorse Road
Ypsilanti, MI 48198
734-482-4386

K & W Cycles
4090 Auburn Road
Utica, MI 48317
586-731-5959

Full Throttle Motorsports
9555 Woodlane Drive
Lansing, MI 48821
517-646-9850

Townline Powersports
6031 North Clio Road
Mt. Morris, MI 48458
810-787-0057

Peacock Ltd.
276 South M37
Baldwin, MI 49304
231-745-4606

Winners Powersports
23979 Allen Road
Woodhaven, MI 48183
734-675-4085

Cycle & Marine Land
3482 Lapeer Road
Port Huron, MI 48060
810-987-3963

Devries Sales, Inc.
10170 Shaver Road
Portage, MI 48024
269-323-2166

Honda East
1230 Conant Street
Maumee OH 43537
419-891-1230

Southwest V-Twin
4390 Chicago Drive SW
Grandville, MI 49418
616-531-9300

Klimmek Sales & Service
1183 South Mapes Road
Mio, MI 48647
989-826-3695

Extreme Power Sports
2572 South Otsego Avenue
Gaylord, MI 49735
989-732-4331
989-826-3695

Dan's Polaris & Victory
18006 Erickson Drive
Atlantic Mine, MI 49905
906-482-6227

YAMAHA

Bright Power Sports
4818 Dix Highway
Lincoln Park, MI 48146-4029
1-866-265-1844

Rosenau Powersports
24732 Ford Road
Dearborn Hights, MI 48127
313-278-5000

Pilgrim Motorsports Yamaha
260 Ann Arbor Road West
Plymouth, MI 48170
734-451-7200

K & W Cycles
4090 Auburn Road
Utica, MI 48317
586-731-5959

Great Lakes Powersports
4211 Fenton Road
Burton, MI 48529
810-233-7800

Townline Sales – Flint
6031 North Clio Road
Mt. Morris, MI 48458
810-787-0057

Ray C's Cycle & Sports
422 Imlay City Road
Lapeer, MI 48446
810-664-4505

Wheels USA
1559 North Lapeer Road
Oxford, MI 48371-2413
248-628-5000

Card's Yamaha
12296 West Brady Road
Chesaning, MI 48616
989-845-7370

Stevens Yamaha Sales
3636 South Huron Road
Bay City, MI 48706
989-684-9872

Wohlfeil Hardware
5818 State Street
Saginaw, MI 48601
989-799-0942

Thumb Motorsports
6466 Van Dyke Road
Cass City, MI 48726
989-872-4077

Cycle & Marine Land
3482 Lapeer Road
Port Huron, MI 48060
810-987-3963

Macomb Powersports
46860 Gratiot Avenue
Chesterfield, MI 48051
586-949-4000

Sandusky Motor Parts
190 East Sanilac Road
Sandusky, MI 48471
810-648-3566

Roseville Yamaha
25838 Gratiot Avenue
Roseville, MI 48066
586-859-2600

Holiday Cycle Sales
4501 Page Avenue
Michigan Center, MI
517-547-3333

Winner's Circle Yamaha
136 Bankers Road
Hillsdale, MI 49242
517-437-7513

Nicholson Enterprises
4405 Jackson Road
Ann Arbor, MI 48103
800-825-5158

Full Throttle Motorsports
9555 Woodlane Drive
Lansing, MI 48821
517-646-9850

Ray's Powersports
959 South Telegraph Road
Monroe, MI 48161
734-241-8444

Magnum Power Sports
6923 Summerfield Road
Petersburg, MI 49270
734-854-6005

Champion Powersports
9700 Belleville Road
Belleville, MI 48111
734-699-3000

East Yamaha
1230 Conant Street
Maumee, OH 43537
419-891-1230

Dexter's Motors
3804 South Adrian Hwy
Adrian, MI 49221
517-263-6050

J & J Sales
475 SE Catawba Road
Port Clinton, OH
419-734-2754

Four Seasons Yamaha
5019 North Grand River Avenue
Lansing, MI 48906-2437
517-321-4601

US 27 Motorsports
5301 North US27
Saint Johns, MI 48879
989-224-8874

Route 66 Powersports
3613 South State Road
Ionia, MI 48846-9477
616-527-0130

Holiday Cycle Sales
4501 Page Avenue
Michigan Center, MI
517-764-3600

M/C Supply
2310 South M37 Hwy
Hastings, MI 49058
269-945-2782

C & C Sports
8090 Grand River Road
Brighton, MI 48114
810-227-7068

Anderson's Sales & Service
1645 South Telegraph Road
Bloomfield Hills, MI
248-858-2300

Kensington Motorsports
56605 Pontiac Trail
New Hudsom, MI 48165
248-446-0000

Shawmut Hills Sales
2807 Lake Michigan Drive NW
Grand Rapids. MI 49504-5856
616-453-5467

Team Alpine
4790 Alpine Avenue NW
Comstock Park, MI
616-784-1221

Quality Service Plus
13035 New Holland Street
Holland, MI 49424
616-399-8444

Boston Motors
4482 Airline Road
Muskegon, MI 49444
231-733-9600

Powers Motor Sports
11995 North Maple Island Road
Fremont, MI 49412-9400
231-924-1924

M & M Motor Mall
2839 Lake Street
Kalamazoo, MI 49048
269-381-5800

Paw Paw Cycle
134 Ampey Road
Paw Paw, MI 49079
269-657-2574

Paw Paw Sports & Marina
5270 Paw Paw LakekRoad
Coloma, MI 49038
269-468-8600

North End Cycle Shop
2426 Cassopolis Street
Elkhart, IN 46514
574-264-0618

Turn One Motorsports
3000 Miller Drive
Plymouth, IN 56463-8084
574-936-9192

Cyclesport Yamaha
Hobart, IN 46342
219-962-4770

C & S Yamaha
4741 East Pickard Street
Mount Pleasant, MI
989-772-5513

Finish Line Motorsports
2284 West US10
Ludington, MI 49431
231-757-8946

Hacker's Yamaha
3901 West Houghton Lake Drive
Houghton Lake, MI 48629
989-366-7015

St. Helen Power Sports
1901 North Saint Helen Road
Saint Helen, MI 48656
989-389-4961

Dave's Yamaha Sales
1655 Plett Road
Cadillac, MI 49601
231-775-3796

Peacock Limited of Baldwin
276 South M37
Baldwin, MI 49304
231-745-4606

Extreme Power Sports
2572 South Otsego Avenue
Gaylord, MI 49735
989-732-4331

T & R Yamaha
215 Main Street
East Jordan, MI 49727
231-536-7211

Schell Auto Center
20468 State Street
Onaway, MI 49765-8665
989-733-8031

Lakes & Trails Power Sports
2229 US Hwy 131 North
Kalkaska, MI 49646
231-258-6767

Woody's Cycle
3424 South F41
Mikado, MI 48745
989-736-8107

T & R Yamaha
215 Main Street
East Jordan, MI 49727
231-536-7211

Brandt's Sport Center
6398 M33 Hwy
Cheboygan, MI 49721
231-625-2567

Great Escapes Motorsports
136 North US 31 South
Traverse City, MI 49684
231-943-9800

Chippewa Motors
3107 South Hwy M129
Sault Ste. Marie, MI
906-632-6651

BSA of Marquette
309 M553 North
Marquette, MI 49855
906-249-3361

Zambon's North Country Sales
2020 Ludington Street
Escanaba, MI 49829
906-789-0360

A-1 Sport & Marine
1212 North Stephenson Avenue
Iron Mountain, MI 49801
906-774-3000

Hancock Bike Shop
115 Quincy Street
Hancock, MI 49930
906-482-5234

Pat's Auto & Sports Center
6440 Hwy M38
Greenland, MI 49929
906-883-3253

Heckel's Eagle River Marina
437 West Division Street
Eagle River, WI 54521
715-479-4471

Lakewood Motorsports
17168 Saint Marys Road
Lakewood, WI 54138
715-276-7067

Tri-County Sports & Equipment
2103 Hall Avenue
Marinette, WI 54143
715-735-9660